The desire that His people take domi which they live began in the Garden of Eden and it is still in effect today. Ed Delph sees our responsibility clearly, and his lucid and penetrating book is a road map that points the body of Christ in the right direction.

—C. Peter Wagner
Presiding Apostle,
International Coalition Of Apostles

My friend Ed Delph is a catalyst for positive change, an inspiration to international Christian leaders, and a visionary who spends himself tirelessly in order to promote the growth and health of the whole church in the whole world.

—John Dawson, President
Youth With A Mission

Church@Community is just what is needed to create an engagement with culture and society that is not accidental but purposeful. Everyone engages with culture; some are shaped by its values, others mindlessly enjoy, or put up with it. This book will teach you the value of serving and blessing rather than simply criticizing—analyzing the darkness. We Christians are good at that. This will help us shine our lights much brighter.

—Gerald Coates
Director, Pioneer Network of Churches
London, England

Since I first met Ed Delph at a conference several years ago, I have come to love him and to appreciate his expansive vision for the Lord's work all around the world. This book points beyond the "clergyfication" of Christianity toward the kind of congregational and community renewal the Holy Spirit is leading the church to embrace today. There is high octane fuel here, so use wisely. But use!

—Timothy George
Dean, Beason Divinity School, Samford University
Executive Director, *Christianity Today*

Ed Delph's *Church@Community* is a priceless reminder that we have to change our thinking before we can change our community. These words are not just the keen insights of a leading strategist in transformation; they are a creative and prophetic challenge to a new generation of leaders to rewrite the old playbooks and release a greater expression of Jesus in the earth. Thanks, Ed, for this helpful and inspiring message.

—David Cannistraci
Sr. Pastor of GateWay City Church, San Jose, California

Church@Community will revolutionize old traditional thinking concerning the purpose of the local church and its relationship to its surrounding community. This book will help church leaders to properly teach people to be the salt of the earth, the light of the world, and the witness of Jesus Christ. Dr. Ed Delph brings a new apostolic kingdom of God concept that is especially relevant to what the Holy Spirit is saying to the church today.

Dr. Ed Delph is challenging the church to change from thinking that the community is for the church to thinking that the church is for the community. This is a paradigm shift that can revolutionize the way the church impacts our cities and nations. God bless you, Ed, for giving us the concepts that align us with God's present truth and challenge for our generation to establish God's kingdom in our community.

—Dr. Bill Hamon
Chairman, Founder, and Bishop of
Christian International Ministries Network
Founder of Christian International Apostolic Network
Author of *The Eternal Church; Prophets and Personal Prophecy; Prophets and The Prophetic Movement; Prophets, Pitfalls, and Principles; Apostles, Prophets and The Coming Moves of God; The Day of the Saints; Who Am I and Why Am I Here?*

Church@Community has come at the right time in this stage of the twenty-first-century church age and reformation. With great biblical wisdom, Dr. Ed Delph presents us with a church in transition from a denominational mindset to a kingdom mindset, from a church growth concept to a community transformation concept. This book will help you take the necessary steps to enter into that process.

—Dr. Hector P. Torres
Hispanic International Ministries

Church@Community burns with Ed's passion to see the church break out of the box. He keeps bringing us back to the irreducible basics that will enable us to be effective in the real world where ordinary people live. He believes that the church really is God's secret weapon to bring about transformation to our cities and nations at every level, in spite of our recent history of ineffectiveness in many places. His book breathes hope and inspires faith, but don't read it if you're looking for a comfortable ride!

—John Noble
Chairman of Charismata,
National Charismatic Leaders Conference

In this book Ed Delph tackles one of the most crucial issues facing the church today—the need for it to be an integral part of the community it seeks to serve in order to be relevant. This is excellent material for anyone who is serious about understanding the way forward for the church in our modern world.

—Brian Pickering
Head of the Australian Prayer Network

Church@Community is a key book for pastors and Christian leaders to read. Dr. Ed Delph provides revolutionary concepts that empower the local church to become relevant in method and message to their community and expand God's kingdom in the twenty-first century.

—Dr. Greg Brown
Senior Pastor, Skyway Church of the West Valley

This book and Ed Delph will forever change the way you understand church and society. What he says really is new, interesting, and true. Read it. Ponder it and do what he says!

—Rev. Alfred H. Ells, MC
Executive Director
Leaders That Last Ministries

Ed Delph came to our church and started a revolution in the way we reach out to the community. I quickly set him up to visit all our network churches in New Zealand and Australia and share his amazing community transformation message. I believe this book would be a good manual for the End-Time harvest.

—Joshua Asafo Avia
Hosanna World Outreach Center
Hosanna Global Network, New Zealand

Dr. Ed has been coming to our church nearly every year for ten years and has helped us tremendously to transition our church towards "A Community for the Community."

—Pastor David Dishroon
Tauranga Worship Centre, New Zealand

When I read *Church@Community,* I gave a sigh of relief...finally here is a book that gives you the "how" to do a thing and not just the "why"! As a speaker and author, like Ed, who speaks around the world, I have seen many cast the vision (the "why") of a thing, but rarely have I seen speakers and authors help us experience the reality of a thing (the "how"). This is a book about achieving results! This is a book to help all finish their race in life. This book is about helping one achieve success in the eight core values of business, ministry, and life. This book is a must read for all who desire to see their dreams become a reality—with intelligent fire.

—Dr. Marcus Hester
Author/Speaker , Chicago, Illinois
The God Factor... Getting the Edge at Work

"When the Cloud went up, they got up and marched." (Num 9:22, *The Message*). Believers in many countries have for some time known that the Cloud has lifted. God is calling his people to shift its focus from the church to the community and recognize that it does exist primarily for its non-members. We are not just out to build a church, but to seek community transformation. In marching after the Cloud I do not know of many better equipped to guide us than Dr. Ed Delph. His new book *Church@Community* is challenging and inspiring and provides useful insights about how a community really functions and about the relationship between the church and other sectors of the community. Dr. Delph has international experience and this book will be just as useful in Europe as in North America. I look forward to recommending it to other pastors and leaders who want to take "The Next Step in Real, Tangible and Lasting Community Transformation."

—Dr. Reidar Paulsen
Senior Pastor, Christ Church in Bergen, Norway
Co-leader of the Pastoral Network in Bergen, Pray Bergen

Ed Delph has been a close friend for years. We share our lives in a pastors' covenant group. Ed is full of passion for the church to be the church, and he lives what he speaks and writes. You will be stirred by this book as I have by Ed personally!

—Dr. Gary D. Kinnaman, pastor and author
Word of Grace Church, Mesa, Arizona

The insights that Dr Delph has for the church today are both timely and strategic. This book will challenge you with the concepts he presents. Thank you, Ed, for making us think about what we are doing!

—Mike Knott
Senior Minister, Elim International Church
Wellington, New Zealand

The impact of the early church was such that the community "esteemed them highly." Ed's insights into the power of the local church to transform their communities is the voice of the Spirit of God speaking to the church today. The hour has come for the church to build bridges into its community.

—Luke Brough
National Leader, Elim Churches of New Zealand

Ed Delph is a gifted teacher with much apostolic insight. You will receive great revelation and a reality check for the church of now in his latest book, *Church@Community*. It will change your paradigm regarding the how and what of church. It is a must read and a now word.

—Apostle John P. Kelly, President
LEAD (Leadership Education for Apostolic Development)

Ed Delph is a twenty-first-century visionary with an apostolic worldview. *Church@Community* should be read and studied for impacting cities and nations. I highly recommend it.

—Apostle Emanuele Cannistraci
San Jose, California

Experiencing the enthusiasm and contemporary cutting edge vision of Dr. Ed Delph was for me an exciting view of how God builds a fire in one man and uses him to transform a generation. It has been my privilege to review his latest book *Church@Community* prior to its publishing. The work has my wholehearted endorsement and recommendation. Every pastor and church leader should not only read the book, but also attend one of Dr. Delph's workshops on the subject. It is my sincere belief that this work will be significant in motivating leadership to reclaim the position of respect and impact that the church should have within our communities and our nation.

—Dr. Richard Drake, Provost
Phoenix University of Theology

It is the habit of the body of Christ to become introspective and thus loose the essence of the message it was meant to carry: the establishment of the kingdom of God in our communities. *Church@Community* effectively confronts this error and is a call to reorient the church toward an outward focus. I highly commend this book as it brings a necessary challenge to the modern church.

—Brent Douglas
Senior Leader, Encounter Christian Centre
Auckland, New Zealand

Church@Community adds several new dimensions to the challenge of community transformation. With fresh language Ed Delph has been effectively encouraging church leaders around the globe to shift focus away from professional clergy-led ministry that exists primarily to serve its members within the walls. The alternative presented by *Church@Community* is steeped in Old Testament and New Testament examples of the people of God living and serving as a predominantly missionary force in the community. The message is as timely as it is fresh. Indeed, a sea of change of restlessness appears to be building among Christian tribes to break out of the institutionalized preferences for predictable comfort. Catch the vision and rationale for a fundamental shift in the nature, function, and mission of the church.

—Dan Reeves
President, Institute of Missional Leadership Teams
Convener, Council of Ecclesiology

As my wife and I travel and speak in Europe, or the United States, we have found that churchgoers are more converted to church than to Christ, and their relationship with doctrine is stronger than their relationship with Jesus. Ed's book is part of God's solution to this problem; an incredible storehouse of information, and revelation. If you want to come to Christ-centeredness, this is a great place to begin. Read the book!

—Rod and Julie Anderson
Founders/Directors
Prayer for the Nations

Dr. Ed Delph has undertaken one of the most significant challenges in our generation... finding the sacred in the secular. As the author of *Learning the Language of Babylon*, I find a kindred spirit in this restless seeker of truth. We cannot delay, for even one more day, the transition that is at hand. A generation must arise and engage the marketplace community with the principles of the kingdom of God. This book will serve as a roadmap on how to get from here to there.

—Dr. Terry M. Crist
Pastor, Citi Church
Scottsdale, Arizona
Author, *Learning the Language of Babylon*

Passion is contagious... truth is challenging... and vision is both inspiring and directional! In his new book *Church@Community*, Ed captures all three. Understanding that the church exists, not to maintain the "religious clubin'" that has become the strategy of much of the church-world, but rather to fulfill the dynamic mission of individual and community transformation, this book will challenge you to the simplicity of "doing the stuff." These truths will inspire ordinary people to a reach for an impacting life at every level of their life. A must read for every believer that has wondered, *How do I and my church make a difference?*

—TONY MILLER
PRESIDENT, DESTINY WORLD OUTREACH

I had the privilege, together with our national leadership, to be ministered to by Ed Delph on some of the themes in this book. Not only does he have the gift of communication and the anointing of the Holy Spirit, the content is so relevant, revealing, and edifying for the church of today. A lifetime's wisdom and experience blend with the inspiration of the Spirit as one is caught up in the pages and fascinating subjects of this book about the church and her divine calling in the community.

—DR. ISAK BURGER
PRESIDENT, APOSTOLIC FAITH MISSION OF SOUTH AFRICA

You are holding an apostolic, prophetic manual for the church in the twenty-first century in your hands. I have come to know Ed Delph as someone who truly loves the church. This book raises the standard for church leaders to seize our greatest moment in history. You will find what Ed has communicated both inspirational and implementable. May this book jolt you to a new awareness of God's intention and purpose for His church.

—ALAN PLATT
SENIOR PASTOR
DOXA DEO, SOUTH AFRICA
PRETORIA, SOUTH AFRICA

Some say the church is dead. Perhaps it's more accurate to say she's comatose or half asleep. Whatever the malady, for too long our churches have been Christian ghettos. For too long they have been self-serving escapist clubs where we take a breather from the harsh and challenging realities of the big bad world. And for too long our members who fail to show at every meeting on the program-driven agenda have been rebuked for their lack of commitment.

Enough. It's time to get up and go—out of your own front door, out of your familiar comfort zone. Our communities will not come to us; we must go to them. We need to be Jesus to real people around us. The people of God have words of life and words of truth from the throne of God Himself. These are the answers for hurting, rootless, and exhausted people around the globe.

In this book Ed will encourage you to engage in your community, in your workplace, in your sphere of influence. I want to encourage you to do so with all your heart, for Jesus' sake.

It's time to unleash the church on the world.

It's time to unleash Jesus into your community.

—Bernard Sanders
Impact Network, U.K.

Dr. Ed Delph's new book *Church@Community* is thought provoking and informative. The interpretation and application of the "Humpty Dumpty" story to our fractured community and our broken world is powerful. The book reminds us that the earth and its fullness is the Lord's; the church and the other four spheres of influence are equally under God's Grace and judgment. *Church@Community* points the way toward community transformation by following God's strategy of building His city. The author has been a clear voice for community transformation as he speaks at conferences and convocations around the world. This book brings his insight and wisdom to another audience. I strongly recommend this book to brothers (and sisters) and others.

—Bishop George D. McKinney
Jurisdictional Prelate and
General Board Member, COGIC
Founder/Sr. Pastor/CEO, St. Stephen's Ministries
San Diego, California

We were privileged to assist in the publication of Ed's first book *Making Sense of the Apostolic*. While small in size, this book was big in impact and relevance. Now we are expectantly awaiting *Church@Community*. Actually I have had a preview and can assure you that this is a great book—great in concept, great in relevance, and great in giving these essential truths back to the church around the world. "Whose time has come" is a phrase often used by Ed in this book—this is truly a "now" book for the church on a mission from God! I join with countless other Kiwis in the South Pacific and say thanks Ed for all of the great work in this book!

—Max Palmer
National Leadership, New Life International
Christchurch, New Zealand

Ed Delph, whose heart is so much concerned about the kingdom of God and the aim to reach the whole world with the gospel, is constantly insisting on the very continuity of meaning between the mystery of faith, the ministry, and the work, with the emphasis that the church is God's kingdom embassy and the voice of God in this world.

Through his frequent and various missions in France, Ed has shown us how good it was to welcome the divine refreshment, but even more excellent to restore the original structure. What a wonderful blessing it has been for me personally and for the whole nation of France to be acquainted with such a man of God, for he is not only accurate on a biblical and spiritual level, but he awakens in us the unction to lead us in our exact and true function.

—Ismaël Sadok
Prophet to the nation of France
Marseille, France

Church@Community is a must-read book for every Christian leader who desires to transition his life and church into a new model for community transformation.

—Mel C. Mullen
Word of Life Churches
Red Deer, Alberta, Canada

It was a privilege for us that our city and church was the first place in Russia where Ed Delph ministered. I have often heard people say that when you come to their conference you will never be the same, but, in fact, nothing changes. Not so with Ed's series on Church@Community. Not only did it bless our city and congregation, it changed our city and congregation. We will never be the same again!

—Viktor Sudakov
Senior Pastor, New Life Church And Church Network
Ekaterinburg, Russia

For too long the church has held an isolationist attitude toward the community around us. Jesus commanded us to let our light shine, to influence our communities in a relevant and significant way for the kingdom of God. Ed Delph teaches us clear biblical principles and offers tremendous insight into the church becoming the church! Not since The Purpose Driven Church has such an important book on this subject come along.

—Jonathan Bernis
President, Jewish Voice Ministries International

Church @ Community

ED DELPH, D.MIN.

CHURCH@COMMUNITY by Ed Delph
Published by Creation House
A Strang Company
600 Rinehart Road
Lake Mary, Florida 32746
www.creationhouse.com

Cover design by Terry Clifton

Library of Congress Control Number: 2004117100
International Standard Book Number: 1-59185-734-1

05 06 07 08 09 — 987654321
Printed in the United States of America

Contents

Acknowledgments

First of all, I need to give thanks to my wife, Becky, who had the chore of making sense of my handwriting and typing this book. What a partner! I also need to thank my children, Kristin, Matthew, and Jonathan, for allowing me to travel so much and fulfill my calling. They have given the most of all. Special thanks to Polly Heller who edited the book before I submitted it to Creation House. Thanks to Pastor Gerald Coates who captured an incredible concept in his book, *An Intelligent Fire*; to Pastor Don Pogue of Joy for All Nations, who provided great ideas on the Queen of the South; to Dr. Harvey Lifsey of Christian Dynamics, who propelled me into my destiny by taking me on my first oversees trip in 1979. His influence and teaching is all through this book.

My life changed significantly after meeting one of the all-time champions of people, Apostle Emanuele Cannistraci. His right words at the right time have been a beacon to me for years. Thanks to Ed Silvoso, John Dawson, and Dr. C. Peter Wagner on your friendship and revelation on community transformation. I don't want to leave out Dr. Richard Drake, Provost of the Phoenix University of Theology, whose encouragement and support lifted my hands at just the right time. The result is this book.

Thanks to all the pastors from New Zealand I have met, hundreds of them too numerous to name, for being the catalysts of this book.

Thanks also to the people of Hosanna Christian Fellowship. This is your legacy. And very special thanks to Allen Quain and Bert Ghezzi of Strang Communications who believed in this book

Finally, I'd like to thank my parents, Edwin K. and Margaret J. Delph. My father imparted to me the core value of excellence and purpose, and my mother's prayers have fueled my whole life.

Foreword

If they can't see us... they won't be us!

Do you realize that the Church and the community are connected? The Church is here for the benefit of the community. The community is where the raw material of the church comes from. The community is where the Bride of Christ comes from. Let me ask those of you in the church a question...

1. How is the community different or better because of your church?

2. If your church was to die, would the community miss you?

These questions are crucial if we ever are to experience community impact and transformation. Years ago God gave the inhabitants of

Jerusalem a strategy on how to transform the city of Babylon. They were to serve God by serving the community. If we had an email address for this strategy, I would call it Church@Community.

The Church-Community Connection

In Jeremiah 29:4–7, God describes what I call the church-community connection. At this time, the inhabitants of Jerusalem had been taken captive by Babylon. The natural reaction would have been for these inhabitants to withdraw. After all, Babylon would be an uncomfortable place for an Israelite to be. Babylon would have been considered very unholy, very sinful, and very anti-God. This describes what many Christians would feel like today in most large cities of the world. The tendency would be to disengage from the city. However, let's look at what God says in Jeremiah:

> Thus says the Lord of hosts, the God of Israel, to all the exiles whom I have sent into exile from Jerusalem to Babylon, "Build houses and live in them; and plant gardens, and eat their produce. Take wives and become the fathers of sons and daughters, and take wives for your sons and give your daughters to husbands, that they may bear sons and daughters; and multiply there and do not decrease. And seek the welfare of the city where I have sent you into exile, and pray to the Lord on its behalf; for in its welfare you will have welfare."
>
> —Jeremiah 29:4–7

God's intention here was for Jerusalem to be greatly involved in the community life of Babylon. His exhortation through the prophet was "build houses, live in them, plant gardens, eat their produce, take wives, have families, have grandchildren . . . multiply there . . . *do not decrease*!" In other words, God was saying "get involved in commerce and the city." God wanted them to start housing companies. God wanted them to be entrepreneurial and start agricultural companies. His desire was for them to multiply in the city. They were to become responsible citizens in the community. While they were in Babylon they might as well be a blessing to Babylon. God gave them the green light to become mayors, magistrates, teachers, provosts, businessmen, educators, involved in the PTA, and to have families and extended families. After all, they were going to be in Babylon for the next seventy years. They might as well be salt and light in the community. God wanted them to engage the community, not 'enrage' the community or 'disengage' from the community. God's strategy then is applicable today. God wants His people to be involved in all five spheres of influence in the community. He needs 'Christians' to be part of and involved in the community's business, government, education, and media/entertainment sectors. His people bring Christian core values into all sectors of the community that enhance the community. In reality, church is wherever they are. Just like the inhabitants of Jerusalem, the present day church needs to be *for the community*, not *against the community*. The perspective the inhabitants of Jerusalem needed to take was one of contribution, not conquest. It is possible and even normal for today's church to be for the city and for God at the same time. How will the other four community spheres of influence know what God is like without people from the church involved in commerce? The Babylonians certainly were not going to synagogues! Therefore, the synagogue had to go to them through those involved in commerce. In the time of Jeremiah, Daniel gave God a face in Babylon. Daniel was a person of influence in a position of influence. He redefined God and the people of God to the Babylonians. He showed the Babylonians by his life and wisdom how to transform a community. His influence was real. His life was exemplary. He changed Babylon's perception of God. He created a positive public relations image of God. He was part of God's plan to put the church of that time into circulation in Babylon. How? Through the business, government, education, and media/entertainment sectors of the community. The 'church at that time' was there for the community, not the community for the church. The church at that time was to be salt and light in the context of the community. The church at that time was to increase and multiply its positive influence. They were to bless the context they live in. The same is true today.

Seeking the Welfare of the City

The last part of this scripture catches us by surprise! Most of the inhabitants of Jerusalem had been taught that Babylon was evil. Now Jeremiah is saying...seek the welfare of Babylon! From a church perspective it would be the same as saying to us...seek the welfare of Los Angeles, Auckland, Delhi, Singapore, London, Paris, or wherever. Look again at God's strategy for influencing Babylon. His people were to seek the welfare of Babylon. They were to pray to the Lord on Babylon's behalf. Why? The Bible says "in Babylon's welfare, the inhabitants of Jerusalem will have welfare!" In other words, the welfare, peace, or prosperity (*shalom*) of Babylon directly affects the people of God. The inhabitants of Jerusalem were to act as intercessors for Babylon, not against Babylon. They were to overcome evil with good. They were to be good citizens in Babylon, not judges of Babylon. They were to be fruit-bearers, not fruit inspectors. They were to see the glass as half full rather than half empty. They were there for the city, the city was not there for them. In other words, the answer to their prayer was...themselves!

The application of this truth should be apparent to all of us reading this book. We, as the people of God, are to be for our cities and communities. We are to act as priests or intercessors praying on our cities' behalf. As a church person, if you live in Singapore, the economy of Singapore directly affects you. In Singapore's welfare, you will have welfare. In Singapore's peace, you will have peace. In Singapore's prosperity, you will have prosperity. Your chances for a profitable and effective business are enhanced as you learn to love Singapore. Your chances for a raise are enhanced as you learn to love Singapore, not hate Singapore. Remember, where there is no love, there is no influence in the city. If you want to be blessed, you bless the context in which you live. God says pray for the welfare of Singapore. Be a part of the solution, not the problem. When Singapore prospers, your family will benefit from the prosperity. It creates better jobs, a higher standard of living, more tithes to the church, taxes to the government, and more money to help the needy. I could go on and on! This is God's strategy for many communities and cities. This is what I call the church/community connection. Please do not *react to* this strategy, *act on* this strategy. Learn to separate the behaviors you may not necessarily agree with in the community from the community. God loves our communities and you can, too! The answer to your communities' behavior is you! God required the inhabitants of Jerusalem to be involved in all five spheres of influence in the community, not just the 'church' realm! Realize the answer to the problem of government is not the 'entity' of government. The real problem is we do not have enough Christians involved in and influencing government for the betterment of the community. In other words, seeking the welfare of your community starts in prayer but ends in community involvement. After all, if they can't see us, they won't be us. The answer to your prayer is you!

The following is a poem I wrote that illustrates the Church-Community Connection.

If We Do Not Shine, Then Who Will Be the Light?

If we do not shine, then who will be the light?
If we do not have influence, then who will be the influencers?
If we do not speak, then who will be the voice?
If we do not lead, then who will be the leaders?
If we do not stay in unity, then who will be the united?
If we do not go to the community, to whom will the community go?
If we do not impart life, then who will be the life imparters?
If we do not show the way, then which way will they go?
If we do not lead against injustice, then who will the downtrodden go to?
If we are not the salt, then who will flavor our community?
If we do not offer salvation, then where will they go to be saved?
If we do not forgive, then where will they go for forgiveness?
If we do not act wisely, then where will they go for wisdom?
If we do not hear the community, then who will the community hear?
If we do not incarnate good citizenship, then who will be the citizens?
If we do not make Jesus known, then who will they go to for a hero?

Introduction

There Is Nothing So Powerful As An
Idea Whose Time Has Come.
—Victor Hugo

Pastor Bruce Benge of Papakura, New Zealand, was praying about his community. In answer to his prayer the Lord said, "Bruce, there is a stronghold of opportunity in your community, and I want you to take a strong hold of it." Community transformation is about taking a strong hold of our communities' strongholds of opportunity.

The late 1980s saw the emergence of a group of leaders with a passion, a revelation, and an unquenchable vision to see communities reached for Christ—transformed, enhanced, and turned into better communities. I and other leaders like George Otis Jr., Ed Silvoso, John Dawson, Dr. C. Peter Wagner, Cindy Jacobs, Roger Mitchell, Ted Haggard, and Mel Mullen, to name a few, were strongly influenced by Argentina's revival in the '80s. The Argentines were experiencing extraordinary results in large-scale community transformations. At the same time, similar transformations began occurring in other parts of the world.

The "culture" of community transformation and some of the components involved in community transformation—such as unity, prayer, spiritual warfare, enabling core values, and prophetic and apostolic issues such as marketplace transformation—have touched the church worldwide. As the revelation continues to unfold, grow, and develop, new components will be added to the existing components and will further enhance and clarify the revelation and core values of community transformation.

An Adventure or a Quest?

An adventure is when a person goes somewhere exciting or exotic and returns. A quest is when a person goes somewhere exciting or exotic and may never return! That is quite a difference. Little did our group know that as we joined the quest for community transformation, the challenge would be so great, so exciting, so filled with potential, and so complex that the quest has changed us forever. Simply put, we may never return—for the better and the greater! We have gone beyond what was expected because we could do no less.

I am encouraged by the thousands of leaders, pastors, intercessors, parachurch organizations, churches, business people, theologians, and even politicians globally becoming aware of the amazing concept of community transformation. I have been in more than 150 countries. I travel nearly every month to at least one country for ministry purposes, and people invariably ask about the topic of community transformation. Indeed, community transformation is an idea whose time has come. This is a quest from which the church will never return! It is a "now" word of the Lord—both biblically correct and spiritually accurate. It is innovative disruption in the nick of time that will change—for the better—the church and its relationship to the community. As I said before, it is an idea whose time has come—and that is powerful!

Moving From Revelation to Reality

No matter what its content may be, most new "revelations" follow the same pattern. Revelations start with the "what"—that which is being revealed—followed by its "why" issues. Finally, those involved in the incarnation and propagation of the revelation address the "how" issues. The what, why, and how issues work together like a three-legged stool—the stool needs all three legs to balance properly.

The following Bible verse illustrates this principle, "By *wisdom* a house is built, and by *understanding* it is established; and by *knowledge* the rooms are filled with all precious and pleasant riches" (Prov. 24:3–4, emphasis added). Notice the three components—knowledge, understanding, and wisdom. Knowledge is *what*, understanding is *why*, and wisdom (which builds or incarnates the revelation) is *how*. Revelation begins with knowledge, but it is absolutely essential to understand the why of the what. When most people understand why, a shift occurs in their viewpoint. Then they are ready for the how. This is where wisdom comes in. Wisdom is the proper application of knowledge through understanding. People who know the hows can build the house (from the foundation up). The revelation becomes reality!

If I were to define this concept by offices, I would say it this way: the prophetic "seers" excel in the "what" and "why" aspects, but are not as gifted in the "how" aspects. That is why we need some apostolic wisdom in the how aspects. Pastor Gary Carter, of the Word of Life Centre in Drayton Valley, Alberta, Canada, calls this moving from a prophetic revelation to an apostolic reality. The purpose of the apostolic is to build what has been revealed, or else the full potential of the revelation will never be realized.

Herein lies the problem I have encountered hundreds of times all over the world. Many of the seers and reporters of the community transformation movement have been very *prophetic*, but not very *apostolic*. They have done an incredible job in revealing and reporting community transformation, creating vision, excitement and forward movement, but have not addressed the how-to-do-it issues in a real and tangible way. I am not criticizing them because their role, as defined by God, is to do exactly what they have done—create movement, be catalytic, cast vision and revelation, and release excitement. That is their role, their assignment. And that is good! However, if we do not follow up on the how-to-do-it issues, the movement will leave frustrated the thousands of leaders, pastors, and people who have embraced this movement. The vision stays in the vision stage.

This is where *Church@Community* comes in. I wrote this book as a response to the issue of *how*. I like to think this book augments what has already been done and adds further application to the revelation. This book is both prophetic and apostolic—it reveals and it builds, addresses the how issues and proposes a set of core values, or the government needed to move the concept of community transformation from an *idea* whose time has come to a *community transformed* whose time has come. This book moves us "from the incredible to the credible," to quote Robert Winters, the prophetically gifted leader of Gatekeepers International Prophetic Network based in Phoenix, Arizona. My heart is to add to, not take away from the very awesome potential of community transformation.

I address the most commonly asked questions:

- How do we get unity among pastors in the community?
- How do you change church culture from church-based to community-based?
- How do we think bigger than just our church?
- What kind of church is required to retain, integrate, and develop new believers who come into the church?
- What are the Kingdom or core-values that enable the vision of community transformation?
- How can we create a burden for our city?
- How does the church relate to business, government, education, and other spheres of influence that play an important part in community transformation?

I also give answers to questions like "How can we make our church grow?" or "How come we are not where we know we can be in our church and community?" These real questions require real answers, or we are in danger of staying in the "unfulfilled potential syndrome." I call it "always learning…never able" (2 Timothy 3:7).

Church@Community is here to enhance what has been started with real and tangible solutions. The alpha is Christ incarnated in all areas of the community. The omega is fulfilled potential—growing churches, growing organizations, growing people, enhanced communities. To say it in biblical language, the community is filled with the knowledge of the glory of the Lord, just like the waters cover the sea (Hab. 2:14) through enabling, life-giving core values. Simply stated, this book is about the reformation of strategic core values that enable the vision of community transformation.

Strength for Today and Bright Hope for Tomorrow

I have written this book to give strength for today to those people investigating or involved in community transformation initiatives so their communities may have a bright hope for tomorrow. Community transformation transcends most fundamental, charismatic/Pentecostal and seeker/leadership church boundaries worldwide. Most churches, church leaders, and pastors—as well as people in other community spheres of influence such as business, government, education, and media—would like to see their communities transformed and enhanced. The church world must understand that they are here for the community, the community is not here for them. It is time for the church to stop using the communities they serve as means to their own ends. Servanthood can take the church where our own individual agendas, theologies, and favorite themes cannot. In the same way, people within other organizational spheres must realize that they must serve their communities rather than expecting their communities to serve them.

For example, I read an amazing article in the November 2002 Hemispheres magazine published by United Airlines. The article was talking about a program called Fantasy Flights which is United's "tradition of giving" around the holiday season to children with life-threatening diseases and disadvantaged kids. United Airlines pilots, ramp service workers, customer service representatives, and air freight representatives volunteer money, time, stocking stuffers, presents, publicity, and fund raising. The children even get a short ride on a United jet or a short taxi! The United Airlines spokesperson Debbie Bridges talks about giving back to the community. She states "Our mission is to communicate United's commitment to community service by supporting programs that improve the communities where our customers and employees live and work." What a statement! United is here to serve the community, not to have the community serve them. There is an important lesson in this for the church.

In the same way United is aware of the community, the church needs to be also. The church world must understand that they are here for the community. Many times it appears to the community that the church world is using them as a means to their own end. I call this..."me Tarzan, you Jane!" We are the boss...you are not. This is not necessarily intentional on the church's part, but we must become more servant oriented. You have to take the low road to get to high places.

CHURCH PASTORS AND LEADERS

I have written this book to church leaders and pastors from all denominations and affiliations. Community transformation is a cause we all can agree upon. And the entire spectrum of denominations from fundamentalists to charismatic/Pentecostals can practice the principles of intelligent fire. Some church cultures stress an intellectual approach to faith, and will respond to the "Intelligent" concept, while others value the experiential aspect of their faith, the "Fire." Without knowing it, many of the church movements and leaders of today's churches have adopted core values that may appear right or religious, but in reality have undermined the church's mission to the community. These values become problematic for crucial issues in community transformation such as unity, relevancy, authenticity, relationships with other community spheres of influence (government, business, etc.), and the full expression of Jesus to the community through local churches. These values create a "disconnect" from the community.

Therefore, I wrote this book with the intention to use theologically sound core values with enough latitude to allow all sides of the church to embrace and develop their own forms of the expression of these core values. For example, the "life and death is more important than right or wrong" concept in Chapter 4 allows the charismatic/Pentecostal to express the core value that is reasonable to him. The same would be true for fundamentalists. I consistently committed to core values or *function* rather than *form*. Most people are tired of and suspicious of the our-form-is-the-only-form type of thinking and writing that is so prevalent in the church at large today.

Intercessors

I also wrote to the tireless and burdened intercessors standing in the gap for loved ones, friends, communities, and countries. Intercessors, here is my challenge: pray in the values! I realize many of you are praying and believing for revival, but as I will explain later in this book, a better strategy would be to pray in the enabling core values that facilitate revival or community transformation. Through prayer, we need to normalize core values that are foreign or "abnormal" to many church leaders. We have to create a culture that enables core values to make community transformation not only possible, but probable! After you read this book, take each core value, wrap it up in prayer, and give it as a gift to your community through prayer.

Business, Government, Educational, and Media Spheres of Influence

I wrote this book also for those who influence secular society. The chapter titled "The Return of the Kings: The Principle of the 11/12 Church" addresses your necessary participation in community transformation and enhancement. The church simply cannot achieve real and tangible community transformation without you.

God has placed churches within communities to cast vision and represent the Kingdom of God. God has placed you also in communities to serve and enhance them with your particular skill set or contributions. If we look at the functional model of the tribes of Israel, only one out of twelve tribes were priests or in full-time ministry. The other eleven were in business, government, education, or other disciplines contributing to the welfare of all the community. What we have learned is that all of the organizational spheres of influence must work together for the benefit of the community. God's vision statement that the earth shall be filled with the glory of the Lord (Hab. 2:14) cannot be fulfilled without you.

The core values that I present in this book will enhance the effectiveness of people working in your organization. These values and principles can be easily adapted to the personnel in your organization. The same is true of individual churches. These core values are universal and may be adapted to enhance the performance of any community organization.

Everyday People

I have also written this book to those who simply want to have a fuller picture of life. If you want to move from unfulfilled potential to fulfilled reality, you will find this book stimulating, yet understandable. These core values develop "world-class" Christians and people with a more complete view of life. You will be enriched, enhanced, and I hope energized. Whether your life is great, good, so-so, or not so good right now, I think this book will add to, not detract from the fulfillment of potential in your life. For those who apply them, intelligent fire core values will shift you from the possibility to the probability of fulfilling your dreams, goals, or aspirations.

The Land of the Long White Cloud—A Land of Intelligent Fire

As I mentioned, I am usually in a different nation every month. As you might imagine, the ideas for intelligent fire come from various countries. The "Kenyan man" story came from Nakuru, Kenya. The "Giving the Church Back to the Community" idea came from a "prophetic" word given by God to Pastor Ken Gott of Sunderland, England. Pastor Mel Mullen of Red Deer, Alberta, Canada, challenged me to develop for his leaders a community transformation series I called *Giving the Church Back to the Community.* Finally, most of the core values and teachings that are in this book came to me while speaking everywhere in New Zealand during the years 2001 and 2002. The Kiwis insisted I keep coming back and give them more intelligent fire. Pastor Brent Douglas of Auckland would not let me get away with anything less than the best. The same is true of hundreds of other Kiwi pastors also.

Therefore, since I dedicate my books to nations, I am dedicating this book to "Aotearoa" or New Zealand, the Land of the Long White Cloud. With great people like the Maori, the Europeans, the Samoans, and everyone else, New Zealand is a nation of people who have and respond to the core values of intelligent fire. New Zealand is truly a land of intelligent fire!

Note: Scripture references throughout this book are quoted from the New American Standard version of the Bible. For the sake of emphasis, in some places I have added italics that do not appear in the original text. References to the Church with a capital "C" refer to the Christian church as a community institution or to the sum total of a community's churches as distinguished from the word "church" referring to a particular local church.

Chapter 1

Divinely Inspired, Specifically Led:

The Principle of Intelligent Fire

In any serious project, the use of undirected human energy is much like lightning itself—it results in merely a brief flash, a lot of noise, and it is occasionally destructive.

—-Grady Daniels

That is quite a concept, is not it? You might be asking, what does he mean by "intelligent fire"? First of all, it will be made real to you in the core value sections of this book. But for now, let me take these two seemingly opposite, even unrelated concepts and put them together for you.

Intelligent fire is where passion and intellect come together, meet together, dance together, and build together. It is the power of the Spirit and the mind of Christ. It is intellect with passion. It is powerful, yet purposeful. It is ordered, intentional, directed, sharp, and passionate. It is passionately strategic. It is having and using the means to arrive at the desired end.

It is a "both/and," not an "either/or." It is where intellect needs fire and fire needs intellect. It is spirit and truth. It is fundamental and charismatic/Pentecostal. It is seeker-sensitive and it is purpose driven. It is the celebration of purpose accomplished by passion and the mind. It is "anointed accountability" enabling the completion of vision. It is more than starting with passion—it is *finishing* with excellence. It is more than academic—it is *strategic*. It is where seeming opposites complete each other, not compete with each other. It is each contributing to and filling up that which is needed in the other to bring both to their full potential. It is where two measures of grace combine to produce grace without measure. It is the job of each part fulfilling its normal, natural, and created function for the accomplishment of purpose. It is a place where the community gets the best of both worlds. It is maximizing resources and minimizing losses. It is the power to get to vision and the vision to get to power for a purpose. It is focus and awareness. It is divinely inspired and specifically led.

It is not being pushed about by wind and waves, but harnessing the wind to propel you to your desired destination. It is not random, unharnessed, or destructive, but consistent, reliable, and purposeful. It is an explosion inside an intentionally designed engine producing horsepower to propel an automobile. It is the power of unleashed gravity-driven water directed through pipes that turn a turbine to produce electricity in a dam. It is the explosion of dynamite strategically placed in a gold mine to open up a vein of gold. It is omnipotence in the form of a baby born in a manger. It is not unrestrained lightning, but constructive electricity flowing through power lines. It is not just sunlight, but sunlight focused through a magnifying glass to produce heat. It is not a mere lump of clay, but clay crafted into a magnificent sculpture by an intelligent and creative artist. Life without intelligence is insanity, but life with intelligence is unlimited!

Fire Is From Venus, Intelligence Is From Mars

Did you ever go to a symphony and hear all the instruments warm up before the concert? Each instrument plays its own tune, in its own key, at its own pace. There is a lot of passion, but it is not directed. When the concert starts and all the music is directed and coordinated by the conductor into an opening tune, that is intelligent fire—goose bump stuff. Intelligent fire takes discord and turns it into harmony and then into one voice. Intelligent fire is architecture—taking the bricks, timber, wiring, roof tiles, and plumbing, and creating a house reflecting the plan of the creator. Intelligent fire is carried by the Nehemiahs of this world for the purpose of repairing broken-down city walls and making them better than before.

Intelligence and fire seem like vastly different concepts, and yet they are symbiotic. Like plants that create oxygen and animals that produce carbon dioxide, the intellect-driven need the "fire" of experience, passion, and Spirit, and the experience-driven need the "fire" of intellect and the mind of Christ. Each has what the other needs, requires, and demands to operate at full potential. Just as the differences between men and women are essential to the survival of the human race, Intelligence must team up with Fire to maximize production.

You probably have heard of Dr. John Gray's book *Men are From Mars, Women are From Venus*. My wife, Becky, says something like, "No, you are both from earth—deal with it!" I would say the same is true regarding the concept of intelligent fire—let's deal with it, constructively, usefully, and joyfully for the sake of the community.

DEEP STRUCTURES

In the context of this book, intelligent fire involves core values that guide and direct essential elements such as a burden to strategically intercede for a city to significantly increase the probability of community transformation and enhancement. It is not just intercession—it is strategic intercession. It is not just a burden, it is the passion of a burden directed in a strategic way. It is assembling, coordinating, and directing all of the elements of community transformation with a focus emanating from the core values of community transformation. Intelligent fire is about adopting core values that enable—not disable—community transformation. Church@Community is the vision; intelligent fire constitutes the values to get to the vision of Church@Community.

I heard a message by Dr. John Maxwell in which he said that core values are deeply held beliefs authentically describing the soul of the leader and the organization. They provide guidelines by which all members are expected to conduct themselves. These values are not open for compromise. Core values are the deep structures in our belief systems that guide our behavior. Core values are internal; behavior is external. Core values are the roots; forms and behaviors are the fruits. Our values drive our behavior. Our core values must change in order for our behaviors to change.

Here are some of my thoughts and what others have said that I think will further develop the concept of values for you. Values are constant. Values are passionate. They touch the heart. They are the essence of the organization. Values are core beliefs that drive the ministry. Remember, while ministry is vision-focused, it is values driven. Some other words we could use for *values* are *precepts*, *choices*, *ideals*, *assumptions*, or *standards*. Values affect decision making, risk taking, goal setting, conflict resolution, problem solving, priorities determination, role clarification, and resource utilization. Values communicate what is important. Values influence overall behavior. Values inspire people to action. Values enable execution of the vision. Values can be the best friend or the worst enemy of the vision. In the context of this book, Church@Community is the vision. The values that enable community transformation are what I call intelligent fire.

Casting vision for community transformation requires both a *vision* change and a *value* change. A vision change without a value change is a recipe for failure. One may get excited with a vision change, but without a value change the vision is defeated before it gets off the ground. Many communities and cities have been captivated by the vision, but after trying it for a short time, have failed, and failed miserably. "It does not work here," is the rhetoric for hundreds of community transformation initiatives all over the world.

We Fall Down, But We Get Up

The problem, as you will see, is not the vision of community transformation, but knowing the core values required to enable community transformation. That is what intelligent fire is all about—revealing, or what I call "revelating," the core value requirements of real, tangible, and lasting community transformation that will unleash its potential. The possibility of community transformation through vision results in the probability of community transformation through enabling core values. My friend, Pastor Bernard Sanders, of Andover, England, says, "Vision sees, core values build." The correct set of core values will "open the gates that the King of glory may come in" (Ps. 24:7, author's paraphrase). Without the revelation of community transformation core values and the integration of those core values in our deep structures, much of our efforts will be a perpetually repeating "groundhog day." Successes will be anomalies and not the rule of thumb. You cannot think 'outside of the box' and live 'inside of the box' and expect great results. Until you reform, you only revisit.

I once heard a story about a frustrated baseball coach having an encounter with a home plate umpire who kept making bad calls. Totally frustrated, he calmly walked out of the dugout, approached the umpire and asked, "Do you get any better, or is this it?" Will community transformation get better? My conviction is we will get better, we are getting better, and the successes will be more and the failures less as we embrace the community transformation core values revealed in this book. However, the revelation has to be internalized in the form of intelligent fire core values. The root is enabling core value; the fruit is community transformation. You cannot change your character just by getting a facelift. In the same way, core values do not necessarily change by getting a vision. The key is to be aware of this principle, so we can use it for the glory of God and the benefit of the community.

WINNING WINESKINS AND WHINING WINESKINS

If you were to ask me what the Holy Spirit is doing up to this point in the twenty-first century, my observation would be that He is moving the church from what I call church-centric to community-centric. Church-centric is when, as far as church people are concerned, the community exists for the church's benefit. Community-centric is when, as far as church people are concerned, the church exists for the community's benefit. Gary Carnahan, my friend and a former board member of NATIONStrategy, says that the Holy Spirit is very quickly reforming the church to make insider information into outsider information. These "reformed" churches and Christians transform communities through enabling relevant ministry emanating from appropriate enabling intelligent fire core values. Transformed churches that have gone through the process of reformation for community transformation will be winning the unchurched, making disciples and influencing their part of the community. They will be redemptively relevant for the sake of the community.

Remember what Jesus said in Mark 2:22, "No one puts new wine into old wineskins; otherwise the wine will burst the skins, and the wine is lost and the skins as well; but one puts new wine into fresh wineskins."

In other words, there is no new wine until there is a new wineskin. In the "wine" of community transformation, the church has to be transformed to produce community transformation. Church transformation produces community transformation. If we can make the church a little better, we can make the community a lot better. Christian-and-church-transformation opens up opportunities into other spheres of influence in the community such as business, government, education, and media for the benefit of the community. Real community transformation is about Christians in church, business, government, education, and media who have real and tangible influence in the community again. It is community transformers taking Jesus in a real and tangible way into their part of their world or sphere of influence for the betterment of the community.

Unfortunately, many church-centric churches want the "wine" of revival their way, in their church, and in their time. Such will be the case of whining churches. Because of their church-centric orientation most of these churches—intentionally or unintentionally—will be on the outside of community transformation looking in, rather than on the inside of community transformation looking out. As a result, these types of churches most often will be critical, arguing over theology, methodology, or personality. Many will get the "Gideon's 300" syndrome—"we are right and the community-centric churches are wrong"—but in reality, there is no new wine without a new wineskin.

Good, Good, Good . . . Good Vibrations

A very contemporary word in the Spanish language is *ondas*. The word means waves or vibes. What are the vibes of community transformation? What does community transformation look like and feel like? What do we mean by community transformation? Is it revival or something greater? Does it last or is it seasonal? Is it inside the church walls reflecting church values, or is it outside those walls, reflected in service within and to the community for the betterment of all in the community? Does everyone go to church when the community is transformed?

First of all, real and tangible community transformation is just that—real and tangible! It is not spiritual wishful thinking or a loud enthusiastic declaration, but incarnated reality. It is much more than revival or something that happens inside the church walls. It is much more than just everyone in the community going to church. It is much more than miracles or signs and wonders.

There is a difference between revival and reformation. I once heard a speaker on apostolic issues say that revival is repainting an old building while reformation is building a new building. Revival is the recovery of breath from a long run while reformation is a whole set of lungs. Revival is awakening a sleeping church while reformation is the dismantling of secular ways, and replacing them with Christian core values. That is quite a difference.

I am not talking about revival in the church's terms or for a validation of a favorite spiritual emphasis or theme. I am not speaking of talking or praying God into doing it *our* way. I am talking about finding out what God is doing, then doing it His way. Look at this verse:

> Seek the welfare of the city where I have sent you into exile, and pray to the Lord on its behalf; for in its welfare you will have welfare.
>
> —Jeremiah 29:7

Community transformation is where the church is relevant, accepting, and inclusive. It is where the church is life-giving, not law-giving. It is where the church, business, government, education, and media adopt Christian core values because these values bring the people of the community up to their full potential. It is where wisdom is building the city. It is where each of the spheres of influence in the community know they exist for the benefit of the community. It is where the church and the people in the church have real influence once again in all spheres of the surrounding community.

While everyone may not go to church, everyone knows the benefits and blessings of living in the city and that God did it. It is Proverbs 11:10–11, "When it goes well with the righteous, the city rejoices" and "By the blessing of the upright a city is exalted." It is where the unchurched are not demonized or marginalized, but loved. The church and Christians "stop in the name of love" before they break God's heart and the community's heart. It is where even the land is affected and may even produce better harvests. It is where we make the community a better place for all, and all the inhabitants of the community benefit.

Will we ever totally get there? Maybe, maybe not, but we can greatly improve the church and our community by learning how to become more community-centric. What causes that kind of shift? The core values that drive our behavior. The very values we will explore in this book.

Lost Opportunities

Through the years I have heard intercessors praying prayers similar to the following: "Oh, Lord, shake the heavens! Bring a revival! Bring all the people into the churches!" Do you realize God answered their prayers?

After the horrifying events of September 11, 2001 in New York City and Washington DC, an amazing phenomenon occurred in the United States. For two or three months, people filled churches throughout the country. However, after a few months many of those who flooded into the churches flooded back out of the churches. I heard many church leaders and church people say something to the effect of, "Oh, the crisis brought them in, but they were not serious or they would have stayed—they just returned to their secular ways."

I am sure some of that is true, but let's ask ourselves a question, "What did they find when they came to church? Was church relevant to them? Were church people aware and accepting? Did we give up our seats for someone else? When they stepped into church, what culture did they find or experience—a 1950s culture or a 2000+ culture? Was it *Leave it to Beaver* or *Third Rock From the Sun*? Did the pastor speak a relevant, life-giving message or was it religious or something that only churched people could understand?

I think you get the message. The truth is that most churches were not prepared, were not redemptively relevant, were not even culturally connected or aware of many of these wonderful people looking for real answers given in a relatable way. The truth is, almost one of every two churches in America did not even address the 9/11 issue. Most just kept on doing their series on Ephesians, Genesis, types and shadows, or whatever. Noted church researcher, George Barna, published the following research results on the 9/11 issue and American culture in the September 3, 2002 issue of his newsletter, the *Barna Update*:

> One reason why there may not be greater evidence of faith impact is because barely half of the nation's churches acknowledged or addressed the attacks in any way during the past year, according to church attenders. Among people who attend Christian churches, 41 percent said their church has done nothing at all since last September to address the attacks or their implications
>
> Just as unexpected were the low percentages of churches that have engaged in particular types of response. For example, only one out of four adults who attend a Christian church (23 percent) said their church had engaged in prayer specific to the attacks; just one out of every six (16 percent) said their church had provided sermons or other teaching related to the attacks; and only one out of ten (10 percent) said their church had provided special services related to the attacks.[1]

What causes that kind of behavior? Deeply embedded church-centric core values that are incongruent with community transformation. The result was missed opportunities. It is interesting that most churches hope they will grow, but the title of author Rick Page's book captures a great truth: *Hope Is Not a Strategy*.[2] What about the churches that were relevant, aware and "in the name of love" stopped being church-centric and had an epiphany of being community-centric and actually changed? I am happy to report that in many of them these crises-driven Americans not only come to church, but stay in church!

That is what community transformation is all about. These churches are seeing and feeling the vibes. What changed the way they conducted church by adopting life-giving community transforming core values? These churches have learned that the church is a community within a community, populated by people of the community for the benefit of the community. They are thinking and acting strategically for the benefit of the community.

What Is Real Revival Like?

If you want to know what a real in-gathering of people is like, just ask many Argentine pastors from the late 1980s. After the Falkland Islands war, the country of Argentina was decimated. The nation had suffered a terrible defeat by the English in this war. The citizens of the country lost their military hope, economic hope (the country was bankrupt), political hope, and even religious hope. As a result, many of the hopeless turned to the Living Hope. Argentines flooded to evangelical churches all over Argentina. The church of one friend of mine, a pastor in Buenos Aires, had a seating capacity of more than three thousand and conducted seven services per day for seven days a week. Do you know how many ushers that takes? How about childcare or janitors? How about the worship team members? How do you keep that preaching schedule up? This particular pastor kept up that schedule for years, and his church probably benefited more than any other church in Argentina for years.

Why did God allow them to experience such a phenomenon? His core values opened the door that the King of Glory could come in!

This pastor created a "silo" that could hold the "wheat" of harvest. He had a wineskin that could hold the wine of harvest with no leaks. He had a winning wineskin, not a whining wineskin.

How about you and I? Are we ready? What if a crisis like that occurred in your country? Would the seekers, unchurched, lost, unbelievers, or whatever you prefer to call them be able to find a place in your church and stay? Could God entrust your church with His harvest?

Investing Time in the Community

You do not spend time in the community, you invest time. By reading this book, you are investing time that will produce and enhance the community-transformation results you desire. Investments are expected to produce results over the long term.

In the next chapter, we will take a look at Nehemiah's recipe for community transformation and further develop the concept of Church@Community for your benefit, your church's or business's benefit, and especially your community's benefit. It is a great investment that is divinely inspired and specifically led.

Chapter 2

Recipes and Rebuilding Walls:

The Principle of Recipe

A measure of grace or grace without measure?

HAVE YOU EVER baked a cake? Have you made a pie or perhaps, macaroni and cheese? Prepackaged ground-beef seasonings, canned soups, cake mixes, and even (perish the thought) homemade meals are combinations of ingredients, not simply one ingredient. Yes, fruits, meat and, so on may be eaten individually, but frankly, I like key lime pie more than a lime by itself, and apple pie more than an apple. Life is about ingredients, a convergence of necessary components that comprise a recipe, a person, a business, or a church. And a healthy diet consists of seven food families. Are you hungry yet?

One Cannot Multiply

Have you ever considered that God enjoys, even demands, diversity—a combination of ingredients, components, persons, or organizations that added together form something wonderful and more complex? You might say that together they birth something bigger than themselves. Simply said, one cannot multiply. Let's consider several spiritual examples: the Trinity (Father, Son, and Holy Spirit), Adam and Eve, priests and kings, the components of the body of Christ (Rom. 12), the offices of the church (Eph. 4), and the ministries of the Holy Spirit (1 Cor. 12). We repeatedly see the truth of Genesis 2:18, "It is not good for the man [or things] to be alone."

From a natural perspective, the same principle holds true. A garden is a *collection* of vegetables; a meal is a *collection* of foods; an organization is a *collection* of people, talents, and resources; even the human race is a *collection* of skin tones, cultures, languages, and perspectives.

Amoeba or Human?

An amoeba is a one-celled organism that has one agenda, itself! It is simple, unaware of any other organism unless it is dinner or has to do with its comfort. Amoebas respond to stimuli and have no power to change anything. They are typical of the lowest form of life—one-celled, one-dimensional, independent and possessing very little awareness of anything other than "their world." They remind me of Judges 21:25: "Everyone did that which was right in his own eyes." Every amoeba does that which is right in its own eyes. That is normal and that is expected—for a one-celled organism.

The higher forms of life are multi-dimensional. Different cells or entities work together for the betterment of all—many times even putting other cells' agendas ahead of their own. They are "others-aware," "others-sensitive" and corporate. Usually they are proactive and can adapt to different environments or stimuli. They have more power because there are more of them. Yes, life is more complex, but far more worth it.

My point is that real life and real answers come from combinations of entities and resources working together create solutions that are more effective in solving real problems. Remember this concept—I will be using it throughout this book. It is a step to a bigger world. I call it "Welcome to a Bigger World—You have Got Mail!"

Community Transformation: The Amoeba or Human Paradigm?

This book is especially for those who want to see their community transformed and enhanced. They realize that most communities, like those in Nehemiah's time, have walls that are broken down and in disrepair (Neh. 1:3). They realize that church, business, government, education, and media/entertainment spheres of influence exist for the sake of the community and not vice versa. These individuals realize that if we can make the church a little better, we can make the community a lot better. Their hearts beat with the passion of giving the church back to the community. They intuitively know that the church is a community with a cause that is the community.

I cannot over-emphasize that the church cannot do it alone. We need the government, the businesses, the educational systems, and so on all working together for the sake of the community—a cause higher than each of these entities' limited spheres, specialties, or causes. The church represents the spiritual side of life, and without Christ life is bleak indeed. Each sphere of influence (church, business, government, education, or media) has its own contributions to make, but each must respect and honor the others' contributions. Each of these spheres of influence has mutually exclusive powers, yet each is not complete without the others. They must be inclusive, not exclusive. Without the visionary or "priestly" role of the church, all of society suffers. The other spheres need to respect and consider the role of the church. The political realm needs the church, business needs the church, education needs the church, and media needs the church. Conversely, the church needs government, government is of God (Rom. 13:1). The church needs business; there needs to be provision for the vision. And the church needs education; Daniel was not afraid of Babylon's universities, and he progressed from uneducated to educated for the purpose of relating to the Babylonians redemptively.

I warned you this book would be reformational! For 1,700 years, the question has been "Will the church be a one-celled amoeba or can we join together with other God-ordained governmental spheres for the sake of Christ's vision of community transformation?" At this point in history, the kingdom of God has to do with the church positively influencing all areas of society with godly core values while honoring and allowing each governmental sphere to operate within its God-given jurisdiction. The church exists to honor the "glory" of each governmental sphere (1 Pet. 2:17), while maintaining her jurisdiction through relationship and influence. The church must to have contact and communication without contamination for the sake of the community. It is not about the church, it is about the community.

If we are to significantly transform the community, we must use a larger wineskin, a strategic way of thinking and a new way of seeing things. It will take intelligent fire.

It Takes a Nehemiah to Rebuild a Jerusalem

For those who do not know the background of Nehemiah, I will briefly set the stage. At the time Nehemiah was written, most of the nation of Israel was in captivity in a place called Babylon. When the Babylonians attacked Israel, they attacked the capital city of Jerusalem. After the captives were taken, the temple, the city, and the city gates were utterly destroyed. One might say the temple held the heart of Jerusalem, the city's buildings comprised the soul of Jerusalem, and the gates represented the body of Jerusalem.

Earlier, the prophet Daniel had prophesied that Israel's disobedience in turning away from God to worship other gods and idols would be punished by a seventy year captivity in Babylon. Near the end of the seventy years, the king of Babylon's cupbearer heard that Jerusalem's walls were burned, torn down, and in total disrepair. The cupbearer's name was Nehemiah. His name means "breath of God" or "comfort from God" and symbolizes the edifying nature of the Holy Spirit. Nehemiah was an apostolic leader in the sense that he had a *building ministry* and was interested in the city returning to its *full, original, normal, and natural state*. With great prayer, anguish of heart, and courage, Nehemiah sought the king's permission to go to Jerusalem and rebuild the gates of the city. To his amazement, the king gave him permission to go on this mission.

When Nehemiah arrived in Jerusalem, his greatest fears were confirmed—the city was in shambles. *The community needed to be transformed.*

What happened next was "revelationary" and revolutionary. It took a *revelation* to create a positive *revolution* for the city.

God gave Nehemiah a strategy for rebuilding the city, for a tangible and lasting transformation. The strategy was like a "recipe" with four vital ingredients that produced a real community transformation.

Nehemiah's Recipe for Community Transformation

Before God sent Nehemiah to rebuild the walls, He sent Zerubbabel to rebuild the temple. Zerubabbel is a type of rebuilder of the church, whereas Nehemiah is a type of community transformer or wall builder—one who has a heart for the community, not just the church.

Let's look at these four ingredients which *all together* result in real and tangible community transformation. As in a cake mix made up of four ingredients, *no single ingredient is the cake.* All are equally essential, but none will produce the end result without the others. If one component is missing, we will have a defective, incomplete cake.

Ingredient #1: A Burdened Heart

> When I heard these words, I sat down and wept and mourned for days; and I was fasting and praying before the God of heaven.
>
> —Nehemiah 1:4

Please notice the statement "...and I wept...for days." Do you see that? God gave Nehemiah a heart for Jerusalem! God gave Nehemiah a deep concern or burden for the state of the community. This is what God has used George Otis Jr. and the "Transformation" videos for.[2] I have talked with George and his heart is burdened for cities and nations. He has a burdened heart for the state of cities locally, nationally and internationally.

That is the main message that comes across through the Transformation videos. It is what George calls the "desperation factor." His primary message is about getting desperate for revival, reaching the city, or what he calls "Community Transformation." Desperation and a desire for change are absolutely essential for reaching a community with the message of Christ. George and The Sentinel Group have done well in getting this first "ingredient" or "burdened heart factor" into the mainstream of Christianity.

I once asked the Lord what our church needed to reach the community and where to start. As I listened in prayer, I heard in my mind the words "deep concern." I have never forgotten that phrase—get a deep concern for the unchurched, and a deep concern for the community! Remember, where there is no love for the community, there is no influence in the community. Do you realize that evangelism programs without a deep concern are like forms without substance, shadows without light? The process of community transformation *starts from the heart and ends in the art.* You cannot have the art without the heart. Community transformation has more to do with *formation* than *information.*

The burdened heart, or deep concern, is the fuel that fires the engine of real and tangible community transformation. It is the burdened heart that enables you to become "all things to all men, so that I may by all means save some" (1 Cor. 9:22). It is the burdened heart that gets you past the barriers of religious forms, sectarianism, governmental hatred and suspicion, demonizing business and money to realizing the community is not here for you, but you are here for the community. Without a burdened heart, you might adopt the art of Willow Creek or Saddleback Community without the *heart* of Willow Creek or Saddleback Community. In my opinion, Bill Hybels and Rick Warren have adopted their forms *because of a burdened heart for the community. They have a passion for the community.*

Here is an example called "A Martyr's Prayer" that shows passion from a burdened heart:

> I am part of the fellowship of the unashamed. I have the Holy Spirit power. The die has been cast. I have stepped over the line. The decision has been made—I am a disciple of His. I will not look back, let up, slow down, back away, or be still. My past is redeemed, my present makes sense, my future is secure. I am finished and done with low living, sight walking, smooth knees, colorless dreams, famed visions, worldly talking, cheap giving, and dwarfed goals. I no longer need preeminence, position, promotions, plaudits, or popularity. I do not have to be right, first, tops, recognized, praised, regarded, or rewarded. I now live by faith, lean in His presence, walk by patience, am uplifted by prayer, and I labor with power. My face is set, my gait is fast, my goal is heaven. My road is narrow, my way rough, my companions are few, my Guide reliable, and my mission clear. I cannot be bought, compromised, detoured, lured away, turned back, deluded, or delayed. I will not flinch in the face of sacrifice, hesitate in the presence of the enemy, pander at the pool of popularity, or meander in the maze of mediocrity. I will not give up, shut up, or let up, until I have stayed up, stored up, prayed up, paid up, and preached up for the cause of Christ. I am a disciple of Jesus. I must go until He comes, give until I drop, preach until all know, and work until He stops me. And, when he comes for His own, He will have no problem recognizing me…my banner will be clear. (Written by a young pastor in Zimbabwe before being martyred for his faith in Christ.)[2]

I think that is all that needs to be said.

How do you get a burdened heart? We will address that in a later chapter, but now let's look at the next ingredient.

Ingredient #2: Bended Knee

> Let Thine ear now be attentive and Thine eyes open to hear the prayer of Thy servant which I am praying before Thee now, day and night, on behalf of the sons of Israel Thy servants, confessing the sins of the sons of Israel which we have sinned against Thee; I and my father's house have sinned.
>
> —Nehemiah 1:6

Look at the tenor of this verse. After his heart became burdened, Nehemiah went to God in prayer. All kinds of prayer are represented in this verse, but especially that which John Dawson calls "identificational repentance." Identificational repentance, or "IR," is the type of prayer that says, "I and my fathers have sinned." Notice that Nehemiah's burdened heart for the city caused him to identify with past sins of his people, again demonstrating the necessity of a burdened heart. God looks at the heart, and even prayer and IR require a burdened heart. IR meetings without a revelation or burden become just another form of godliness with little power.

On the contrary, prayer with a burdened heart, and especially prayers of repentance for current and past sins, can greatly influence a city's or nation's destiny. That is the message of John Dawson's wonderful book, *Healing America's Wounds*. Many revelatory books on prayer have been written recently. Some of the authors I would suggest are Cindy Jacobs, Dutch Sheets, Dr. C. Peter Wagner, and Ed Silvoso. Indeed, the prayer movement across the world is increasing dramatically.

THE GREATER THE PRAYER, THE GREATER THE POWER

Why is prayer a necessary ingredient in Nehemiah's recipe? The answer is simple—prayer releases spiritual power; the greater the prayer, the greater the power. Prayer links the burdened heart to strategic thinking and action. Prayer connects the heart to the mind and hands. Someone once said that ministry is doing what God just said in a prayer. Jesus was able go through Calvary because he had prayed at Gethsemane.

During my pastorate of twenty-two years in the metro-Phoenix area, my constituency often asked me one question: "Why was there so much power in the books of Acts?" I would take them to the book of Acts and show them these verses:

> These all with one mind were continually devoting themselves to *prayer*.
>
> —ACTS 1:14, EMPHASIS ADDED

And they were continually devoting themselves to the apostles' teaching and to fellowship, to the breaking of bread and to *prayer*.

—Acts 2:42

Now Peter and John were going up to the temple at the ninth hour, *the hour of prayer*.

—Acts 3:1

And when they had prayed, the place where they had gathered together was shaken, and they were all filled with the Holy Spirit, and began to speak the word of God with boldness.

—Acts 4:31

And at the hands of the apostles many signs and wonders were taking place among the people; and they *were all with one accord* in Solomon's portico.

—Acts 5:12

But we will devote ourselves to prayer, and to the ministry of the word.

—Acts 6:4

And falling on his knees, he cried out [*prayed*] with a loud voice, "Lord, do not hold this sin against them!" And having said this, he fell asleep.

—Acts 7:60

Now when the apostles in Jerusalem heard that Samaria had received the word of God, they sent them Peter and John, *who came down and prayed for them,* that they might receive the Holy Spirit...Then they began laying their hands on them, and they were receiving the Holy Spirit.

—Acts 8:14–15, 17

But Peter sent them all out and knelt down *and prayed*, and turning to the body, he said, "Tabitha, arise." And she opened her eyes, and when she saw Peter, she sat up.

—Acts 9:40

> And Cornelius said, "Four days ago to this hour, *I was praying* in my house during the ninth hour; and behold, a man stood before me in shining garments, and he said, "Cornelius, *your prayer* has been heard and your alms have been remembered before God.'"
>
> —Acts 10:30–31

> *I was in the city of Joppa praying*; and in a trance I saw a vision, an object coming down like a great sheet lowered by four corners from the sky; and it came right down to me.
>
> —Acts 11:5

> So Peter was kept in the prison, *but prayer for him was being made fervently by the church to God.*
>
> —Acts 12:5

> And while they were ministering to the Lord and fasting, the Holy Spirit said, "Set apart for Me Barnabas and Saul for the work to which I have called them." Then, *when they had fasted and prayed and laid their hands on them*, they sent them away.
>
> —Acts 13:2–3

> And when they had appointed elders for them in every church, *having prayed with fasting*, they commended them to the Lord in whom they had believed.
>
> —Acts 14:23

Do you see the common denominator in all these verses? *Prayer* is one of the reasons there is so much power in the book of Acts. In Chapter 1, the early church continually prayed; in Chapter 2, they broke bread and prayed; in Chapter 3, Peter was on the way to a prayer meeting when he said, "Silver and gold have I none…in the name of Jesus, walk." In Chapter 4, the church did not have an earthquake, they had a prayer quake. In Chapter 5, they were all with one accord in Solomon's portico; in Chapter 6, they devoted themselves to prayer and living out the Word. In Chapter 7, while Stephen was being stoned, he prayed the same prayer as Jesus—"Father, forgive them." In Chapter 8, the Samaritans received the Holy Spirit *following prayer*; in Chapter 9, Dorcas was raised from the dead *following prayer*; in Chapter 10, the

Samaritans received the Holy Spirit *following prayer*; in Chapter 11, Peter recalled the great white sheet vision. When did he receive it? At the hour of prayer! In Chapter 12, Peter was in jail. What did they do? They had a prayer meeting! In Chapter 13, the first apostles and missionaries were sent out *following prayer*. In Chapter 14, the first elders were picked out from among the church *after prayer*. And when you choose an elder, you had better pray!

Prayer was a powerful component in the book of Acts, prayer was a powerful component in Nehemiah's time, and prayer is a powerful component or ingredient in community transformation today. It is part of the recipe—a very important part. Prayer alone, however, is usually not "the" factor, but it is an important factor in real, tangible, and lasting community transformation. The same is true of a burdened heart. In most cases, these two ingredients, when added to the next two ingredients of our recipe, greatly increase the probability of community transformation. This book is about moving from the *possibility* of community transformation to the *probability* of community transformation by following a model "recipe" that utilizes *all the ingredients* necessary to "bake the cake."

Intelligent Fire

What I call the next two ingredients in Nehemiah's recipe for rebuilding the walls of the city constitute intelligent fire—keys to real, tangible, and lasting community transformation.

The final two ingredients are strategic in increasing the *success* and *probability* of community transformation. As I noted earlier, much significant work and "ingredient recovery" has been done in the areas of the burdened heart and bended knee. A strong revelation has been producing a consistent and reliable burden for our cities and intercession for our cities. This is what I call "passionate fire." But now, to our passionate fire we need to add intelligent fire, which encompasses the last two ingredients of our recipe. Indeed, passionate fire without intelligent fire is incomplete, just as intelligent fire without passionate fire is incomplete.

Many of us are aware of passionate fire. Let's add some intelligent fire to our arsenal. I want us to get all the tools in the toolbox! So the rest of this book will concentrate on the last two ingredients of the recipe for community transformation. These last two ingredients enable us to have Church@Community.

Ingredient #3: A Clear Mind

> And I arose in the night, I and a few men with me. I did not tell anyone *what my God was putting into my mind to do for Jerusalem* and there was no animal with me except the animal on which I was riding.
>
> —Nehemiah 2:12

Mind. That word is a blessing to some and a stumbling block to others. In my twenty-eight years as a Christian, I have been in both sides of the church. To the fundamentalist, the mind is equated with right theology and generally conservative ways of thinking. Truth, as their minds perceive it, is to be guarded at all costs, even at the expense of fragmenting relationships or criticism of "wrong theologies." The core value of these Christians is "being right." This is what sometimes turns into truth decay. In the name of rightly dividing the Word, many "defenders of the truth" have wrongly divided the church. The result is endless arguments and theological micromanaging while the community looks at this and says, "Wazzup with them?"

On the other hand, Pentecostal/charismatics often sacrifice the mind on the altar of experience. Many of these well-meaning Christians have a knee-jerk reaction to anything cerebral or intentional. They replace the mind with "the Spirit," which many times, unfortunately, is a license to do just about anything. Logic, planning, learning, and strategic thinking are marginalized while the community looks at this and says, "Wazzup with them?" As they say, "I have been there, done that, got the t-shirt—on both sides."

I have looked at the church from both sides, and guess what? There are great aspects on both sides. I am a *Bapticostal*! Jesus said "worship the Father in spirit and truth" (John 4:23, author's paraphrase). We can have both *passionate fire* and *intelligent fire*! It is not an either/or proposition—it is a both/and! Both passionate fire *and* intelligent fire are required to increase the intensity and frequency of real, tangible, and lasting community transformation.

A Clear Mind Is a Strategic Mind

When Nehemiah said, "I did not tell anyone what God was putting into my mind to do for Jerusalem" (Neh. 2:12), he was referring to a strategy for repairing the walls of the city. It was not about doctrine, theology, or apologetics—it was about strategic thinking for a purpose. What was the purpose? To repair the walls of the city. He had the "mind of Christ" (1 Cor. 2:16) concerning a strategic plan to repair the walls. One family would repair one section of wall, another family a different section, this place would need an extra armament, and so on. (See Nehemiah 3.) Nehemiah was a builder, a repairer of the breach for the sake of the community. To use Pastor Rick Warren's vernacular, Nehemiah was purpose-driven. Everything Nehemiah did had a plan which fit into a strategy for quickly rebuilding the walls for everyone's benefit—even the "unbelievers."

This is a very necessary ingredient in making the "cake" of city transformation. Remember, *prayer* connects the heart to the *mind* for a purpose! Great leaders such as Pastor Rick Warren, Pastor Bill Hybels, Dr. John Maxwell, and others have captured the concept of the "clear mind." They have given us the powerful revelation of being a *meaningful specific* rather than a *working generality*. Nehemiah was "spirit-led" and "purpose driven." He had a convergence of the Holy Spirit and the mind of Christ. He could see the big picture, determine the issues, communicate them in a way that all could understand, and he was not afraid to work with his people.

Most of today's successful churches have leaders who realize they must be strategic for the sake of the community. Everything they do is for a purpose. These church leaders understand the principles of strategic thinking and the necessity of the convergence of many components, not just one component. As a result, the churches they lead are multi-dimensional, not one-dimensional. They think strategically, they have a clear mind with a clear goal for the sake of the community. This is what I call intelligent fire! They have the "fire" of excellence and going beyond what is expected because they can do no less.

We will explore the concept of intelligent fire more in Chapter 5. Let's go on to the fourth ingredient—another strategic component of intelligent fire.

INGREDIENT #4: CALLOUSED HANDS

> And I told them how the hand of my God had been favorable to me, and also about the king's words which he had spoken to me. Then they said, "Let us arise and build." *So they put their hands to the good work.*
>
> —NEHEMIAH 2:18

Let me share with you a truth. I created this saying while I was waxing eloquent to a group of singles one Wednesday evening: impression without expression leads to depression! Do you realize Nehemiah could have a burdened heart, could have prayed all day and even had a strategy to rebuild the walls, but ultimately all these ingredients had to become real and tangible action or work? Somebody ultimately had to do God's plan, not just proclaim God's plan. Somebody had to "put their hands to the good work." As we know, faith without works is dead. (see James 2:17.)

Jesus knew the reality of "calloused hands." As Luke 10:2 says:

> And He was saying to them, "The harvest is plentiful, but the laborers are few; therefore beseech the Lord of the harvest to send out laborers into His harvest."

Jesus was telling His intercessors to pray for harvesters. A harvest can be harvested only by a harvester, or someone who *works*! Prayer can ripen a harvest, but only a harvester can harvest a harvest. To use another illustration, fish do not make a regular habit of jumping into the boat—it takes a fisherman! Fishermen fish, they incarnate, they work, and they harvest! Unfortunately, many Christians today make a declaration, pray a prayer, or "bind and loose" in their minds, hoping that a miracle will happen. They want to receive a miracle without work, catch a fish without fishing, or harvest a harvest without using a sickle. While fish may occasionally jump into a boat, that is the exception, not the rule of thumb. God has called us to do more than live off winnings from spiritual lotteries.

Living life by the exception greatly reduces our potential effectiveness. Standing in a boat in the ocean opens up the possibility of catching a fish, but using a fishing pole with the right bait and dropping the bait into the water moves us from possibility to probability. in the community transformation context, harvesters doing the work of the harvest greatly increase their effectiveness when coupled with a burdened heart, a bended knee, and a clear mind. Calloused hands are the expression of a burdened heart, a bended knee, and a clear mind. Without calloused hands, we have impression without expression that leads to depression, or unfulfilled potential. The *impression* of passionate fire has to "incarnate" in the *expression* of intelligent fire—a clear mind *and* calloused hands.

We will return to the concept of calloused hands in the chapter called "Incarnationally Challenged—The Principle of The Tiger's Head, The Mouse's Tail.

So there you have it—a convergence of ingredients that together produce something that none of them alone could produce! It is Welcome to a Bigger World—You have Got Mail! It is moving beyond the amoeba stage and developing into a sophisticated, effective, thinking organism with purpose and awareness.

Nehemiah was someone who had the best of both worlds, and it transformed his community. He was not one dimensional, pushing his favorite theme to the detriment of the city. He understood that each of the four ingredients has a "measure of grace," but when all four were added together, they produced a "grace without measure."

The Chart Attack

This first chapter concludes with a chart of these four ingredients and how they work together.

Each ingredient has a "measure of grace."

This chart represents the mind of Christ, honoring all the ingredients, valuing all the ingredients, and integrating all the ingredients

<table>
<tr><td>Ingredients of Nehemiah</td><td>Mark 12:30
Love the Lord</td><td>Attribute</td><td rowspan="3">Passionate Fire</td><td rowspan="5">Favor with God

“Word became Flesh”

Favor with Man</td><td rowspan="5">Christ through the church to the community</td></tr>
<tr><td>1) Burdened Heart (Neh. 1:4)</td><td>Heart</td><td rowspan="2">1) Revelation
2) Prophetic
3) Priestly
4) Initiation
5) Spiritual
6) Spirit</td></tr>
<tr><td>2) Bended Knees (Neh. 1:6)</td><td>Soul</td></tr>
<tr><td>3) Clear Mind (Neh. 2:12)</td><td>Mind</td><td rowspan="2">1)Reality
2) Apostolic
3)Kingly
4)Completion
5) Natural
6) Truth</td><td rowspan="2">Intelligent Fire</td></tr>
<tr><td>4) Calloused Hands (Neh. 2:18)</td><td>Strength</td></tr>
</table>

for a purpose—real, tangible, and lasting community transformation. Each ingredient alone does not carry the weight or grace for a permanent shift in the community. The most each ingredient can cause individually is a temporary shift in the community. This is why many of the early attempts at community transformation were partially successful and usually for a short time. Most were based on one or perhaps two ingredients. That is like calling the flour and eggs the cake! However, we are getting better, growing in the revelation and becoming aware of a much bigger picture. We are building the airplane while it is flying.

In the next chapter we will start with defining the Five Mutually Exclusive Spheres of Influence that God has created to bring a community or city to its full potential. We will look at how communities work best. We will depart from the church only way of thinking, or what I call church-centric, to a community way of thinking, or what I call community-centric. We will look at strategic alliances, mutual collaborations, and supporting casts for the sake of the community. The next chapter is about an old friend, Humpty Dumpty. He represents a picture, a vision, an engineering feat designed by God to bring a city to fullness. He is a picture of what a city looks like when it is done, whole, or complete. If we are concerned about community transformation, we had better know how a community works best.

Chapter 3

The Fall and Rise of Humpty Dumpty:

The Principle of Strategic Alliances, Mutual Collaborations, and Supporting Casts

Humpty Dumpty sat on a wall
Humpty Dumpty had a great fall
All the king's horses and all the king's men
Could not put Humpty back together again.

Who Was Humpty Dumpty?

Humpty Dumpty was a colloquial term used in fifteenth century England to describe someone who was fat or obese—giving rise to lots of theories pertaining to the identity of Humpty Dumpty. However, in this case the question should be not who was Humpty Dumpty but what was Humpty Dumpty? Humpty Dumpty was in fact an unusually large cannon that was mounted on the protective wall of St. Mary's Wall Church in Colchester, England. It was intended to protect the Parliamentarian stronghold of Colchester, which was temporarily in control of the Royalists during the period of English history described as the English Civil War (1642–1649). A shot from a Parliamentary cannon succeeded in damaging the wall underneath Humpty Dumpty causing the cannon to fall to the ground. The Royalists, "all the King's men," attempted to raise Humpty Dumpty on to another part of the wall, but even with the help of "all the King's horses" failed in their task and Colchester fell to the Parliamentarians after a siege lasting eleven weeks.

Did you ever wonder why all the king's horses and all the king's men could not put Humpty Dumpty back together again? Perhaps it is because they never asked the King who made the king!

Everywhere I go in the world, people have heard the nursery rhyme of "Humpty Dumpty." In Singapore, Norway, South Africa, or the Pacific Islands, Humpty Dumpty is the famous "egg" who had a fall. His tragic end is that he could not be put back together again. He went from whole to fragmented, and from peace to pieces. His destiny was wasted. He was doomed to underachievement, never even coming close to the potential he had as a "whole" Humpty Dumpty.

Humpty exemplifies the pathos of starting strong and finishing weak. Somehow this little four-line rhyme has been indelibly etched into most people's minds throughout the world. Its story catches us by surprise and leaves lots of questions unanswered. Ultimately, I think it causes us to ask questions. Who was Humpty Dumpty? Why was he sitting on the wall? How did he fall? Was he pushed? Did he lose his balance? Who are the king's horses? Who are the king's men? Finally, was this fall really a life-ending event, or were the king's horses and men not skillful enough? It sounds to me like they tried but could not quite fix poor Humpty. There is a lesson to be learned here, but what is it?

Lots of questions and very few answers. The simple children's rhyme leaves us hanging, conjecturing, and wanting this fate not to happen to us. No one wants to end up fragmented, abandoned, and doomed to underachievement and unfulfilled potential.

A City Whose Architect and Builder Is God

In December 2002, I began to seek God's wisdom regarding how He designs a city or community in the natural. I was impressed with Hebrews 11:10, 16:

> For he was looking for the city which has foundations, whose architect and builder is God...But as it is, they desire a better country, that is a heavenly one. Therefore God is not ashamed to be called their God; for He has prepared a city for them.

I figured there had to be a way cities and communities were designed by God "...on earth as it is in heaven" (Matt. 6:10). How does God see communities and cities? How do communities work best? What are the spheres of influence in cities and communities? What and who are the pillars in the foundation of a city here on earth? What does it take to transform a city from underachieving to a city that is doing well for its inhabitants? What does a city whose architect and builder is God look like? Why are there so many problems in our communities? Why are our communities underachieving in most all areas? What is the Church's role in the community? Is the Church the only influencer in a community?

As I sought the answers to these questions in the Bible, in thought and in prayer, I was impressed by the Lord that our communities and cities are like Humpty Dumpty. Our communities have had a great fall. Our communities are fragmented. The walls of most cities are broken down with large gaping holes like Jerusalem Nehemiah's time.

The key spheres of influence God has placed in each city to help that city be all that it can be are separated from each other. The "king's horses" and the "king's men" in a community cannot put the community back together again in this separated, fragmented state.

Can Humpty Dumpty be reconstructed and resurrected? My answer is yes, if we will work together and ask the King. After all, God is the Architect and the Builder of great cities.

How Communities Work Best

If we really want to see communities transformed God's way, we must look at the blueprint of cities the way God made them. I will use layman's terms and the metaphor of Humpty Dumpty to illustrate five spheres of influence in every city and community and how they all work together for the benefit of the community.

Here on the wall sits Humpty Dumpty, or the community or city in which you live. Notice how Humpty is labeled with five mutually exclusive spheres of influence designed to serve the community. The following five spheres of influence exist within every community:

1. Church
2. Education
3. Government
4. Media/entertainment
5. Business

Some sociologists say there are three community spheres of influence, and others may identify as many as ten or eleven. I chose these five because they are both broad and specific. Someone may ask, "Where is the military?" My answer would be *government*. Another may ask, "Where is science?" My answer would be in *education* or *business*. Another might ask, "Where is sports?" My answer would be *media/entertainment*. I think these five categories are specific enough yet broad enough to cover the spectrum of societal influences in our communities.

Observing Humpty Dumpty, you can see that the church is not the only sphere of influence in a community. God has placed all five of these entities in the community for a specific purpose and to complete specific tasks in their areas of authority. The strategic alliance of these spheres of influence is absolutely essential for a community to be all it can be. Each of these entities is essential to the well-being of any community. Each has a specific purpose and contribution to make in and to our communities. None of these spheres of influence exists for itself. They all exist for community enhancement and the betterment of their communities.

Community transformation occurs when community reformation occurs. Community reformation is each of these spheres of influence becoming aware of its function and the necessity of strategic alliances, mutual collaborations, and sometimes taking a supporting role for the benefit of the community. Ultimately, each sphere of influence must start with the following premise:

We (spheres of influence) are here for the community; *the community* is not here for us. We are smaller "communities" with a cause, which is the community. The community is not a means to our end; it is the end in itself.

I realize there are many opinions regarding these entities that cloud the real issue of why each was created. In the eyes of many people all over the world, the church seems judgmental and irrelevant. Many do not like government or the media. Let's try to move beyond opinions and examine the genuine roles and contributions of each of their vital spheres of influence.

Now, using the analogy of the body, let's explore what each sphere of influence contributes to a community.

THE CHURCH IS THE HEART

What is the church's contribution in and to a community? What does "The Church is the Heart" mean? I believe the church contributes the essential character and core values necessary for the community to operate. Values determine behaviors. These essential core values release individuals, families, and the community to be all they can be. Values such as respecting others, keeping one's word, authenticity, diversity, honesty, integrity, others-centered morals, caring, compassion, behaviors with boundaries, and so on are absolutely essential for a community's well-being. Lacking these essential core values, a community, city or nation will be faced with corrupt corporations, sexual scandals, lawless behavior, and political tyranny. People will struggle with low self-esteem and disabling issues that are expensive to repair both emotionally and fiscally. Many will not fare well, but will be on welfare. People will use each other as means to their own ends. Ultimately, everyone in the community loses and underachieves.

It is the church and the Judeo-Christian ethic that enhances any community. Ask any businessperson if they would prefer to have a lazy employee or a productive employee? Ask any educator if they would prefer to teach a compassionate student or an indifferent student? Ask any mayor if he or she would prefer to serve a tolerant citizen or a prejudiced citizen? Ask any media/entertainment telecaster if they would prefer to hire a reporter who is thorough or one who is negligent? Where do all these values originate?

As the brochure of the Character Training Institute of Oklahoma City, Oklahoma, says, "Character determines success." The church in its purest form takes care of widows and orphans, feeds the poor, offers real and tangible service to the community, and insists on full potential. The values of integrity, wisdom, interdependence, others-centeredness, decisiveness, sensitivity, and compassion started with the church and remain the church's contribution to any great community. This is what I call the heart.

I know what you are thinking here: wouldn't it be great if we could have churches like this? I will address that later on in this book.

Throughout history, the church's role in its purest form has contributed enabling core values that enhance the community. While some of these values require self-control, discipline, and faith in God, they give much more to a community than they will ever take. These values are a means to an end, not the end in itself. They enable, they empower, and they transform under-achieving communities into communities closer to fulfilling their potential. The church and these values in their purest form are life-giving, not law-giving. These values are purpose-driven and transforming, and transport a community to peace, prosperity, purpose, and eternal life.

Let's move on to the next community sphere of influence.

EDUCATION IS THE BRAIN

Education is crucial to any community, city, or society. The brain is an amazing tool designed to be filled with knowledge, understanding, and wisdom. The book of Proverbs talks about knowledge in a positive way:

> A wise man will hear and increase in learning, and a man of understanding will acquire wise counsel.
>
> — PROVERBS 1:5

> Give instruction to a wise man, and he will be still wiser, teach a righteous man, and he will increase his learning.
>
> —PROVERBS 9:9

> Also it is not good for a person to be without knowledge, and he who makes haste with his feet errs.
>
> —PROVERBS 19:2

> There is gold, and an abundance of jewels; but the lips of knowledge are a more precious thing.
>
> —PROVERBS 20:15

A wise man is strong, and a man of knowledge increases power.
—PROVERBS 24:5

According to Isaiah 11:2, Jesus had the spirit of knowledge. God spent forty years and a whole generation schooling Israel in the ways of knowledge. The nation of Israel was totally ignorant after four hundred years of slavery in Egypt.

One reason people become slaves is a lack of knowledge. The "educated" generally rule and have more wealth, health, and stealth. That is why God gave His people a forty year education in the wilderness. Not only did He give them a spiritual education, He gave them an education in moral laws, ethics, hygiene, government, civil responsibilities, relational, and marital responsibilities and even animal husbandry. God knew that if His people were going to be leaders, they would have to be educated. They would have to learn, become knowledgeable in heaven's and earth's ways, and learn to be focused yet aware of others and their surroundings. By the time the old generation passed away, the new generation of Israelites was one of the most "high tech," educated, and spiritually aware nations in the world. God knew His people would perish for lack of both spiritual and natural knowledge so He took them to school to become educated.

It is important to note that *both* spiritual and natural education and knowledge are needed for a community to be all that it can be. Without education, people drink brown water and become sick. Without education, people become victims of their surroundings, victims of their culture, and victims of their oppressors. Education is part of man filling the earth and subduing the earth. Education allows people in the community to focus and become more aware of their society's needs. Consider this: all over the world since history began, wherever education has been lacking, communities have underachieved. Education is a friend, not an enemy.

In April 2003, I was speaking at the Breakthrough Conference in Wellington, New Zealand. Pastors Mike and Jeannie Knott host this wonderful conference each year. I was speaking on the concept of education/knowledge and Humpty Dumpty. After the message, a "Kiwi" lady ran up to me crying. She was a teacher at a school in Wellington.

She told me that this was the first time she had heard education not "demonized" from the pulpit. (She did not go to Mike's church.) She cried in amazement that a church speaker would honor rather than dishonor education as were her previous experiences.

Having been a pastor for more than twenty-three years, I knew where she was coming from. Church culture tends to demonize any sphere of influence other than itself. In a later chapter of this book, I will explain why that is the case. However, her point is profound. If we, as the Church, will not honor other spheres of influence God has placed in a community, how can we expect them to honor the church?

Education is essential to our communities. Without education, any community will underachieve. However, education is a means to an end, not the end in itself. Ultimately, it serves the community so that the community can achieve its destiny and potential. God made it that way.

Government Is the Skeleton

Government's role can be likened to the skeleton of any community, city, country, or society. Romans 13:1 states that government is of God, and Romans 13:4 says that government is a servant of God.

> Submit yourselves for the Lord's sake to every human institution, whether to a king as the one in authority, or to governors as sent by him for the punishment of evildoers and the praise of those who do right.
>
> —1 Peter 2:13–14

> Honor all men; love the brotherhood, fear God, honor the king.
>
> —1 Peter 2:17

> They said to Him, "Caesar's." Then He said to them, "Then render to Caesar the things that are Caesar's; and to God the things that are God's."
>
> —Matthew 22:21

A skeleton provides the framework on which to build a body. Government provides the chain of command and leadership in a community. Government sets up the boundaries by which all of the community, city, or country live. Government collects taxes that bring infrastructure to a community. Government is appointed by God to be the "avenger of wrong" and protects the community from those who would bring calamity and lawlessness to the community. Government protects the vision of the community. Government exists for the community, not vice versa. Government is the means to the end of an effective, safe, opportunity-laden, and productive community. Government is a servant, not the master. Government's main role is to ensure the achievement of potential of the community.

Government is the way it is because of why it is. Government's role is to serve vision, protect vision, and collect the tax to achieve the vision. Without the role of an effective government, lawlessness abounds. Prices and taxes go up. Crime ascends to impossible-to-achieve-anything levels. Without government, every community sphere of influence and every citizen are affected negatively. When governments stay within their boundaries or assigned areas, the whole community benefits. Conversely, when the government is not effective or biblical, the whole society suffers.

Media/Entertainment Is the Eyes, Nose, Ears, Mouth, and Nerves

Media/entertainment represents the senses of a community. Media operates much like the nerves in a body. Media reports what is going on in the community. Within the community, media gives us feedback just like the eyes, ears, nose, mouth, and nerves do in our bodies. Media/entertainment facilitates communication and community awareness just like our senses facilitate our body or self-awareness. Media is an outlet for the arts, sports, news, and other essential information necessary to the well-being of any community. Much like the scribes and historians of Old Testament times, media/entertainment has the role of being a reporter of news, not the maker of news. Without the essential core values that the church brings into the equation of the community, media will become agenda-driven. Media will politicize and distort news. Media will become the end rather than the means to an end. Ultimately, media must report the news, not "make" the news. Media/entertainment exists for the community, not the community for the self-seeking agenda of the media/entertainment sphere of influence.

Let me give you an example. If the media/entertainment sphere of influence is agenda-driven rather than core-value driven, all of the community underachieves. The community will be affected adversely. That is like your foot "reporting" to your brain that it hurts when it does not hurt. You would be adjusting your whole life to something that is not real. Conversely, if your foot is hurting and the nerves do not report it, even worse calamity can befall your foot. The results are catastrophic. Just ask anyone who has lived in a government-controlled community that permits only one-way, distorted, and contaminated communication.

Arts, sports, news, and other forms of communication are absolutely essential to the welfare of any community. When communication fails, the country is soon to fail also. We need to have good news (see Romans 10:15), and accurate, non-biased news or we will subsist on entertainment rather than news. We will become market-driven or politics-driven to the detriment of the whole community. Like the nerves in a body, media/entertainment provides an important, necessary, and non-negotiable function. Just like the scribes and historians reported the history and laws of Israel, we need the twenty-first century scribes also.

Now let's consider the last, but certainly not least, of the five community spheres of influence.

BUSINESS IS EVERYTHING ELSE

One of the biggest contributors to underachieving communities and countries is the lack of business and business opportunities. Without successful and profitable business, jobs are few and far between. When there are no employment or expansion opportunities, all the other spheres of influence suffer.

> But you shall remember the Lord your God, for it is He who is giving you power to make wealth, that He may confirm His covenant which He swore to your fathers, as it is this day.
>
> —DEUTERONOMY 8:18

In every community, business and people employed by businesses are created and designed by God to have an enormous role in the creation of wealth in a community. The ability to create goods and services, make a profit, provide employment, pay taxes for the benefit of the community, tithes to the church, and pay school tuitions, make business absolutely essential in community transformation and enhancement.

Get the picture? Profit is not a dirty word, it is a good word. Profit allows expansion and the purchasing of new products, goods, and services that create sales and profit in other businesses that employ people down the line. Businessmen are essential "kings" in the production of wealth that finances schools, churches, community centers, arts and music, and most other community institutions. All of these contribute to the welfare of the community.

Without the creation of wealth, most of the countries in Africa have suffered. Statistics like 70 to 80 percent unemployment make the apostle John's statement of prospering in all ways (3 John 2) more of a wish/dream than a reality. While some might say that wealth gets in the way of spiritual life, I would counter with the lack of wealth creates even more spiritual life problems in people.

In any event, healthy business is a blessing to most any people, community, or country. The power to create wealth advances the Kingdom of God in a very significant way.

Honoring the Entities

So here we have the community spheres of influence:

- Church
- Education
- Government
- Media/Entertainment
- Business

All of these entities or spheres of influence were created by God to serve and enhance the community. We see that the Church is not the only sphere of influence, but it is one of the spheres of influence in a community. This is the way God designed cities and communities to operate. It is His design, not ours. It is "on earth as it is in heaven" whose architect and builder is God.

This design was effectively used by the early settlers in the United States, New Zealand, and other countries of the world. As a result, communities grew in character, prosperity, employment, and spirituality. While these were still problems, the communities were generally much more efficient, effective, crime-free, and civil than most of today's cities. That is what each sphere of influence operating by Judeo /Christian core values can do.

Effective communities formed by "honoring the entities" now need to be transformed back to their original, normal, natural, and most effective state. However, the road to community transformation requires all five of the spheres of influence, not just one of the spheres of influence. Whether the Church likes it or not, strategic alignment and mutual collaborations with government, business, education, and media/entertainment spheres of influence are "prerequisites" to real, tangible, and lasting community transformation. The Church cannot do it alone.

Why are our communities underachieving? Perhaps Humpty Dumpty can further reveal the cause to us.

Was Humpty Dumpty Pushed?

There is a bumper sticker in America that says, "Humpty Dumpty was pushed!" That sentiment plays to the victim mentality currently pervading most cultures, but I do not think that is the issue in Humpty's case.

The rhyme says Humpty Dumpty had a great fall. According to the

Bible, what comes before the fall? Most of us know that pride comes before a fall. The Bible confirms that in Proverbs 16:18. I propose that through the years, these spheres of influence began to separate from each other and individualize. In other words, a sphere of influence began to think it was *the* sphere of influence. That is called pride.

Rather than integration, disintegration developed leaving communities to choose a part rather than the whole. Each sphere began to define diversity by its own calling, agenda, or ethos causing Humpty Dumpty or the community to fall with the effect of creating a win/lose, us/them, right-or-wrong, good-or-evil attitude among the vital spheres of influence. I call this phenomenon "Me Tarzan, you Jane." The result is one-upmanship, distrust, and competition. The survival of the fittest. The object becomes winning and maintaining power rather than serving the community. So now we have the five spheres of influence in the community whose roles and responsibilities are very different, each thinking that they are right and the others are wrong. If you reduce the rhetoric, each is screaming, "I'm right and you are wrong!" The truth is, each is right—partially. However, the truth also is that none alone can bring a community to fullness, completeness, and purpose.

When *a* sphere of influence thinks it is *the* sphere of influence, everyone loses. The problem is one of scope—too narrow a scope. The Church was never designed to exist by itself. The Church has a mission and needs a context. The Church is not the end, the Church is a means to an end, which is influence in and to the community.

The community needs what the Church brings to the table. The same is true of the government, business, education, and media/entertainment spheres of influence. Each sphere of influence needs what the other spheres contribute. In Bible language, the concept would be that the heart is for the body, not the body for the heart. The brain is for the body, not the body for the brain, and so forth. As my friend Pastor Kelly Varner says in his book entitled *The Corporate Anointing*, "It is the whole body or nobody!"[2] Anything less leaves all the king's horses and all the king's men trying, but unable to put Humpty Dumpty back together again.

No-ing the Community or Knowing the Community

Let's take a look at the church's role in the American context. I realize people from many nations will read this book, but I am told that what I am about to say is fairly typical in most Western nations.

Noted researcher George Barna recently conducted a poll on the seven top influencers of American culture. The shocking result (to church people) was that the church sphere of influence was not even listed in the top seven influencers.[3] Not long ago there was cooperation among and working relationships with the other four community spheres of influence for the sake of the community. However, in the 1960s government (the political realm), education, business, and media/entertainment began to disconnect from the church. Some of this disconnect was due to the fact that the church had become institutionalized, judgmental, non-relevant, and had lost its ability to contextualize in a changing world. As the other spheres began to marginalize the church, the Church began to marginalize the other spheres. The Church would preach against business, government, media, and education saying that they were of the devil and so on.

As a result of this disconnect, the Church has limited passport or influence in the community. In effect, the other community spheres of influence have taken over the determination of cultural and individual values, and the Church is angry, hurt, and marginalized. The Church has individualized from *itself* and the *community*. We have been no-ing the community when we ought to have been knowing the community. Using the analogy of a baseball game, every time we "get up to bat" for the community, we already have two strikes against us. It is hard to "hit a home run" for the community with the pressure of two strikes against us in the community's eyes. However, the real problem was that the Church "swung" at two balls or pitches it could never have hit. The real loser in this "at bat" is not the Church, but the community.

"Intergracing"

Let me ask you a question. What has the United States learned that Europe has not…yet? What is a main contributing factor to the influence of the United States? I call it "Intergracing." Intergracing is different from integration. Integration is trying to make everyone and everything the same. Intergracing is honoring the boundaries of the "diverseness" of other races, nations, genders, and spheres of influence yet allowing them all to birth something bigger than themselves individually. It is discovering what we all can do together rather than apart.

Before the United States became a nation, America was a collection of states, not an alliance of states. Each state had a "measure of grace" and its own unique contribution and provincial issues. In a sense, each state was its own individual entity and identity. Each state had the option to remain independent of the others, but to our founding fathers, that seemed to be a recipe for failure. What did these states do? They entered into a strategic alliance, mutual collaboration, even sometimes taking a supporting role in the cast considering other states' needs more of a priority than their own. Many times the stronger helped and supported the weaker to benefit all in the alliance. In the process, the grace of each state and the needs of each state were honored yet joined together in an alliance that multiplied each state's "grace." Each remained a state while becoming a member of a nation or republic.

To this day the states are joined in some areas (money, executive government, military, etc.) yet unique in others (state government, state taxes, etc.). The point here is profound. The United States government has to honor the boundaries and sovereignty of each state while governing in the larger scope of events and issues. The Church participates in similar "intergracing." In one sense all Christian churches are one. In another sense, we are many. Just like the nation of Israel in Old Testament times, we are tribes and we are a nation. The concept of intergracing takes time, some patience, and the ability to see a both/and type of thinking. It has been a benefit to the United States and has multiplied the influence and effectiveness of the country.

Throughout most of its long history until recently, the nations of

Europe maintained a different way of thinking. Europe remained a plethora of individual countries. Strategic alliances, mutual collaborations, and supporting casts were based on political expediency and tended to be short lived. Each country seemed to spent most of its time, energy, and resources trying to outdo the others. Rather than "honoring the entities," each country dishonored the "entities," weakening all of Europe for centuries.

In recent years, Europe has discovered the principle of intergracing and the benefits thereof. The powerful Airbus Industries, a mutual collaboration among England, France, Germany, and Spain, has caught up to Boeing in sales of commercial jetliners. For years, because of each country's small size, the manufacturing capacity of the commercial aircraft industry was small. However, as national pride and selfish individualism decreased, the potential of strategic alliances, mutual collaborations, and supporting casts increased. The rest is history.

More recently, France and Germany, despite their differences, have amazed the world by their united stand against the 2003 war in Iraq. I am not saying they were right or wrong. The point is to show the power and influence of strategic alliances, mutual collaborations, and supporting casts.

The Church must not try to "be government" at this point in history. That is Jesus' job later on. When the Church tries to be the government, it is moving the boundary mark established by God. The Bible says that government is of God. God, in effect, is saying, "honor the king" (Rom. 13:7); the government is a significant other with significant "druthers" that I have called it to do; do not go beyond the boundary that I have given you; I have not given you its assignment; I have given you *your* assignment. If you offend the government, you offend Me, and that sets into motion cause-and-effect issues that will limit your contribution and influence in the community. (See Deuteronomy 27:17.)

The same would be true if the government tried to move the Church's boundary marks. The ultimate loser is the community. That is why this chapter is so important to all of the community. If we do not know each other's contributions and graces given by God, we will be stepping all over one another trying to "gift-project" and conform all the other community spheres of influence into our image. The result is underachievement, misunderstanding, one-upmanship, distrust and, consequently, "cities who are in great distress and reproach" (see Nehemiah 1:3).

We need to understand that as significant brothers, no matter which one of the community spheres of influence we are, there will be significant others with significant druthers that we need for the benefit and enhancement of the community. That is why we honor the entities!

Significant Brothers and Significant Others With Significant Druthers

Let's apply the concept of intergracing to the concept of community transformation and apply what we learned about the United States and Europe. For example, the Church has two realms that she needs to be aware of. I call this concept "Significant Brothers and Significant Others." Both the brothers and the others have significant "druthers." Each has significant contributions to make to a community—contributions that need to be included, not excluded. The Church's brothers would be other churches in the community who are Bible based and orthodox in their beliefs. They could belong to many denominations and many church movements. They are all part of the Body of Christ. This is what I mean by the church sphere of influence.

The "others" are the other four community spheres of influence. The Church was designed by God to have authority in its sphere, and to have influence in and with the other spheres. The Church was never created to dominate the other community spheres of influence. As a matter of fact, when the Church has tried that, it offends God, offends the others' spheres, and becomes a curse to the Church (as in, the Crusades).

> Cursed is he who moves his neighbor's boundary mark. And all the people shall say, "Amen."
>
> —Deuteronomy 27:17

Normalizing the Abnormal Which Should Be Normal

Community spheres of influence were meant to complete one another not to compete with one another. The Church trying to be the government is trouble. The government trying to be the Church is trouble. Education needs essential Church core values or it will underachieve. Also, the Church could use education's contribution in church. Get the picture? The key to real, tangible, and lasting community transformation is discovering what all these spheres can do together for the community while honoring and including each sphere is contributions. Healthy communities come from healthy spheres of influence working together in strategic alliances and mutual collaborations for the betterment of the community. Ultimately we and our families benefit. As Jeremiah 29:7 says, "And seek the welfare of the city where I have sent you into exile, and pray to the LORD on its behalf; for in its welfare you will have welfare."

A healthy community provides the context for employment and enjoyment through the deployment of essential core values enabling the community to "be all that it can be" for the benefit of all. The Church is very strategic to the community when a community is more like Babylon than Jerusalem. The community needs the Church to pray on its behalf, as well as to work on its behalf for its welfare. Anything less than that is a lose-lose situation for the community. Our community's prosperity provides a context for our prosperity. Our community's peace provides a context for our peace. Our community's ability to solve problems provides a context for the problem to be solved in our lives. This relationship was re-confirmed by Paul in 1 Timothy 2. What a challenge, huh?

So here we have the possibility, even probability, of normality—a city whose architect and builder is God. So, if we can make the Church a little better, we can make the community a lot better. The same is true for the other spheres of influence. If all the spheres of influence get a little better, the community will be a lot better! Every entity exists to add value to, not to take value from, the community.

We now see the same phenomenon of strategic alliances in America with more and more frequency. For example, look at the alliance between Taco Bell and Pizza Hut. How about Baskin-Robbins Ice Cream and Dunkin' Donuts? I have seen Chevron gasoline stations and McDonald's restaurants in the same building. I could go on and on. Some of these alliances are owned by the same parent company, but many are not. These alliances are not "covenant" relationships like marriage. The Church working with the government or other sphere of influence is not a covenant. This is not an "unequally yoked" issue. This is the sharing of mutual resources, callings, and graces for the sake of the community. The Church or any other of the four spheres of influence by itself cannot transform the community.

NATIONStrategy

In response to the incredible potential, as well as the challenge of community transformation, I started a non-profit organization called NATIONStrategy in May 2001.

Our mission is unleashing the potential of communities through the strategic alliance of church, business, government, education, and media/entertainment to the benefit of all in the community.

Our vision is envisioning and empowering today's leaders and influencers in church to be tomorrow's leaders and influencers in the community.

Our strategy to fulfill our mission and vision is communicating a specific set of core values that encourage and empower churches to partner with other churches and community spheres of influence for the betterment of the community.

Simply stated, our assignment is to "revelate" the vision, values, and strategies to "put Humpty Dumpty back together again." That is what this book is all about.

Tomorrow's Community Today

Remember the king's horses and the king's men who were not going anywhere because they were eternally busy trying to put Humpty Dumpty back together again? Let's see what could happen if they asked the king. At this stage in the book, Humpty is still in five pieces, but before we put him back together again we had better address some strategic issues. It will not be enough to get a vision, learn about the spheres of influence in the community, and expect the community to be changed. I have already mentioned that vision is not so much the issue as the values. Community transformation will be very limited without a strategic core value transformation.

Community transformation requires the right values in the right people—the King's men. In a real sense, this book reveals the core values the twenty-first century church should adopt and apply. I want to "revelate" tomorrow's values *today*. Let's pick up the "ondas" of community transformation.

The King's Men Will Ride Again

The King's men will ride again if they know where to begin. Their old way of doing things will never work. They need a new mindset, a new set of core values so that when they begin to help put the community back together. They will need Church@Community core values or what I call intelligent fire.

Chapter 4

Giving the Church Back to the Community:

The Principle of No Deposit, No Return

The church is the only organization in the world that exists primarily for its non-members.

It is amazing to me how many churches want a return from the community without putting a deposit into the community. They would like revival, but do not understand the principle of 'no deposit, no return.' Let me illustrate what I mean by this.

Upon arriving in Wellington, New Zealand in October of 2003, I thought I would test the principle of no deposit/no return at a local bank. I walked into an ANZ Bank and asked for my interest on the million dollars I deposited in their bank. She said, "What?" I said, "I'd like my interest on the million dollars I put into your bank." She asked, "What is your name?" I replied, "Edwin Delph." She looked in her computer and said, "We do not show you as ever making a deposit in this bank." I replied very emphatically, "But I did in the spirit!"

She looked at me questioningly. I said, "I made it in prayer and even prophesied it into existence." As she picked up the telephone to call the police she said to me, "Sir, we do not show that you made a deposit into this bank, therefore you do not get a return!"

Actually, that never happened. I was tempted to try it but was afraid I would end up in jail. However, there is a principle to be demonstrated in this illustration. The principle is that natural man cannot understand the things of the Spirit. Why would you expect them to? The Son of God became the Son of man...the Word became flesh...the invisible became visible...the intangible became real, tangible, and lasting because that is where the community is, and that is what the community requires. The church is called like Jesus to make a real and tangible deposit in the community. Like Jesus, the church gives God a face. Giving the church back to the community bridges the gap between God and man. Otherwise, the community could say, "we are attending your churches...in the spirit!" This book is about how to make a real, tangible, and lasting deposit into the community producing favor with God and man.

Write the Book!

In May 1999, I was speaking in London, England, at a conference that literally changed my life. In fact, the revelation I received at this conference is what propelled the writing of this book. As I was escorted into the conference, the ushers seated me by my good friend, one of the other speakers at the conference, Cindy Jacobs. As we were listening to another speaker, Cindy began to speak these words to me in a whisper: "Write the book, write the book, WRITE THE BOOK!" I think God was setting the table for what would happen in the next day or so.

The conference was hosted by Prayer for the Nations, or PFN. Rod and Julie Anderson are the leaders of this wonderful movement of intercessors in the European context. The speakers included Ed Silvoso, Dutch Sheets, Cindy Jacobs, Ken Gott, John Dawson, and me. The message that affected me the most was delivered by Ken Gott of Sunderland, England. I recall his story and message as if they took place yesterday. I want to share the main idea of the message with you. But I will need to give you some more background on Ken Gott first.

Pastor Ken's Sunderland church was known worldwide for being the "Toronto" church of England. Thousands of people from all over the world have gone there to be ministered to at his "river" services, in which Christians receive prayer, laugh, and get spiritually refreshed. Ken has an incredible ministry of touching Christians with the presence of God. That is what his church was known for at that time, this is what Ken has written books on, and this is Ken's gift to the world. His identity and "passport" into the churches of the world was based upon his incredible God-given ministry. His church was a refreshing venue for years.

However, as Ken spoke at the conference he shared something that was to change the emphasis of his church dramatically.

"GIVE THE CHURCH BACK TO THE COMMUNITY"

Ken spoke on the following message he had recently heard from God, "Okay, you have had your fun, now give the church back to the community!"

I was stunned! God was telling Ken that it was all right to be a source of refreshing, a "river" church, a Toronto export center *for a while*, but that time had come to an end. God had wanted them to be an "inward church for a time, but now it was time to give the church back to the community. There was a reason and a season for God's refreshing the Christians, but now there was a new reason and a new season—the *community*.

There is such a time as *this*—Esther 4:14, but also such a time as *that*! It is crucial to know the *this-es* and the *thats*. God was calling Ken's church to lay down its life, pick up the cross, and follow Him. It was time to move Jesus beyond the church walls. It was time to realize that the community is not here for us, *but we are here for the community*. God was teaching Ken and his church that the church is a "community" with a cause, which is—the community!

During the refreshing season, God was making the church a little better so He could make the community a *lot* better. The Word of God contained in Ken's church had to incarnate and move into the neighborhoods of Sunderland. Like Jesus, the Living Word in their church needed to become flesh (real and tangible) and dwell in them (Sunderland). The presence on the inside of the church had to become the presence on the outside of the church. Look at Ephesians 3:10:

> In order that the manifold wisdom of God might now be made known through the church to the rulers and the authorities in the heavenly places.

The manifold wisdom of God (Christ) is to be made known through the church to the powers which reflect themselves in the neighborhoods and community. Notice that the apostle says Christ...through the church, not to the church exclusively. God was telling Ken, *here is my apostolic mandate to you—Christ through the church to the community!* Or even more specifically, Christ (the manifold wisdom of God) to the church, then through the church to the community.

Ken went on to share how as a result of this "word," his congregation changed locations, tore down the walls that surrounded his church, started feeding the poor, evangelizing, and so on. Now that is risky—that is entrepreneurial and reformational, but especially that is incarnational! They had to move from church-centric to community-centric! I am sure the change in emphasis upset many in his church, and perhaps even in the world, but remember something that Israel forgot: we are blessed to be a blessing.

> Now the Lord said to Abram, "Go forth from your country, and from your relatives and from your father's house, to the land which I will show you; and I will make you a great nation, and I will bless you, and make your name great; and so you shall be a blessing; and I will bless those who bless you, and the one who curses you I will curse. And in you all the families of the earth shall be blessed."
>
> —Genesis 12:1–3

Today, many Christians' and many churches' sole purpose is to be blessed, be filled, to "have church" inside the church walls (us four and no more, and everybody else out the door). We tend to want our own version of being a habitation for God, rather than filling the earth with the knowledge of the glory of the Lord. We teach people how to be Christians at church, but not in their marriages, at their schools, in their jobs, and with their neighbors. Our version of church is what happens on Sunday within the walls. But may I suggest that real church is what happens Monday through Saturday *outside* the church walls. The saints go marching in without ever *marching out*. God is saying to the church, "You are blessed on Sunday so you can be a blessing to the community on Monday, Tuesday, Wednesday, Thursday, Friday, and Saturday." God blessed the Jews on the Sabbath so they could be a blessing to the nations on the non-Sabbaths. God is saying to churches, leaders, and Christians today, "You do not hold a revival—you turn it loose!"

GOD'S VISION STATEMENT

Community transformation is an idea whose time has come—and that is powerful. There is a "leadershift" from the church to the community and from inward to outward. We are beginning to understand that the community is not here for the church, the church is here for the community. God is opening the eyes of our hearts to see that one goes into the presence of God in church so he can go out with the presence of God in the community. In a real and tangible way, we are beginning to make God's priority our priority. It is not "When the Saints Go Marching In," it is "When the Saints Go Marking Out"! We do not hold a revival—we let it go!

Now let's consider the theology of community transformation and who is to accomplish it. Today it seems as if every organization has a vision, mission, or purpose statement. Do you realize that God has a vision statement also? (I think He started this trend first!)

God's vision statement is found in Habakkuk 2:14:

> For the earth will be filled with the knowledge of the glory of the Lord, as the waters cover the sea.

That is what God said in Genesis 1:28:

> And God blessed them; and God said to them, "Be fruitful and multiply, and fill the earth, and subdue it; and rule over the fish of the sea and over the birds of the sky, and over every living thing that moves on the earth."

The earth will be filled as the church evangelizes, converts, disciples, and works until every people group has heard of the knowledge of the glory of the Lord. The end, as Jesus called it in Matthew 24:14, will not come until the whole world has heard or has knowledge of the glory of the Lord.

What is the knowledge of the glory of the Lord?

In talking about the vision statement of God, "the earth shall be filled with the knowledge of the glory," let's define the word vision. I once heard vision defined as "a compelling picture of a preferable future that motivates you to perform." *Vision is motivational.* When you see it, you should change or move. *This vision of God moved Him to send Jesus.* With what did He send Jesus? The *glory.*

> And the Word became flesh, and dwelt among us, and we beheld His glory, glory as of the only begotten from the Father, full of grace and truth.
>
> —John 1:14

> I glorified Thee on the earth, having accomplished the work which Thou hast given Me to do. And now, glorify Thou Me together with Thyself, Father, with the glory which I had with Thee before the world was.
>
> —John 17:4–5

> In these last days has spoken to us in His Son, whom He appointed heir of all things, through whom also He made the world. And He is the radiance of His glory and the exact representation of His nature, and upholds all things by the word of His power. When He had made purification of sins, He sat down at the right hand of the Majesty on high.
>
> —Hebrews 1:2–3

The glory is simply what God is like. The knowledge of the glory is *knowing* what God is like. God wants the whole earth to know what He is like, so He sent His Son to show the earth what He is like. Jesus stated the reality in John 14:9, "He who has seen Me has seen the Father." God wants to make Himself known.

The glory is not a what, it is a *Who.* The whole world needs to have a real and tangible opportunity to know about Jesus, the glorious Son of the Father, who came to start the process of "that the earth may be filled with the knowledge of the glory of the Lord just as the water covers the sea" (Hab. 2:14). The world, the community, and the inhabitants of the earth need a vision of the glory of God. That glory is in God's son, Jesus. When *all* see Jesus, they are seeing God. Jesus was the governmental vehicle of God's vision of making Himself known. Jesus said in John 12:32, "And I, if I be lifted up from the earth, will draw all men to Myself."

HERE COMES THE BRIDE

Now that Jesus has been lifted from the earth, who will bring to the world a vision of the knowledge of the glory?

> And the glory which Thou has given Me I have given to them; that they may be one, just as We are one; I in them, and Thou in Me, that they may be perfected in unity, that the world may know that Thou didst send Me, and didst love them, even as Thou didst love Me.
>
> —JOHN 17:22–23

> And whom He predestined, these He also called.
>
> —ROMANS 8:30

> To whom God willed to make known what are the riches of the glory of this mystery among the Gentiles, which is Christ in you, (the church) the hope of glory.
>
> —COLOSSIANS 1:27

The church is to look like Jesus, act like Jesus, and demonstrate Jesus. God's strategy to get His vision fulfilled is first through Jesus, then through us, the church, and ultimately to the entire community.

The early disciples were successful in this.

> And the disciples were first called Christians in Antioch.
>
> —ACTS 11:26

They walked like Christ, talked like Christ, had character and love like Christ, evangelized like Christ, and ministered like Christ. They looked like Christ in character, ministry, and mission to the whole community and the nations. God's strategy to fulfill His vision was simple. The gifts of the Spirit and the fruit of the Spirit were for the purpose of accomplishing the *mission* of the Spirit. They literally filled the earth with the knowledge of the glory of the Lord.

> You have filled Jerusalem with your teaching.
>
> —ACTS 5:28

> First, I thank my God through Jesus Christ for you all, because your faith is being proclaimed throughout the whole world.
>
> —ROMANS 1:8

> The preaching of Jesus Christ...has been made known to all the nations, leading to obedience of faith.
>
> —ROMANS 16:25–26

The church made known the manifold wisdom of God to the rulers and authorities in heavenly places. How did they do it?

> In order that the manifold wisdom of God might now be made known through the church to the rulers and the authorities in the heavenly places.
>
> —EPHESIANS 3:10

The church was conformed to Jesus. When the inhabitants of the earth saw the church, they saw Jesus and they saw the knowledge of the glory of the Lord. And they were evangelistic—they filled the whole earth at that time with the knowledge of the glory and lo, He was with them always. (See Matthew 28:20.) However, if we do not *go*, there is no "lo"!

Dr. Pete Miller of Phoenix, Arizona has come up with a definition of the mission of the church that I have found helpful. His definition is "presenting all people with a real and meaningful opportunity to become conformed to the image of Jesus." When Christians reflect Christ in character, ministry, and mission, the world gets to see incarnated versions of what Jesus was like through us and through the church. The key is to "make Him known" in and through the church. Why? As the Bible says in John 12:32, when Christ is lifted up He will draw all men to Himself. Dr. Miller points out very correctly this demonstration has to be to all people and be real and meaningful. Let's look at God's strategy to do that.

The Ultimate Neighborhood Activist

Let's look at one of the most strategic verses in the Bible:

> And the Word became flesh, and dwelt among us, and we beheld His glory, glory as of the only begotten from the Father, full of grace and truth.
>
> —John 1:14

Do you realize Jesus was the ultimate neighborhood activist? If I were to shorten John 1:14 according to its meaning, I would paraphrase it like this, "the seed incarnated in the neighborhood." Jesus could have stayed in heaven with the Father and the Holy Spirit (a great church!), but He chose to leave His "church" and incarnate or become real and tangible in the earth's neighborhood.

As I said earlier, Jesus is spiritual, Jesus is natural, but Jesus is especially incarnational. His mission was to connect the message with the audience, not just preach to God, the Holy Spirit and the angels. God's crowning creation was in trouble—in sin—and Jesus *did* something about it. Remember, salt cannot flavor what it does not touch. The people of earth had problems and Jesus had the solution. The strategy the Godhead chose was incarnation—the Word had to become flesh and move into the neighborhood. The answer was contact and communication without contamination. The Son of God strategically became the Son of Man. Impression without *expression* leads to *depression*. Jesus found a need and met it, even though it required leaving His comfort zone for a while. Jesus gave the church back to the community, or neighborhood.

Connecting the Message With the Audience

Do you know the church is the only organization in the world that exists primarily for its nonmembers? That is what makes the church different, it exists for others. The church is here to facilitate every person, every city, every country, and every continent to operate at their full potential. The church should not like underachievement, like the Godhead does not like underachievement. God sent the church to be a part of the community for the better. How do we help the community? By being involved in the community, in circulation, having influence, and providing solutions to some very difficult issues through Christ's wisdom.

My friend, worship leader Godfrey Birtrill from England, wrote a song called "Outrageous Grace" that very powerfully points to the necessity of Christians and churches "incarnating" in the community. These are the words of his song:

> There is a lot of pain, but a lot more healing.
> There is a lot of trouble, but a lot more peace.
> There is a lot of hate, but a lot more loving.
> There is a lot of sin, but a lot more grace.
> Outrageous grace...outrageous grace!
>
> Love unfurled by heaven's hand.
> Outrageous grace...outrageous grace!
> Through my Jesus I can stand.
>
> There is a lot of fear, but a lot more freedom
> There is a lot of darkness, but a lot more light.
> There is a lot of cloud, but a lot more vision.
> There is a lot of perishing, but a lot more life!

Outrageous grace ... outrageous grace!
Love unfurled by heaven's hand.
Outrageous grace ... outrageous grace!
Through my Jesus I can stand.

In the context of this song, the pain is on earth, but heaven has the solution—healing. The trouble is on earth, but heaven has the solution—peace.

The rest of the verses follow in the same manner. The Word became flesh and dwelt amongst them. The seed incarnated in the neighborhood and connected the solution with the problem. God's strategy was to "give the church back to the community." Where sin opened the door to underachievement, grace closes the door to underachievement, but Christ must incarnate through the church to the community. (See Ephesians 3:10.) The church was put on earth to add value, not to take away value from the community. The church is here to bring Jesus into its part of the community, city, and world.

The same is also true of individual Christians. We are here to bring Jesus into "our" part of the world in a real and tangible way. We cannot hide in church and touch the community at the same time. I repeat—salt cannot flavor what it does not touch. Salt needs to be in circulation. We need to connect the message with the audience. I once heard John Wimber, the founder of the Vineyard movement of churches, say something like, "Get out of the seat and onto the street." That is where the church and Christians can regain their rightful influence into the community. It is time to quit being "incarnationally challenged" to the peril of the community.

CHURCH-CENTRIC OR COMMUNITY-CENTRIC?

One of my biggest challenges as an international speaker each year is shifting the mentality of those leaders from "church-centric" to "community-centric." In 2002, I spoke 209 times in formal settings at leadership conferences or church services all over the world. Many of the sermons, lectures or talks were on the subject of what it takes to be community-centric. Community-centric means being aware that the church is part of the community, placed within the community by

God to enhance the community or make it better.

The church is a necessary part of a community, but it is only one part of the whole community. The image and attitude the church reflects to the community directly affects the influence we have within the community. In other words, the way the church sees the community is the way the community sees the church. Becoming aware of our community is a visionary concept that will begin to change the way we conduct church.

In a very short time, churches, Christians, and those involved in the church culture tend to become church-centric. They begin to think that the community exists for them, not that they are there for the community. They tend to focus on the church only. In essence, the church becomes its own culture, separating from the community and eventually even separating from itself. This inward focus undermines the mission of Jesus and God' s vision of the earth being filled with the glory of the Lord. A church-centric focus undermines real and tangible community transformation, to the peril of those living in the community. In the next chapter, I will address why this happens.

I have often posed the question, "Why would you be a Christian fellowship when you could be a church for the community?" A Christian fellowship generally serves the "found," a community church serves the "lost and found." The potential in a community-oriented church is much greater than that of a Christian fellowship. I have even seen church leadership teams change the name of the church they serve to reflect their heart for the community. My friend, Pastor John Kordon of Glendale, Arizona, and his church leaders changed their church's name from Victory Church to Camelback Community Church. Pastor John chose to be a "lake" rather than a "pond."

Abram was extremely aware of what he and his nephew, Lot, looked like to the inhabitants of the communities around them:

> Now Lot, who was moving about with Abram, also had flocks and herds and tents. But the land could not support them while they stayed together, for their possessions were so great that they were not able to stay together. And quarreling arose between Abram's herdsmen and the herdsmen of Lot. The Canaanites

> and Perizzites were also living in the land at that time. So Abram said to Lot, 'Let's not have any quarreling between you and me, or between your herdsmen and mine, for we are brothers. Is not the whole land before you? Let's part company. If you go to the left, I will go to the right; if you go to the right, I will go to the left.' Lot looked up and saw that the whole plain of the Jordan was well watered, like the garden of the LORD, like the land of Egypt, toward Zoar. (This was before the LORD destroyed Sodom and Gomorrah.) So Lot chose for himself the whole plain of the Jordan and set out toward the east. The two men parted company.
>
> —Genesis 13:5–11, NIV

Notice that Abram did not want the conflict between his herdsmen and Lot's herdsmen to affect the public relations image of God's people in a foreign land. He was very aware that strife, conflict, and arguments among the people of God could and would affect the inhabitants of the land negatively. Even though he, being older, had the right to his first choice of the land, Abram deferred the choice to Lot to preserve peace and a good public relations image to the community. He was aware that the *Canaanites* and *Perizzites* were looking at the way he and Lot conducted themselves in a crisis situation. The "community" was watching the "church." Would Abram and Lot be different from them or the same or perhaps even worse?

Spies Sent by God

I have often said that my family members are spies sent by God to hold me accountable.

My wife, Becky, and my children, Kristin, Matthew, and Jonathan, watch everything I do. When I push that yellow light that is close to turning red, my son Jonathan (our prophet) lets me know about it right away. I call Becky my "government." She has special built-in "radar" that keeps me honest, aware, and under control in a redemptive way.

Similar to my family watching me, the community watches the

church. The community watches to see how we behave with each other and with those outside of the church community. People in the community have "radar" that senses issues like, do we care about others or are we here to serve ourselves? They are very good at discerning whether we are using them or serving them. They know when we are self-centered or others-centered, and if we are using them as a means to our own ends.

In my opinion, most churches are not even aware of the community and the effect we have on and in the community. This is demonstrated in our actions, not our rhetoric. If we are not aware of this, we end up with a disconnect from the community and the biggest public relations problem in the world. This affects our mission in a very negative way with the end result that we never live up to our potential. The possibility of community transformation then becomes greatly reduced also.

Do you realize we do not have church splits or divisions in churches for the sake of the community? We have good pastor-to-pastor relationships and good church-to-church relationships for the sake of our community. We get along and work together for the sake of the community. We are aware of and relevant to those we serve for the sake of the community. We pay our bills on time and have integrity in working with others for the sake of the community. We love one another, have good marriages, and do our best in raising our children for the sake of the community. We are not racially prejudiced for the sake of the community. We are holy, have good character, and live authentically for the sake of the community. We are outward-oriented for the sake of the community. We are non-religious and pro-Jesus for the sake of the community. We bless and curse not for the sake of the community. We might even give up our way of doing the type of church we are comfortable with for the sake of the community. Jesus did!

This was also the core value the apostle Paul consistently exhibited.

> To the weak I became weak, that I might win the weak; I have become all things to all men, that I may by all means save some.

> And I do all things for the sake of the gospel, that I may become a fellow partaker of it.
>
> —1 Corinthians 9:22–23

> Give no offense either to Jews or to Greeks or to the church of God; just as I also please all men in all things, not seeking my own profit, but the profit of the many, that they may be saved.
>
> —1 Corinthians 10:32–33

Becoming community-centric provides an opportunity for the church to become conformed to Jesus not only in character and ministry, but also in mission—like Abram, who could have asserted his authority and right, but chose to defer to Lot for the sake of the community. Paul emphasizes this same truth in 1 Corinthians 6:1–8 concerning the issue of Christians bringing their lawsuits to a community court system because, among other things, the community is watching. How we, the church, behave toward each other directly affects the community both positively and negatively. Remember what Jesus said regarding our witness to the community:

> By this all men will know that you are My disciples, if you have love one for another.
>
> —John 13:35

> That they may all be one; even as Thou, Father, art in Me, and I in Thee, that they also may be in Us; that the world may believe that Thou didst send Me.
>
> —John 17:21

If our behavior is excellent *among* the unchurched, it releases the glory and the testimony of God into the community. Remember, God's vision statement is "the earth shall be filled with the glory of the Lord." This cause-and-effect principle is literally put into the hands of the church. It is our responsibility to be aware of our "audience" because what the church does directly affects the community. We give the church back to the community by our actions, not our rhetoric.

Abram realized that and he was a friend of God. He realized the testimony of behavior among God's people does not just stay in the church, it trickles out into the community. He was community-centric, that is, aware of the community or (dare I use the word) market! He wanted nothing to stand in the way of connecting the message with the audience by both word and deed. He caught God's heart for the world. His passion for God led him to God's compassion for people, and an excellent testimony "among the gentiles." No gentile was going to blaspheme God because of him. (See Romans 2:24.)

This whole concept is summarized perfectly in 2 Corinthians 6:1–3 (emphasis added):

> And working together with Him, we also urge you not to receive the grace of God in vain—for He says, "At the acceptable time I listened to you, and on the day of salvation I helped you"; behold, now is "the acceptable time," behold, now is "the day of salvation"—*giving no cause for offense in anything, in order that the ministry be not discredited.*

Notice, we work with one another—person-to-person and church-to-church—and God for the salvation of many in our communities. Our task is not to "discredit" the ministry in any way. That is the heartbeat of real community transformation.

Future Bride

A few years ago as I was listening to a worship cassette called "Stoneleigh" by Pastor Terry Virgo's New Frontiers network in England, a certain spontaneous song captivated me. As I reflected on the words in this song, which spoke of the mystery of the Father seeking a bride for His Son, I began to understand another important aspect of salvation from God's perspective. He wants to get His Son married. Now, most theologians would agree that His Son's bride is the church. (See Ephesians 5:23–32; Revelation 19:6–9.) God will not give His Son a partial bride, and Jesus will not return until every person who is supposed to be the bride has responded to the Father's call.

An incredible story of the mystery of the Father seeking a bride for His Son is our church's worship leader and lead guitar player, Alan Wells. During his late teenage years and early twenties Alan was the lead-guitar player of an extreme rock band. He wore the make-up, had a very feminine appearance, and had (let me say it this way) *extremely* long hair. At that point, he was future-bride. I remember his mother giving me pictures of him during that time in his life. She was the one who applied his make-up! To illustrate the concept of future-bride, we projected his picture on our nine-by-fifteen-foot screen at our church. Underneath his picture I placed the caption "Can this be saved?" Most of our church did not even recognize him. Then, we put up his present-church picture. Our church got the message! Alan moved from future-church to present-church, from future-bride to present-bride. He is one of my favorite people in the world. It does not matter what form a person comes in, salvation belongs to our God!

Community transformation is about the mystery of the Father seeking a bride for His Son. Community transformation is about creating a spiritual and natural climate that positively contributes to the formation of the bride of Christ. Oh...the mystery!

Salvation Belongs to Our God

Community transformation begins with personal transformation, one person at a time. If you want to change your community, it happens as the present-church in the community has influence in all areas of the community leading to salvation. Whom God calls and how He calls them is none of our business because salvation belongs to our God! Giving the church back to the community is our job—the modus operandi is God's.

God gives the church power for missions. Read Acts 1:8:

> But you shall receive power when the Holy Spirit has come upon you; and you shall be My witnesses both in Jerusalem, and in all Judea and Samaria, and even to the remotest part of the earth.

God's power is not the end in itself but a means to an end—missions both close and far. God uses his power to confirm the *message*, not the messenger. Salvation belongs to our God. His house is a house of prayer *for the nations*. A house of prayer is the means, not the end. A house of prayer is community-centric, not church-centric. We were blessed in order to be a blessing for the community. The church's blessing is not for itself, but for the community!

Let's conclude this chapter by looking at Acts 16:10:

> And when *he* had seen the vision, immediately we sought to go into Macedonia, concluding that God had called *us* to preach the gospel to *them*.

Pastor David Cannistraci of Gateway City Church in San Jose, California, taught me the following spiritual truth. Notice the pronouns in this Scripture. The pronoun progression is *he... we... us... t hem*. The response to the Macedonian's call started with God's vision and one person, Paul, having an epiphany or revelation of the vision. Notice how God was turning the church inside-out at that time. As Paul shared God's vision, the others (we) *immediately* agreed and entered into or took ownership of God's vision (us). Where did they go? The answer is to *them*, the Macedonians. They did not argue, delay, vote, or dispute! Why? They realized that salvation belongs to God! They gave the church to the Macedonian community. This vision moved from a *he*, to a *we*, to an *us*, to a *them*! They filled that area of the earth with the knowledge of the glory of the Lord. The Word became flesh in them and moved into the Macedonian neighborhood. They connected the message with the audience. They had had contact and communication. They participated in the mystery of the Father seeking a bride for His Son. They gave God a face in Macedonia. They became all things to all men so that some might be saved. They realized that salt cannot flavor what it does not touch. They realized that the church is a community with a cause, which is the community.

My prayer is that all over the world the present-church people would have an epiphany of "Giving the Church Back to the Community." Let's not just grow a church, let's grow the community! I thank God there is a group of Pauls who are seeing the present-day

Macedonian call of community transformation. I am looking forward to the time when the vision takes on momentum and becomes a he to a we to an us so we can reach *them*! The Alan Wellses of the world are waiting. Salvation belongs to the Lord!

Anglers or Commercial Fisherman, Gardeners or Farmers?

Giving the church back to the community requires the church to see the community in a whole new way. The church was never called to be an angler. What do I mean by that? An angler goes fishing when he feels like it. An angler views angling as a sport rather than a means of existence. An angler fishes every once and a while depending upon his time, the weather, his comfort, and his finances. A commercial fisherman on the other hand is going for volume. He is willing to get wet, endure bad weather, and get seasick. He knows his life depends on it. He will change, adapt, and brave the elements to catch fish. He is willing to become "all things to all men" as the apostle Paul was to catch fish. The world would be a much different place if the church became serious about "fishing."

The same is true concerning gardeners and farmers. Gardeners are amateurs. Most gardeners grow small amounts of food using the food mostly for themselves. Their lives or livelihood do not depend on it. However, a farmer is serious about both quality and quantity. His livelihood depends on it. He is there to harvest a harvest. He is not there to pick out a head of lettuce or two.

In my opinion, these are great analogies for the church. The church is to be commercial fisherman, not anglers; farmers, not gardeners. The gardener or angler approach is the result of being church-centric. A farmer or commercial fisherman approach requires a community-centric mindset. One cannot have harvest and be church-centric at the same time. One cancels out the other.

The next chapter is about understanding that any vision must have congruent values that enable the vision. In the case of community transformation we must have right values that enable community transformation, not disable community transformation. As

I said before, you cannot have a huge catch and be an angler at the same time. Let's learn about the principle of vision and the values or "government" necessary for the church to put the pieces of Humpty Dumpty back together again. This principle, if applied, moves us from the possibility of community transformation to the probability of community transformation.

Chapter 5

TURNING UNFULFILLED POTENTIAL INTO FULFILLED REALITY:

The Principle of Vision and Government

The fulfillment of the potential of community transformation is dependent upon appropriate and enabling core values. Giving the church back to the community is not about vision, it is about values.

CHURCH@COMMUNITY CORE VALUES require that the last two elements of Nehemiah's recipe be applied for real, tangible, and lasting community transformation. Let's look at the following verses:

> So then you are no longer strangers and aliens, but you are fellow citizens with the saints, and are of God's household, having been built on the foundation of *the apostles and prophets*, Christ Jesus Himself being the corner stone, in whom the whole building, being fitted together is growing into a holy temple in the Lord; in whom you also are being built together into a dwelling of God in the Spirit.
>
> —EPHESIANS 2:19–22

I categorize the first two elements, "a burdened heart" and "a bended knee," as prophetic values, or passionate fire, and the second two, "a clear mind" and "calloused hands" as apostolic values, or intelligent fire. God is looking for the *whole house*, the *whole council* (see Acts 20:27), or what Paul calls in Ephesians 4:13 "the fullness of Christ." We are to grow up in all aspects into Him. (See Ephesians 4:15.) In other words, God needs the "full house" to open the community up to the King of Hearts. That is why we need to add apostolic values to prophetic values. Both are necessary and both, by themselves, are incomplete! Without both, the potential of *real* and *lasting* community transformation will never be fully realized.

Let's now focus our attention on intelligent fire—the "clear mind" and "calloused hands." I can explain the concept of intelligent fire by relating an incident that happened to me in Nakuru, Kenya.

Every Kenyan's Vision

In January 2000, I was speaking for Pastor Mark Kariuki of Nakuru, Kenya. This is the city in Kenya where the pink flamingos congregate by the thousands in famous Lake Nakuru. Pastor Mark had scheduled me to speak at one of the church's lunch hour "fellowships." The church rents a movie theater during the week at lunchtime, and the people come to get fed "the Word of God" for lunch. I had been to Kenya many times in the past, and while I have a tremendous love and respect for the Kenyans, I had noticed a tendency of Kenyans to be full of vision, but lacking the follow-through to ever see their vision fulfilled. This tendency exists in people all over the world. But I must admit, despite my love for the Kenyans, their lack of follow-through in many cases was getting to me. I want them to get to their purpose, vision, and destiny!

As I prepared for the lunch hour message, none of my old messages would "resurrect." The issues of *vision* and *government* with the Kenyans were too much on my mind. Finally, the Lord gave me an idea, a revelation, a principle that has changed my life as well as thousands of other lives around the globe. The beginnings of Church@Community were also birthed out of the land of *Hakuna Matata*, which means "no problem" in Swahili. God showed me that there was, indeed, a problem, or "matata." He showed me how to help many Kenyans identify the problem.

First of all, let me say that many Kenyans have a vision to win the marathon in the Olympics. Kenyans are great long distance runners. It is a source of national pride, and Kenyans have in their DNA the capacity for long distance running. It is a grace from God, a redemptive purpose, and a divine enablement that has been proven race after race for years. The world—especially the Kenyans—knows it. Remember, this was January 2000, and the Sydney, Australia Olympics was going to start in a few weeks.

I started my message with a question: how many Kenyans here have a vision to win the marathon at the Olympics? The scene following this question was wildly enthusiastic and positive! Over one thousand Kenyans stood up, screaming, dancing, going crazy. We had a revival! It took me over ten minutes to calm down the crowd! Then, after they quieted down, I asked the next question: how many people here think that Kenyans have it in their DNA to win the marathon at the Olympics? You guessed it! The theater exploded with shouting, joy, and celebration. It took me (as I recall) fifteen minutes to quiet the "revival." I could have gone back to my hotel at this point and we would still have "had church." Then I asked the last question: what if you have a Kenyan who has a vision to win the marathon at the Olympics, and he/she has it in their DNA to win the marathon, but *who never practices*. Will he/she win the Olympic marathon? You guessed it—the theater was quiet. No revival, the celebration stopped! I thought they were going to run me out of town!

A Vision Ungoverned Leads to Frustration

Here is the problem with the Kenyan I used as the example. He/she has a core value or "government" issue that undermines vision rather than enables vision. You cannot win the Olympic marathon and at the same time be lazy, eat wrong, or not have a coach. The Kenyan's lack of self-government will lead him to frustration and failure and unfulfilled potential. Obviously, there are Kenyans who have a good vision as well as good government, or else no Kenyan would ever win the Olympic marathon.

The point is that vision and government were always meant to work together. Government is a vehicle for the fulfillment of vision. Vision by itself cannot and will not achieve our objective. That Kenyan who never practices will never win the Olympic marathon, even though he has it in his DNA! His self-government issues will undermine him every time. The fulfillment of potential requires appropriate and enabling governmental core values.

Good Vision/Poor Government

Here is the problem with most people, churches, and organizational spheres. Generally, we are good at creating vision, but lack the appropriate government to get us to the vision.

What about the man who wants to have good "abs" (abdominal muscles), but never works out or exercises? Great vision, *but* the wrong government for the vision. What about the person who wants to graduate with honors from college, *but* never does their homework? Or the woman who wants to weigh 125 pounds, *but* who loves snacks? What about the pastor who wants to have a big church, *but* does not serve the people, invest time leading, or study the Bible? What about the person who wants to be a "great" intercessor, *but* cannot focus on prayer? How about the person who wants to be a great worship leader or musician, *but* never practices? What about the man who wants a big savings account, *but* spends everything he gets and more? How about the person who wants to be a good employee and get a promotion, *but* comes to work late and unfocused? Will he/she ever get to their vision? What about that husband who returns from a Promise Keepers meeting and wants to be a great husband, *but* cheats on his wife? What about a church that wants to "take the city," *but* is exclusive and ends up competing with other churches? What about the Christian who wants to be a "good neighbor," *but* leaves his front yard a mess?

Will these people ever get to their vision? The answer in all but a very few cases is no! Why? The core values, or government, of these people disable the vision rather than enable the vision. In my opinion, they have good vision but incompatible core values for the vision. These people will be loaded with frustration caused by governmental values that are incompatible with what they want to accomplish. Simply said, they lack the self-government to get to their vision.

ALWAYS LEARNING, NEVER ABLE

In 2 Timothy 3, Paul describes what the last days will be like. The first seven verses give us further revelation of the concept of vision and government.

> But realize this, that in the last days difficult times will come. For men will be lovers of self, lovers of money, boastful, arrogant, revilers, disobedient to parents, ungrateful, unholy, unloving, irreconcilable, malicious gossips, without self-control, brutal, haters of good, treacherous, reckless, conceited, lovers of pleasure rather than lovers of God, holding to a form of godliness, although they have denied its power; and avoid such men as these. For among them are those who enter into households and captivate weak women weighed down with sins, led on by various impulses, *always learning and never able to come to the knowledge of the truth.*
>
> —2 TIMOTHY 3:1–7

In these verses, Paul mentions the principle of "always learning and never able."

In other words, people in the last days will be pursuing the *vision* of "the knowledge of the truth," but lack the *government* to ever arrive at or achieve it. Governmental core values like lovers of self-adequacy, boasting, or unloving disable the vision rather than enabling the vision. The result is pretending, claiming, declaring, or holding to a form of godliness "although they have denied its power." How do they deny its power? The government or core values are wrong for the vision of "coming to the knowledge of the truth."

As a result, people in the last days will be always learning but never able. They will be a society of frustration and unfulfilled potential. Like the Kenyan in our example, they will possess a vision but lack the government to fulfill the vision. The problem is that the frustration caused by the lack of government leads to much worse things down the road.

I fear this same issue applies to many Christians, churches, businesses, and organizations also. There is a lesson here: we need appropriate and enabling core values or government to get us to our vision, dreams, and goals. We will not get there *by vision alone*. Remember, without a vision the people perish (Proverbs 29:18), but without the people the vision perishes. As in our recipe on community transformation, it will take more than a burdened heart or a bended knee. It will take a clear mind and calloused hands to make the vision of real, tangible, and lasting community transformation a reality. A clear mind means getting the mind of Christ regarding the enabling core values or government that will be the correct vehicle to community transformation. A clear mind has the ability to get the hands to the good work. *A clear mind takes an impression and turns it into an expression*. A clear mind is always learning *and* always able. Why? The right core values are applied to the right vision. The result is moving from dream to done, revelation to reality, invisible to visible, declaration to actualization, implied to applied, theology to biography, and spiritual to the natural. What we envision becomes reality!

"Shirt, I Iron You!"

Unfortunately, many Christians and church leaders do not understand the correlation between vision and government. This is demonstrated in what I call the "Satan, I bind you" phenomenon. I once heard a cassette tape by the late Pastor John Wimber where he talked on binding. As I recall he was saying, "Satan, I bind you," is like saying, "Shirt, I iron you." If I carry his thought a little further, it is like saying, "Floor, I vacuum you," "Food, I eat you," "Wife, I kiss you," or "Book, I write you." I have tried the book-I-write-you approach, and it did not work!

What these well-meaning people have failed to realize is the principle of vision and government. Actually, Jesus addressed the process of binding in Matthew 18:15–20. He was teaching his disciples that binding is more than what the Pharisees and rabbis did in the temple, that is, holding their breath, and mentally declaring, "Sinner, I bind you." Jesus, His disciples, and the people of Israel knew this practice very well. Jesus said, in effect, that if you want to "bind" a "sinner" and "win your brother," you must have not only the vision of binding, but also the government of binding.

> If your brother sins, go and reprove him in private; if he listens to you, you have won your brother. But if he does not listen to you, take one or two more with you, *so that by the mouth of two or three witnesses every fact may be confirmed*. And if he refuses to listen to them, tell it to the church; and if he refuses to listen even to the church, let him be to you as a Gentile and a tax collector. Truly I say to you, whatever you shall bind on earth shall be bound in heaven; and whatever you loose on earth shall be loosed in heaven. Again I say to you, that if two of you agree on earth about anything that they may ask, it shall be done for them by My Father who is in heaven. For where two or three have gathered together in My name, I am there in their midst.
>
> —MATTHEW 18:15–20 (EMPHASIS ADDED)

According to these verses, you bind a sinner by following these steps:

1. Going alone and talking to him (real and tangible).
2. If he does not receive you, taking one or more others and talking to him (real and tangible).
3. If he refuses to listen, telling it to church (real and tangible).
4. If he refuses to change, treating him as a tax-gatherer (real and tangible).

Those steps are real and tangible expressions of government to get to the vision of binding a sin and winning your brother. Real ministry and turning unfulfilled potential into fulfilled reality require the spiritual to express itself within the natural. You cannot "camp out" in "vision land"! You bind a "spirit" of hunger by getting organized, getting some food, and going to where people are and feeding them! Notice in Matthew

18 how vision and government were congruent, enabling, and in synch. The government enabled the vision, not disabled the vision. The principle of vision and government together opened the gates that the King of Glory could come in. (See Psalm 24:7.)

Governmentally Challenged

If I were to assess the situation of the Kenyan at the beginning of this chapter, I would say he was "governmentally challenged." He figured out had the vision, but he was not able to incarnate it. His lack of government impeded the impression from becoming expression! The result could be depression.

Before going further into the guiding principle of this book, I want to clearly define "vision" and "government."

Remember, vision is a compelling picture of a preferable future that motivates one to perform. Vision is motivational. It is where God wants us to be—it is the dream of His heart. When we have a compelling picture of a preferable future, it motivates us to *go*. Vision has to do with the eyes. Let's look at how God motivated Abram to leave Ur of the Chaldees (Babylon) to a more preferable future, that is, Israel.

> And the LORD said to Abram, after Lot had separated from him, "Now lift up your eyes and look from the place where you are, northward and southward and eastward and westward; for all the land which you see, I will give it to you and to your descendants forever. And I will make your descendants as the dust of the earth; so that if anyone can number the dust of the earth, then your descendants can also be numbered. Arise, walk about the land through its length and breadth; for I will give it to you."
>
> —GENESIS 13:14–17

Notice "lift *up* your *eyes*... *look* from the place where you are." In other words, *"Here is your more preferable future, Abram!"* That vision is what motivated him to go where no man had ever gone before. So vision gets us on our way, but it takes government to make sure we get there! I will say it again— many people, leaders, organizations, and churches have vision, but the key to achieving vision is the vehicle of government (the correct set of core values to get to the vision).

I am referring here to the *principle* or *concept* of government. Government is the vehicle with the authority to use the power to fulfill the vision or purpose. A study of Romans 13 reveals to us that:

1. The principle of government is from God, and established by God (verse 1).

2. Government is a *minister* of God to you (verse 4).

3. "Rulers" are servants of God (verse 6).

4. He who resists governmental authority is opposing a principle of God (verse 2).

5. Peter exhorts us in 1 Peter 2:17 to *honor* governmental authority.

6. As God takes vengeance to serve, preserve, and protect vision (Romans 12:18–19), so does government as our avenger of wrong. (See Romans 13:4.)

7. From Romans 13, we conclude that government is a vehicle ordained by God to:
   a. protect vision
   b. serve vision
   c. collect the tithe or tax to accomplish the vision

What I want you to understand here is the principle, concept, and function of government. Please do not think in terms of various governmental *forms*, such as national governments, boards, or elders. You need to grasp the *principle of government* and how it is God's agent or vehicle on earth to accomplish vision. When I refer to the principle of government in this book, I mean *the authority and power to fulfill the vision*.

Government's primary role is that of a *minister* or *servant*. What is a minister? Webster's Third International Dictionary defines the word *minister* as "one who acts under the orders or authority of another."

Used as a verb, it means, first, "to serve or officiate in worship," and second, "to attend to the wants and comforts of someone; to serve; to do things needful or helpful." In principle, therefore, it is government's job to make sure that the vision gets done. Government attends to the wants of vision, serves vision, and acts under the authority of vision. Government needs a purpose or vision. It is not an end in itself.

Therefore, good government is the protector of the vision, *not* the *perfector* of the vision. Government exists for vision, not vision for government.

Head and Shoulders

I will summarize with six key principles of government:

1. Government is a servant; it ministers to vision.
2. Government requires agreement with vision.
3. Government is a means to an end, never the end in itself.
4. Government is created by God to carry out vision.
5. Government is the vehicle; vision is the driver of the vehicle.
6. Vision is the "eyes," government is the "shoulders." Eyes are above the shoulders.

Do you realize that Jesus was the government or vehicle to carry out God's vision of "Thy Kingdom come. Thy will be done, on earth as it is in heaven" (Matt. 6:9–10)?

Look at Isaiah 9:6–7:

> For a child will be born to us, a son will be given to us; and the government will rest on His shoulders; and His name will be called Wonderful Counselor, Mighty God, Eternal Father, Prince of Peace. There will be no end to the increase of His government or of peace, on the throne of David and over his kingdom, to establish it and to uphold it with justice and righteousness

> from then on and forevermore. The zeal of the Lord of hosts will accomplish this.

Notice "*government* will rest on *His shoulders*. That is why Jesus said, "Not my will, but Thine be done" (Luke 22:42). Jesus knew He was operating in a governmental capacity to serve a vision, God's vision. "My food is to do the will of Him who sent Me, and to accomplish His work" (John 4:34). Jesus was a vehicle to serve and protect vision, and He had the power and authority to *do the vision*. He was *the* enabling government or "shoulders" to serve God's vision. Because He was in agreement with God's vision, unfulfilled potential became fulfilled reality. He took the God's vision from dream to done, from revelation to reality, and from idea to incarnated.

In Genesis 2 and 3, Adam could have but did not want to serve God's vision. His was a case of government trying to determine the vision. Jesus, as the last Adam, came to protect God's vision, serve God's vision, and use His power and authority (shoulders) to achieve God's vision. He had the right core values to accomplish the vision!

I will finish this chapter with a conceptual chart to help correlate and connect the principle of vision and government.

Description of Vision and Government

Vision	Government
Eyes/head	Shoulders
Sees	Does/builds
Prophetic	Apostolic
Power to see	Power and ability to do
Individual	Requires a vision to partner with
What is being served	Servant/minister
End/goal	Means to an end
Intangible	Real and tangible
Impression	Expression
Provider of the vision	Finisher
Built to be fast/catalytic	Built to last

Mothering/birthing	Fathering/establishing
Thermostat	Air-conditioning unit
Priest	King

To verbalize one of these pairs as a simple illustration, imagine vision as the thermostat, but government as the air-conditioning unit—it has the power to get things done, to carry out the vision of cooling the house to seventy degrees.

In the next chapter, we will explore how the principle of vision and government works in a practical way, and how this principle determines the outcome of a vision. This book presents my vision of real, tangible, and lasting community transformations—lots of them. I believe that Kenyan marathon runner can turn his unfulfilled potential into fulfilled reality *if* he has the right values. The same holds true of "normalizing" community transformation *if* we have the right values. Church@Community has to do with the discovery and application of appropriate core values or government that enables the vision of real, tangible, and lasting community transformation. These enabling core values are the vehicle that turns the unfulfilled potential of real, tangible, and lasting community transformation into fulfilled reality. One of the main themes of Church@Community is understanding how vision and government partner to enhance the community.

Chapter 6

Visionary "Drivers" in Governmental "Vehicles":

The Principle of Agreement, Unity, and Abundance

The two become one, the one becomes many.

What could I possibly mean by Visionary "Drivers" in Governmental "Vehicles"? Vision drives the vehicle while government is the vehicle. Cars exist for the purpose of getting their drivers to their desired destinations. The car is the means to an end, not the end in itself. However, it takes the right vehicle to get the driver where he wants to go. I would not take a Cadillac on a road that is a challenge for a four-wheel drive Jeep. That Cadillac will end up frustrating everybody. The fault, however, does not lie with the Cadillac; it lies with the driver. He picked the wrong vehicle for his desired destination.

Good leadership and good stewardship of vision are about discovering the right vehicle for getting where you want to go. I believe those interested in community transformation have the right vision for what God is doing today. The key is discovering the right government, core values, or vehicle to arrive at the destination. That is what I call intelligent fire. In this chapter, we will explore some very real examples of how this principle works, and at the end discover why it works.

Directional Vehicles in Business

Let's imagine a long established and successful corporation wanted to change its corporate vision. Their old vision was to be the most profitable of all the corporations that produce a certain line of products in the United States. For many years they had accomplished that goal. Through these years, they sold their products to a very select group of customers in their industry. They were only interested in those customers that would pay their bills in thirty days or less and had a perfect credit rating. They were not interested in selling to "marginal" companies which did not fit their exact criteria. For many years, their values and their vision worked together to accomplish what they were after.

Now, here comes the new vision. The management now wants this company to be the sales leader in their particular industry for the whole United States. That is quite a vision and quite a change for the company. Perhaps the original owner's son took over!

What will happen if this company adopts the new vision of being the sales leader in their industry but does not change their old values? Let me explain. If they kept their old "government" of all bills paid within thirty days and the perfect credit requirement, would they accomplish their new vision? The answer is, of course, no. Why? Because the government is not in agreement, nor congruent or adequate to fulfill the new vision. It is a full-sized Cadillac trying to go where only a Jeep can go. As a result, the new vision will stay in the dream stage and never get to the done stage. And remember, a vision unmanaged leads to frustration.

This company will have to change more than vision to accomplish this new vision. They will have to change their government or credit values also. They will have to discover the right values or government to enable the new vision not disable it. The company's credit policy will have to be changed to allow sales to other customers also. Not every customer is a "perfect" pay. However, they can be good customers. They also can be customers that can increase sales significantly. The management will have to rethink issues such as how much risk to take, credit policies, and profitability. They will have to loosen up their credit policies. A vehicle or new government will need to be established that enables the new vision. The vision and government will need to be congruent and in agreement. Hopefully, after this process is done, they will have a match of a visionary "driver" in a governmental "vehicle."

In doing that, they just made the new vision possible rather than impossible!

Take My Debt, But Leave My Credit Card

Remember the man from Kenya? He has the vision, he has the DNA, but his lack of self-government disables the vision. The man who wants good abs, but never works out, will he get to his vision? How about the person who wants to graduate from college with honors, but never does his homework? Remember the woman who wants to weigh 125 pounds, but who consumes snacks? How about that pastor who wants to have a big church, but does not serve his people, invest time leading, or study the Bible? Remember the person who wants to be a great worship leader or musician, but never practices ("Piano, I play you!")? What about that person who wants a big savings account, but spends everything he gets (take my debt, but leave my credit card)? That man who wants to get the promotion and the raise, but comes to work late and unfocused, will he realize his vision? Remember the man who wants to be a great husband, but keeps cheating on his wife, will he be successful? Finally, how about that man who wants to be a good neighbor, but leaves his front yard a mess? Will these well-meaning people ever get to their vision? The answer is no, as long as their self-government or core value set remains incompatible with the vision or goals they want to achieve.

Following is a chart with three categories: vision, disabling behavior/wrong government, and enabling behavior/right government. Obviously, there are many causes for disabling government. They could include such things as ignorance, childhood hurts, habits, or negative shaping events, but ultimately, after someone goes through the necessary remedial process, he or she needs to be functional enough to adopt the enabling core value. Take a few moments to look at the chart:

VISION/GOVERNMENT CORRELATION CHART

VISION/ GOVERNMENT	DISABLING BEHAVIOR/WRONG GOVERNMENT	ENABLING BEHAVIOR/RIGHT GOVERNMENT
Win Olympics	Does not practice	Practice/self-control
Have good abs	Does not work out	Works out/self-control
Graduate from college with honors	Does not study or do homework	Studies/does homework/ self-control
Weigh 125 pounds	Consumes snacks	Limiting snacks/ self-control
Have big church	Does not serve, invest time, study	Serve, invest time, study self-control
Great worship leader	Does not practice	Practice/self-control
Have savings account	Spends everything he makes	Moderates spending/self-control
Wants promotion and raise	Comes to work late and unfocused	Arrives on time or early/ focused/ self control
Be great husband	Cheats on wife	Remains faithful and loving/self-control
Be a good neighbor	Leaves front yard a mess	Clean up and cares how his neighborhood looks/self-control

Although a person may have many reasons for his disabling behavior, ultimately he must arrive at the correct behavior, which comes from the appropriate governmental convictions or core values. The purpose of this chart is not to explore the "why" of the behavior, but to show the correlation between vision and government that enables or disables a vision, desire, or goal.

I desire to make this very important foundational principle as sharp and clear to you as God has made it to me. Remember, a vision ungoverned leads to frustration. Real, tangible, and lasting community transformation is a wonderful vision, but without the enabling government or core values, the victories will be few and false starts many. My heart's desire here is to achieve the full potential of community transformation.

Chip Off the Old Block

It is easy to see the vision/government correlation in my own home. I am the visionary in the house, and my wife Becky is government. It is easy for me to get way out in "visionland." My church even bought me a baseball cap with "Delphland" embroidered on the front. That was their way of saying "Hold on, let's consider how we are going to get there, if we want to get there at all!" My wife has what I call "the brunette anointing." She is solid, has good borders, and generally makes sure that we stay on earth. To borrow from the title of this book, she is real, tangible, and lasting (meaning she will be there!). Becky has been a great helpmate to me in finishing what I start and making sure the "power and authority" to fulfill the vision are there in a practical way.

Our two boys, Matthew and Jonathan, are microcosms of Becky and me. Like me, Matthew is a visionary, and Jonathan is governmental like Becky. As you can see, we have an "interesting" but fairly effective household. Each of us has what the others needs. Remember, opposites attract then negotiate the differences.

Matthew, our visionary, has just turned sixteen. We have noticed he tends to be a dreamer, has big ideas, wants to make lots of money, and even wants to be a youth pastor, but is "governmentally challenged" when it comes to studying. His paradigm is "homework, I write you" or "test, I study for you!" He is into miracles on test day. He tends to be like the person who wants to win the lottery—big money, big cars, big stuff—but no work, no government, and living life by the extreme exception rather than the rule of thumb.

Something happened, however, to change Matt. Let's just say, Matt has a vision—it is called driving. And his government was not congruent with the vision. In fact, getting a D disqualified him from getting to his vision both from an insurance perspective and from a parental perspective. Therefore, the government in our house set up some borders to enable Matt's vision of driving the car. The policy is, "If you have Ds, there are no keys." It is amazing how quickly Matt got a "revelation" on the issue of government to achieve the vision. As I write this book, Matt is doing great. He is a fine, young man who is beginning to understand the principle of vision and government, and that government will get him and keep him where he wants to be. Matt is a visionary driver in a governmental vehicle. Also, I thank God for insurance companies who give a discount for a B average. It is the insurance company's fault and not ours for once!

Vision and Government in the Bible

Let's look at some verses in the Bible and see how this principle works in spiritual issues.

Example 1

> But have nothing to do with worldly fables fit only for old women. On the other hand, discipline yourself for the purpose of godliness; for bodily discipline is only of little profit, but godliness is profitable for all things, since it holds promise for the present life and also for the life to come.
>
> —1 Timothy 4:7–8

We see here that the vision was not discipline, but godliness. Paul is saying that discipline or government was never the end in itself, but rather a means to an end—getting to the vision of godliness.

Godliness was the vision, and discipline the government. Godliness was the eyes, and discipline the shoulders. Notice that the shoulders are always below the eyes, unless the person is a mutation or upside down. However, it is interesting to note that the vision of godliness does require the government of discipline. Godliness is a visionary driver in a governmental vehicle. I realize some have made bodily discipline their vision, but frankly, this is of little profit. Usually, making bodily discipline the vision creates obsessive-compulsive behavior on the part of those pursuing that vision. I will say it simply— godliness is profitable for all things, but it requires a partner or something to agree with. That partner is the government of discipline!

Example 2

> You husbands likewise, live with your wives in an understanding way, as with a weaker vessel, since she is a woman; and grant her honor as a fellow heir of the grace of life, so that your prayers may not be hindered.
>
> —1 Peter 3:7

As we look at this verse, we see that the vision is that the husband's prayers would not be hindered. If his government is not living with his wife in an understanding way and, therefore, not honoring her, he will never get to God's vision of his prayers being heard and answered. His government disables the vision. This is why many times our prayers do not get answered.

Jesus says in Matthew 5:23–24, "If therefore if you are presenting your offering at the altar, and there remember that your brother has something against you, leave your offering there before the altar, and go your way; first be reconciled to your brother, and then come and present your offering." In other words, get your government in line with what you want to accomplish. Do not "come to the altar" with a disabling government. In the case of 1 Peter 3, the husband's prayers answered is the visionary driver, and honoring her and living with her in an understanding way is the government vehicle. The same is true for women also. If you are an intercessor operating in a disrespectful way and lacking understanding of your husband, your prayers will eventually be hindered. Why? Your government disables your vision or your desire.

Example 3

> And the glory which Thou hast given Me I have given to them; that they may be one, just as We are one; I in them, and Thou in Me, that they may be perfected in unity, that the world may know that Thou didst send Me, and didst love them, even as Thou didst love Me.
>
> —John 17:22–23

Many of you may disagree with my analysis of this verse. Do you realize the purpose of glory is to create unity? Jesus' glory and, therefore, God's glory is never to be used as an end in itself. Jesus says that glory is the government and unity is the vision. In other words, glory is never to be what we seek but is simply the means to an end, or unity. Glory is the shoulders and unity is the eyes or vision. God's glory is given to us for the purpose of unity. The glory in heaven produces the unity of the Trinity!

When that glory comes to earth, it is meant to produce unity or right relationships with people, in marriages, among churches, and with the community. Many churches that seek the glory are marked by disunity, church splits, and spiritual favoritism. Why? These well-meaning churches are trying to make the government the vision. Let's quit misusing God's glory, and honor what He is trying to do with it—*unity*. Unity is the vision, and glory is the government, not vice versa.

Now notice verse 23—the purpose of unity is to produce evangelism. Here unity becomes the government, and evangelism—"that the world may know that Thou didst send Me"—becomes God's vision. Unity is the governmental authority and power—or enabling core value—to enable the vision of evangelism and community transformation. Psalm 133 suggests the same principle. When brothers dwell together in unity, there the Lord commands the blessing—*life forever*. The vision is life forevermore, and the government is brothers dwelling together in unity. This is what I call purpose-driven glory and unity.

When you start to become aware of this revolutionary principle, you begin adding intelligent fire to your passionate fire. Remember, God won the fight, and the community is the prize!

Example 4

> But you shall remember the Lord your God, for it is He who is giving you power to make wealth, that He may confirm His covenant which He swore to your fathers, as it is this day.
>
> —Deuteronomy 8:18

Let's analyze this verse. What is the vision and what is the government? The vision is that God may confirm His covenant (establish His Kingdom) and the government is the power to make wealth. God uses money to establish His Kingdom. Money is the government, and confirming His covenant is the vision. Money is the means to an end, never the end in itself.

Making money the vision and using God's Kingdom to do it is a major violation of vision and government. That is when you start using God as a means to your own ends. The problem is, sooner or later, it catches up to you. Money is a wonderful servant, but a terrible master. The power to make wealth for the purpose of establishing God's Kingdom is getting the right vision with the right government. Money is the servant of the vision of confirming His Kingdom. Establishing God's Kingdom is the vision, and money is the governmental vehicle.

Example 5

> You know that David my father was unable to build a house for the name of the Lord his God because of the wars which surrounded him, until the Lord put them under the soles of his feet. But now the Lord my God has given me rest on every side; there is neither adversary nor misfortune. And Behold, I intend to build a house for the name of the Lord my God, as the Lord spoke to David my father, saying, "Your son, whom I will set on your throne in your place, he will build the house for My name."....And the Lord gave wisdom to Solomon, just as He promised him; and there was peace between Hiram and Solomon, and the two of them made a covenant.
>
> —1 Kings 5:3–5, 12

The vision was to build a house for the name of the Lord. David had the vision of building the house, but Solomon would have to be the government to fulfill the vision. Why? The passage says that David was disqualified because of "the wars that surrounded him." It is even more clear in 1 Chronicles 28:3, which calls him a man who "has shed blood." Even though David was a man after God's own heart, he was a man of war. It is one thing to be in a war, it is another thing for war to be in you. Evidently, at some point in David's life he crossed that line, and God knew it. God knew that David was the wrong vehicle for the vision of building His house. Solomon was a man of wisdom and of peace (v. 12). His name even means peace. God invented the principle of "wisdom builds the house" (see Proverbs 24:3), not *warfare* builds the house. In fact, Ecclesiastes 9:18 says that wisdom is better than warfare.

So we see that wisdom was the right vehicle for building the house of the Lord. The vision was to build a house for the name of the Lord. The governmental power and authority that built the house was wisdom. If someone tries to build the house of the Lord by warfare, the governmental vehicle disables the vision rather than enables the vision. In Solomon's case, wisdom and peace were the vehicle, and building the house of the Lord, the vision. The result was that the Temple was built. This very important governmental issue that will be further developed later on in this book.

Functional National Government

The principle of vision and government is being incarnated in the country of Afghanistan even as I write this book. On September 11, 2001, an event took place that shocked the world. I was in New Zealand at the time, and I will never forget that early morning when several pastors from the Elim denomination woke me up. I was in Auckland speaking at Elim's national conference.

"Wake up mate! Look at the television—you will not believe what is happening in your country," they said. We all watched the television in shock as the images of that morning were screened over and over again. This attack on the vision of the United States illustrates perfectly the principle of visionary drivers in governmental vehicles.

The vision of the United States of America can be summed up

this way: "Liberty and justice for all." On September 11, there was an attack on this vision. Remember, government is a means to an end. Good government has the authority and power to protect vision, serve vision, and collect the tithe or tax to accomplish the vision. (Romans 13). Government's job as a vehicle is to have the infrastructure, the integrity, and strategies in case of emergency to make sure the vision is protected, served, and accomplished. So what is government's role in the case of September 11, 2001? Obviously, if it is a good government, it should do what it was created to do—protect the vision. That is the reason the military of the United States is in Afghanistan. Real government is that which has the power and authority to carry out vision.

As I write this chapter, I am in the country of Uganda. Once the "Pearl of Africa," Uganda is slowly rebuilding. I believe it is rebuilding because it has a government that is starting to serve the vision of the country. During Idi Amin's time, the government rebelled against vision and became "the end" rather than a means to an end. The results were disastrous.

The issue of vision and government and their proper roles is probably why much of Africa has so much unfulfilled potential. When government is self-serving, tribal, and corrupt, the result is that the vision of liberty and good standards of living will not be achieved. This has been a hard lesson for many Africans, South Americans, and developing world governments to learn. Most of these nations have the same potential and, in many cases, more potential than most European countries, but have not had a revelation about getting the right government for their visions. Most of their constitutions and bill of rights documents (vision) would be similar to those of "developed nations." The problem is not in their vision statements, the problem is in the government. Vision statements without enabling government are rhetoric. I love Proverbs 29:18: "Where there is no vision, the people are unrestrained." We all need direction. However, the opposite is also true. Without the people (enabling government), the vision perishes!

All I have to say is "Watch out world" when the developing world discovers and implements what the developed world has known for a while—the revelation and correlation of visionary drivers in governmental vehicles.

Purpose-Driven Theology

In March, 2002 I was in Chicago at the Willow Creek Community Church. I was there for the National Association of Ecclesiology annual meeting. This group consists of denomination presidents, seminary presidents, heads of church networks like Willow Creek, and the heads of some large parachurch organizations. Dr. C. Peter Wagner asked me to represent the New Apostolic Reformation churches at this council, a task that I was happy to do. My friend, Dan Reeves of Reeves Consultants, is the convener. The vision of this very amazing group is to discover and focus on our similarities as churches and movements, rather than our differences, and ultimately to discover what we all can do together for the United States.

At this council, several large seminaries are represented, such as King's College and Seminary with Dr. Paul Chappell, Dallas Theological Seminary with Dr. Darrell Bock, Asbury Theological Seminary with Dr. Howard Snyder and Dr. Tom Tumblin, Wheaton College with Dr. Mark Talbot, and Liberty University with Dr. Elmer Towns. During our meetings, I heard several of these seminary representatives use the term "purpose-driven theology." I was ecstatic over the use of this term—which was adopted from Rick Warren of Saddleback Community Church—because it described exactly what theology is meant to do. Theology is a means to an end, not the end in itself. Theology exists for a purpose, or—to use my vernacular—for a vision. The vision of theology is to help people to be better Christians by knowing the Person of God accurately. Theology exists for the vision, not vice versa. Frankly, this has been the problem for many seminaries and theologians. Rather than being the servant, theology became the master, an end in itself. You might say theology is a wonderful servant, but a terrible master. Theology is a governmental vehicle whose purpose is to propel people like you and me to the vision of knowing God better.

Even church government is not an end in itself, but a vehicle to serve vision, protect vision, and to make sure that the local church has the funds to accomplish the vision it is there to serve. Church eldership, the governing board—or whatever a church calls its government—exists to be the "shoulders," making sure the church is within the law of its nation both legally and financially. The government of the church is also meant to protect the vision of the church. Without enabling and functioning church government, a church will stay in the "unfulfilled potential loop." It will be like the man from Kenya—great vision, but lacking the government to ever get to the vision.

Agreement, Unity, Abundance

You might be asking, "Why does it take two entities to complete a task?" Why does it take vision *and* government? What is the principle dictating the partnership of vision and government? The answer is the amazing principle of agreement, unity, and abundance!

I first heard this principle at a Christmas banquet in December 2001 through my good friend, Pastor Derone Robinson of Word of Abundant Life Church in Phoenix, Arizona. God used Pastor Derone to reveal to me why visionary drivers require governmental vehicles.

Remember Genesis 2:18, "It is not good for the man to be alone." Up to that point, God said everything was "good." However, he saw something in man that was incomplete or inadequate and "not good." God knew that one cannot multiply. God knew no person or entity is complete enough to exist alone. After all, God Himself is actually composed of three different aspects of Godhead existing in such unity that one cannot tell where these individual aspects begin or end. These aspects are three, yet One. In the Bible, the Hebrew word *Elohim* describes this three-yet-One concept. Elohim is used in Genesis 1:26, "Let *Us* make man in *Our* own image." There is even an aspect of God that is corporate, plural, and a convergence of attributes and aspects. Therefore, it should be no surprise that God said, "We shall make a helpmate or completer for Adam; she shall be called woman" (Gen. 2:23). Eve was custom made for Adam, and Adam was custom made for Eve.

Then God said an amazing thing in Genesis 2:24, "And they shall become one..." Later, the two becoming one resulted in the one becoming many, or a family. God further developed this principle in Matthew 18:20, "For where two or three have gathered together in My name, there I am in their midst." What God is saying is that one man, entity, or concept alone is incomplete. It is true that we all need others to complete us, grow us, mature us, and bring us to full potential or fruition. We were designed to be corporate, patterned after the Father. Let *Us* make man in *Our* image!

Two or Three to Agree

Throughout this book, I will refer to the following pattern I have observed in Scripture:

1. Agreement—which takes at least one partner to agree, complete, and enable.

2. Unity—the product and power of agreement between or among two or more partners.

3. Abundance—the outcome of unity as a result of an enabling partnership in agreement.

I will explain it this way: the two became one, the one became many. See the pattern? This is a guiding principle designed by God for people, marriages, businesses, governments, education, and all other organizational spheres. It is called the principle of agreement, unity, abundance. The two became one, the one became many.

Let's use Adam and Eve as an example. Adam and Eve were two that became one and had a family. The two became one, the one became many. Using Psalm 133: as an example, we find the same principle is true, "Behold, how good and pleasant it is for *brothers* to dwell *together* in unity...for there the Lord commanded the blessing—life forever" (vv. 1, 3). Here again is the principle, the two (brothers) became one (unity) and the one became many (commanded the blessing). The brothers had sufficient agreement to create unity, which in turn created the commanded blessing.

Even wicked Nimrod in Genesis 11:6 knew this principle. He gathered all his partners into a united force to build the tower of Babel. As a result of the partners' unity, the tower was being completed at a very rapid rate (abundance). The Lord took notice and said, "Behold, they are one people, and they all have the same language. And this is what they began to do, and now nothing which they purpose to do will be impossible for them."

What principle did Nimrod know? When brothers dwell together in unity, there is accomplishment of purpose. Abundance is the fulfillment of purpose. In each of the above cases, the two became one, and the one became many. There were two or three to agree.

I could go on with examples like Gideon's 300, or the assembling of David's army in 1 Chronicles 12, but I think you get the message. The point is you have to start with at least two. There has to be agreement before there can be unity! Paul asserts this concept even in arriving at the truth: "Every fact is to be confirmed by the testimony of two or three witnesses" (2 Cor. 13:1). Agreement emanates from an act of the will and incarnates in the miracle of unity. Unity in turn creates abundance, or fulfillment of purpose.

It Is Not Good for Vision to Live Alone

Let's return to our concept of vision and government, visionary drivers in governmental vehicles. The principle of agreement, unity, abundance, shows us the importance of first, having a government in the first place, and second, having a government that is in agreement with and thus enabling the vision. Vision needs a vehicle to transport it to abundance.

Remember what I said earlier: a vision ungoverned leads to frustration. Without a vision, the people perish, but without the people (government), the vision perishes. Many visionaries fail because they do not know this principle. Their logic seems to be, "God gave me the vision, all I need is God, God is my partner." Please realize that God wants to incarnate Himself *in others* for your benefit! They are there to sharpen you, hold you accountable, help you think through the vision, develop your relationship skills as well as task skills to accomplish your vision. Remember it takes the agreement of two or three to have abundance or the accomplishment of purpose.

This principle has major ramifications that affect the pastor and his church government elders, relationships with the community and government, church to church relationships, marriage relationships, and business partnerships. I will discuss more of this principle in the next few chapters. For now, please remember the goal of this book is to get you, the church, and the community operating to full potential. I want to move us from revelation to reality, dream to done, theology to biography, intangible to tangible, implied to applied, impression to expression, and from declared to achieved. The door to actualization is through the vision and government principle. I want that man from Kenya to win the Olympic marathon. I also want you, your church, and your community to win the destiny that the Lord has for you and them. That is why we need intelligent fire!

And Now, Intelligent Fire Core Values

The reason for this book is to maximize the potential of real, tangible, and lasting community transformation. I also believe that it is God's vision. In the next eight chapters, I will discuss the governmental core values that need to be shifted or changed in church life to enable the vision of community transformation. As we have learned, we need to have agreement and unity in the vision and government realm so we can get to the abundance of real, tangible, and lasting community transformation. It is not just a matter of leadership, it is a matter of "leadershift"!

Chapter 7

The Man Who Made the Fish Sick:

The Principle of Life-and-Death or Right-or-Wrong

It is better to light a light than to curse the darkness.

Now we are getting into the real meat of this book. This is the "boiler room" where we can find the real power or government to reach our communities. Remember that our values drive our behavior. The Church@Community core values are the enablers or vehicles to get us to God's vision of community and, ultimately, national transformation. Values are the air-conditioning unit, while the vision of community transformation is the thermostat. A thermostat informs us of the need to change. The air-conditioning unit responds with the power to fulfill the need. Enabling core values move one from revelation to reality and from implied truth to applied truth. If we want real, tangible, and lasting community transformation, we must have—within the church and within each of us individually—the "right stuff." It is more than wishing and hoping and dreaming and praying—it is values that drive our attitudes and actions toward life-giving community transformation. Hold on, deliverance is coming!

Life and Death, or Right or Wrong

In March 2001, I was speaking at a large community transformation rally in Glendale, Arizona. Pastor Greg Brown of Skyway Church had invited more than forty churches in the area to this event. The group of leaders and churches is called Cities for Christ. The atmosphere was electric and eclectic with churches ranging from conservative denominational to "radical" nondenominational. We had come together for the sake of the community and surrounding areas. More than one thousand people were there, including many area pastors, leaders, and parachurch leaders.

I delivered a message titled "Giving the Church Back to the Community." I actually ended up throwing about one hundred pounds of corn kernels on the attendees to illustrate a point—God wants His Word, or seeds, in circulation, planted in the community. In community transformation, a key principle is truly "no deposit, no return."

At the end of the meeting, I said something I will ever forget to Cheryl Sacks of Bridgebuilders International Leadership Network. Cheryl, a powerful prayer mobilizer, has organized, equipped, and released hundreds of intercessors in churches across Arizona. She lives and breathes prayer. The goal of her ministry is to make sure intercessors are praying intelligently and strategically. What I said to her may shock you (especially if you are an intercessor), but read carefully and do not react, because everything will turn out just right in the end.

I said, "Cheryl, I have heard you have six hundred intercessors praying for revival in Arizona? If that's all you're praying for, then you may want to think again." Cheryl and I have known one another for years, so she instantly knew by the strength and severity of my question that I was trying to make a point. Now, Cheryl is always looking for fresh information to help intercessors pray more strategically. In fact, her mission statement is to connect Christians to relevant information enabling focused, informed intercession. I knew I had her attention.

She said, "So, Ed, what are you trying to say?"

I replied, "If 90 percent of the churches and pastors in Phoenix believe that doing 'right or wrong' is more important than 'life or death,' why would God ever give us revival?" I went on to explain the following story from Matthew 9:9–13:

> And as Jesus passed on from there, He saw a man, called Matthew, sitting in the tax office; and He said to him, 'Follow Me!' And he rose, and followed Him. And it happened that as He was reclining at the table in the house, behold many tax-gatherers and sinners came and were dining with Jesus and His disciples. And when the Pharisees saw this, they said to His disciples, 'Why is your Teacher eating with the tax gatherers and sinners?' But when Jesus heard this, He said, 'It is not those who are healthy who need a physician, but those who are sick. But go and learn what this means, *I desire compassion, and not sacrifice*, for I did not come to call the righteous, but sinners.
>
> —Matthew 9:9–13

Jesus sat down and ate with the tax-gatherers and sinners while the Pharisees stood at the door and worried about "contamination." Why? Jesus held the core value that life-and-death is more important than right-or-wrong. He knew He was sent to seek and save "that which was lost" (Luke 19:10). His core value or "government" of *life-and-death is more important than right-or-wrong* enabled Him to have *contact and communication without contamination*. Jesus knew that Matthew's soul was more important than the Pharisees' religious hang-ups. He knew Matthew would never fulfill his destiny, neither earthly nor heavenly, without someone making "first contact."

Meaningful Specific or a Working Generality?

The point I was trying to make with Cheryl was this: I "guesstimate" that 90 percent of the churches in Phoenix by their actions demonstrate a belief that right and wrong is more important than life or death. The result is a disabling government that tends to impede revival or community transformation rather than release or empower it. This is not intentional, but is more a product of Western-based church culture. The 90 percent estimate probably holds true for most cities or communities throughout the Western world.

Christians and churches demonstrate their values by what they do, *not* by what they say. Most churches would say that life and death is more important than right or wrong, but their behavior, both inside and outside the church, reflects the core value of right or wrong. This behavior is not intentional, but our "cluelessness" is hindering our efforts to get to where God wants the church to be. I believe that is why so many pastors and churches are not effective in community transformation. Their right-or-wrong core value is disabling community transformation rather than enabling community transformation. Remember the principle of agreement—community transformation requires agreement. Without agreement, they cannot have unity. Without unity, they will not achieve the "abundance" of community transformation. They may have the vision of community transformation, but their government is not in synch with their vision.

My suggestion to Cheryl was this: "Let's rally those same intercessors and equip them to pray even more strategically." I suggested that her intercessors should pray that the church in Phoenix, Arizona, would undergo a core value shift from right-or-wrong-first to life-and-death-first.

"Let's use the power of prayer to shift us to core values that enable community transformation," I continued. "Let's pray in the values or right government that opens the gates that the King of Glory may come in. Let's have our prayer be, as someone I heard say at a conference I attended, a 'meaningful specific rather than a working generality.' Let's activate some strategic informed purpose-driven intercession. Let's pray in the values. Let's get our core values working for us rather than working against us!" Remember, there will be very limited community transformation until the church has a core value transformation.

I think by the time Cheryl and I finished talking we were even more on the same wavelength. We need prayer, but not just any kind of praying. We need strategic intercession. We also need intelligent fire, or the appropriate and enabling core values that can get us to real, tangible, and lasting community transformation.

EVERY SINNER HAS A FUTURE, EVERY SAINT HAS A PAST

Recently, while browsing through a Christian bookstore in Christchurch, New Zealand, I saw a book by an Australian author titled *Every Sinner Has a Future, Every Saint Has a Past.* That statement captures the heart of God, the passion of Jesus, and the mission of the church. We are all—both the "saints" and the "aints"—on an even playing field. There is a place where the lost and the found converge. That place is called the "foot of the cross."

That is why my friend Apostle John Kelly says that the church is a "lost-and-found department." As Pastor Ted Haggard says, the church is here on earth to "win the lost at any cost." A constant core value of the Willow Creek Association of Churches is that lost people matter to God, and therefore ought to matter to the church.

Our concern must be demonstrated in action, not in rhetoric. "Giving the church back to the community" is looking at people through grace-healed eyes. We are here to love the lost like Christ loved the lost. The truth is, we cannot serve those whom we hate, do not understand, or are afraid of. You cannot have a passion for God without having compassion for people. One should not happen without the other. The unchurched are not the enemy, they are *victims* of the enemy. It is time to start looking at the unchurched the way God looks at the unchurched. Jesus won the fight, and we all—both churched and unchurched—are the prizes.

Think about these questions: how does a church or a churched person live out the ramifications of the above paragraph in everyday actions? What is the fuel that moves a church or a churched person from a church-based (inward) life to a community-based (outward) life?

Such changes come through a *core value* shift, from right-or-wrong first, life-and-death-second, to life-and-death-first, right-or-wrong-second. I am not saying right-or-wrong issues are not important, but I believe these values are secondary in importance.

Let's consider an example. A fisherman catches the fish first, and *then* cleans it, not vice versa. Most churches want the fish to be cleaned first, then caught. The church is to be fishers of men, not fishers of sin if we are to reach our communities for Christ. My question to Cheryl still stands: if our core value is that the fish has to be cleaned first, then why would God ever send a revival or community transformation? We would not treat these newly-converted people with honor or respect. They would be more of a *bother* than a *brother*. They would be more *sinister* than a *sister*. There would be no room for them in the "inn" of our church. We would be like the Kenyans trying to win the Olympics without practicing.

Intelligent Fishing

The Pharisees' attitude regarding Matthew the tax gatherer was "there is no room in the inn." Why? Wrong core values for being a blessing to the Gentiles. If you want to be a burden to the Gentiles, the right-or-wrong core value first is totally appropriate. The problem is that it is not Christlike. On the other hand, because Christ had the core value of life-and-death first, right-or-wrong-second, there was plenty of room in the inn for Matthew and the whole world. His core value enabled community transformation, rather than disabling it. His primary core value opened the gates that the King of Glory could come in.

The apostle Paul held the same core value. He declared it and lived by it: "I have become *all* things to *all* men, that I may by *all* means save some" (1 Cor. 9:22). Notice the "all means" idea. Paul never worried about the various *forms* of community transformation; he was concerned about the *function* of community transformation. He wanted to connect the message with the audience. When life-and-death is your first priority, it does not matter which form of evangelism you use. How many with the core value of right-or-wrong have said that evangelism can only happen *their* way? The right-or-wrong mindset causes arguments about power evangelism, friendship evangelism, seeker sensitive, Billy Graham crusades, or whatever. The result is disabled community transformation. We argue over the XYZs rather than doing the ABCs.

The truth is, there are many forms of evangelism. The key is to use the appropriate form in the appropriate context. Using the fishing example again, Jesus says in Matthew 4:19, "Follow Me, and I will make you fishers of men," and in Luke 5:10, He says to Simon, "Do not fear, from now on you will be catching men." Fishermen use different types of lures in different lakes. Also different types of fish are attracted to different types of lures in different lakes. For example, "power evangelism" may work wonderfully in the African context. The seeker-sensitive form of evangelism may be the "lure" the fish are biting on in the American context (especially in the Phoenix, Arizona, area). Friendship evangelism may work best in the European context. The point is, "by all means." Let's use what works—all things, all men, all means. The purpose of fishing is to catch fish, not argue over lures. I will address this concept in more depth in the "Clueless In Seattle" chapter.

The core value of life-and-death-first empowers churches, leaders, and Christians to find the best "lure" and use it. Pastor Bill Hybels of the huge Willow Creek Community Church in the Chicago area exemplifies a leader with the life-and-death-first, right-or-wrong-second core value. He identified what the fish were biting on in his area of the country and adapted to the fish, not vice versa. The result is a genuine community church with genuine community influence. However, if Bill Hybels were in Africa, my guess is he would adapt to what the "fish" in Africa are biting on. His form does not determine how he will reach the unchurched, his core value does. In the language of the vision-and-government concept, the *vision* is to catch fish, the *government* is life-and-death-first. Remember our principle: agreement, unity, abundance.

NO, UH UH, NO UH UH, NO, NO, NO, SO FORGET IT!

Speaking of fishing, what happens when a prophet's attitudes and behavior are driven by the right-or-wrong core values? What are his actions like? What does the church act like, feel like, and look like when right-or-wrong rather than life-and-death is their first and most important core value? What does that value look like to the community, city, or country to which he or she was sent? Is the right-or-wrong core value a badge of honor, or a recipe for failure? The Bible tells the story of a prophet like that. His name is Jonah. Usually spoiled fish make men sick, but this spoiled man made the fish sick. As one of the great African-American preachers has said, "Jonah was so small spiritually a guppy could have swallowed him!" We should not, however, pick on Jonah because much of the church has acted the same way towards their community. Why? Whether intentionally or unintentionally, these churches' core values are law-giving, not life-giving.

Look at Jonah 1:2–3:

> "Arise, go to Nineveh the great city, and cry against it, for their wickedness has come up before Me." But Jonah rose up to flee to Tarshish from the presence of the LORD. So he went down to Joppa, found a ship which was going to Tarshish, paid the fare, and went down into it to go with them to Tarshish from the presence of the LORD.

That is quite a verse. Notice God's heart for the city of Nineveh and contrast that with Jonah's heart for the community. The result of Jonah's heart, attitude, and behavior was "he fled *from* the presence of the Lord." God was trying to get Jonah into His will and presence, and Jonah was trying to get God into his will and "nonpresence." That is what the right-or-wrong-first core value rather than life-and-death-first core value can potentially do to you. The result was "Nineveh, we have a problem!" As I said earlier, you cannot serve whom you hate. The result was a whale of a taxi ride right back into God's presence and redemptive purpose for the city. I call this Community Transformation.

After a "beach landing," God returned Jonah, the church-centric prophet, to Nineveh a second time. Let's look at some more verses in this story.

> "Arise, go to Nineveh the great city and proclaim to it the proclamation which I am going to tell you." So Jonah arose and went to Nineveh according to the word of the LORD. Now Nineveh was an exceedingly great city, a three days' walk. Then Jonah began to go through the city one day's walk; and he cried out and said, "Yet forty days and Nineveh will be overthrown." Then the people of

> Nineveh believed in God; and they called a fast and put on sack-cloth from the greatest to the least of them.
>
> —Jonah 3:2–5

> When God saw their deeds, that they turned from their wicked way, then God relented concerning the calamity which He had declared He would bring upon them. And He did not do it.
>
> —Jonah 3:10

> But it greatly displeased Jonah, and he became angry. And he prayed to the Lord and said, "Please Lord, was not this what I said while I was still in my own country? Therefore, in order to forestall this I fled to Tarshish, for I knew that Thou art a gracious and compassionate God, slow to anger and abundant in lovingkindness, and one who relents concerning calamity. Therefore now, O Lord, please take my life from me, for death is better to me than life."
>
> —Jonah 4:1–3

> Then the Lord said, "You had compassion on the plant for which you did not work, and which you did not cause to grow, which came up overnight and perished overnight. And should I not have compassion on Nineveh, the great city in which there are more than 120,000 persons who do not know the difference between their right and left hand, as well as many animals?"
>
> —Jonah 4:10–11

That is what I call preaching, and a community transformation all by a very reluctant prophet with a bad attitude and a spirit of prejudice. The whole city believed in God. It made Jonah so mad, he had a death wish. He wanted the Jews or his own country to get right with God first, and then maybe he would go to Nineveh or the Gentiles.

As you can see, Jonah's world revolved around Israel and the law. In today's language, he was church-centric (Israel), not community-centric (Nineveh). Jonah's right-or-wrong core value determined his reaction to the will of God for a city that desperately needed Jonah's God. However, Jonah did not want to give God to them. He had the equivalent of the pharisaical attitude of the Jewish elite when Jesus said in Matthew 23:13, "But woe to you...because you shut off the kingdom of heaven from men." Jonah was supposed to make it hard to go to hell in Nineveh, but instead his attitude and actions would have made it easy to go to hell in Nineveh.

God was saying that abnormality is being a worshipper of God. Normality is being a worshipper of God *and* a deliverer of men. Abnormality is having a passion for God. Normality is having a passion for God *and* compassion for people. Unbelievers are not the enemy. Unbelievers are *victims* of the enemy. The amazing thing to me is that God could use even someone with a bad attitude and no faith to change a whole city for the better.

In my opinion, the story of Jonah and his great success at community transformation is the exception rather than the rule of thumb. This story is the anomaly—the end of the bell-shaped curve—but it illustrates several important lessons. First of all, let's never lose hope in Christians and churches who refuse to do God's will of giving the Church back to the community. Second, we should never give up hope in a generation of people who seemingly refuse to turn back to God. If Nineveh, "whose wickedness has come up to God," could be transformed, so could your community, city, county, country, or continent. Finally, we must realize that God has the ability to bring correction and salvation to the unchurched. There is no hopeless community, only Christians and churches who have become hopeless about their community.

When Right Becomes Wrong

Where did Jonah get this attitude? What stopped him from evangelism and community transformation? The same thing that stops many other churches from real and tangible community transformation. It is the same issue that stopped the Pharisees from eating with the tax gatherers. Once again, it is the right-or-wrong core value that drives our believers. The truth is, as far as Jonah was concerned, they were sinners, unholy, unclean, and "dogs" (Matt. 15:26). He was afraid he might become contaminated. His opinion of himself and the Jews was "We are the holy people, God's elect and chosen people."

God said, "Arise and go to Nineveh, they are in sin and they need me." But Jonah becomes angry and, in effect, says, "Lord, we want to keep our religion pure...with us Jews. We are right and they are wrong—me Tarzan, you Jane! We are good, they are evil; we are winners, they are losers; we are saints, they are heathens." Sound familiar? This attitude froze evangelism, community transformation, and Israel.

Remember, this is a picture of a dysfunctional Israel. This is not the way God intended Israel to be. God wanted to bless all nations through Israel. Actually, God gave Israel the *privileges* and *responsibilities* of the Great Commission and community transformation in Genesis 12:1–3:

> Now the Lord said to Abram, "Go forth from your country, and from your relatives and from your father's house, to the land which I will show you; and I will make you a great nation, and I will bless you, and make your name great; and so you shall be a blessing; and I will bless those who bless you, and the one who curses you I will curse. *And in you all the families of the earth will be blessed.*"

God said to the future Israel that they were blessed so they could bless others. Israel was blessed to be a blessing to the nations. God's order was to "go forth from" their country, things they could relate to, and even their "father's house." They were to be community-centric, *not comfortable.* They liked the part of getting blessed, becoming a great nation, making their name great, and God cursing those who curse them. Those were the privileges and they liked that. However, along with privileges came the responsibilities. God asked them to get out of the seat and onto the street or "go forth." God said, you are to be a blessing, you are like seed planted in the field of the earth, produce and give away the blessings or fruit of blessing to the nations.

In other words, God was saying to Israel, "When you go forth, I will go forth." Noteworthy to me is if Abram and the future Israel did not go forth, God would not go forth. Get the message? In today's church, if we do not "go forth," God will not go forth, at least, as the general rule of thumb. Consequently, we have the "great omission" rather than the Great Commission. Commission means God and man are working together to proclaim God's name throughout the earth (Romans 9:17).

One becomes frozen even though chosen when he forgets, ignores, or is unaware of what God's heart is; "He is not wishing for any to perish" (2 Peter 3:9). As I have said earlier, you do not hold a revival, you let it go. Unfortunately, in Israel's case at the time of Jesus, the right-and-wrong core value ruled. The result was that Israel became proud, obstinate, possessive, law-giving, and ingrown. The result was a culture of exclusiveness that would never allow them to become a blessing to all nations. Community transformation was undermined.

This exclusive worldview caused Jesus to transfer the privileges and responsibilities of the Great Commission from the Jews to the Gentiles. Let's read these verses:

> Jesus said to them, "Did you never read in the Scriptures, THE STONE WHICH THE BUILDERS REJECTED, THIS BECAME THE CHIEF CORNERSTONE; THIS CAME ABOUT FROM THE LORD, AND IT IS MARVELOUS IN OUR EYES"? Therefore I say to you, the kingdom of God will be taken away from you, and be given to a nation producing the fruit of it.
>
> —MATTHEW 21:42–43 (EMPHASIS ADDED)

> I say then, they did not stumble so as to fall, did they? May it never be! But by their transgression salvation has come to the Gentiles, to make them jealous.
>
> —ROMANS 11:11

Who was the nation producing the fruit? The Gentiles, or what would later be called the Church? Do you realize that Jesus put His trust in the Church to do what Israel did not do? The Church has been called to bear fruit that remains in our character, in our ministry and especially in our mission to the world. The Church has been blessed to be a blessing. Community transformation is about Christians in the Church and its individual churches to sow the blessing of God, not to hoard the blessing of God. We cannot be like Jonah, the Pharisees, or the Jewish elite. We must not become proud, obstinate, possessive, law-giving, or ingrown, creating cultures of exclusiveness.

Denominations, leaders, and churches who individualize will eventually become frozen in law-giving, church-centric core values. The result will be that God will give immense blessing and members to other churches who will reach the community, not just other Christians. The frozen churches will be jealous of community-centric churches just as the Jews were. Remember God's principle: "Give unto abundance, hoard unto poverty." No deposit into the community, no return from the community.

Two Different Trees, Two Different Destinies

When Jesus mentions fruit in reference to the Jews and Gentiles, it should remind us of the Garden of Eden. Remember, there were two trees in the garden. One tree produced the fruit of life while the other tree produced the fruit of "godship." Godship is when someone other than God determines what is right or wrong, what should or should not be, what is fair or unfair, and in effect becomes judge of all. That is what God calls the knowledge of good and evil. Read the following verses:

> And out of the ground the Lord God caused to grow every tree that is pleasing to the sight and good for food; the tree of life also in the midst of the garden, and the tree of the knowledge of good and evil.
>
> —Genesis 2:9

> Then the Lord God took the man and put him into the garden of Eden to cultivate it and keep it. The Lord God commanded the man, saying, "From any tree of the garden you may eat freely; but from the tree of the knowledge of good and evil you shall not eat, for in the day that you eat from it you shall surely die."
>
> —Genesis 2:15–17

> Now the serpent was more crafty than any beast of the field which the Lord God had made. And he said to the woman, "Indeed, has God said, 'You shall not eat from any tree of the garden'"? And the woman said to the serpent, "From the fruit of the trees of the

> garden we may eat; but from the fruit of the tree which is in the middle of the garden, God has said, 'You shall not eat from it or touch it, lest you die.'" And the serpent said to the woman, "You surely shall not die! For God knows that in the day you eat from it your eyes will be opened, and you will be like God, knowing good and evil." When the woman saw that the tree was good for food, and that it was a delight to the eyes, and that the tree was desirable to make one wise, she took from its fruit and ate; and she gave also to her husband with her, and he ate. Then the eyes of both of them were opened, and they knew that they were naked; and they sewed fig leaves together and made themselves loin coverings.
>
> —Genesis 3:1–7

As we think this concept through, let's be aware that God tells Adam and Eve about two different trees and two different destinies. The order in which God talks of the trees is very prophetic. The first tree He mentions is rooted in God's life and produces the fruit of God's life. The second tree is rooted in the knowledge of good and evil and produces the fruit of knowing good and evil from man's limited perspective. *The root determines the fruit*.

If Adam and Eve had eaten from the tree of life, their destiny would have been rooted and "fruited" in life. When Adam and Eve ate from the tree of the knowledge of good and evil, their destiny became "you shall surely die." In effect, God was saying, "Adam and Eve, you do not have the big picture; you only know a very small part of the big picture. However, you think your knowledge of the small picture is the big picture. You will think your world is the world." In other words, when Adam and Eve operated by the principle of right-or-wrong rather than life-and-death, they thought they would be God when, in reality, they only knew a small percentage of God. They would think the trunk of the elephant was the elephant, and describe the elephant that way. They were limited with just enough knowledge to make themselves dangerous to the rest of the world as well as to themselves. That is why the Bible says in Genesis 3:22–23:

> Then the Lord God said, "Behold, the man has become like one of Us, knowing good and evil; and now, lest he might stretch

> out his hand, and take also from the tree of life, and eat, and live forever"—therefore the Lord God sent him out from the garden of Eden, to cultivate the ground from which he was taken.

God did not want a world where judgment triumphs over mercy, but a world where mercy triumphs over judgment (James 2:13). Remember, it is God who is omniscient (all-knowing), not man. Judgment in the hands of sin-affected and sin-influenced man is inherently dangerous to all. Knowledge is not necessarily the issue, it is how people use the knowledge with others, whether churched or unchurched. That is what God is concerned with. Knowledge in the control of God and the stewardship of man is life-giving. Whether churched or unchurched, man's knowledge is limited, and in his control it has the potential to cause death through the vehicle of judgment. Remember, the two different trees have two different destinies for us, our neighbors and our communities. Every graveyard in the world confirms that the serpent was a liar and God is a good theologian.

WHO TOLD YOU THAT YOU WERE NAKED?

When Adam and Eve ate the fruit of the tree of the knowledge of good and evil (right and wrong), their eyes were open, they found fault with one another, and knew that they were inadequate in some way. What did they do? They went to Saks Fifth Avenue to buy the latest suit to cover up their inadequacy. They could not be authentic anymore, only exposing part of themselves from time to time.

Look at the results of the right-or-wrong core value in Adam and Eve's lives:

- Fear—They hid themselves from God and each other (v. 10).
- Denial—They made themselves loincloths to "cover" themselves (v. 7).
- Guilt—They hid from God (v. 10).
- Played God—"Who told you that you were naked?" (v. 11).

- Blamed God and mankind—"The woman whom You gave me" and the devil made me do it (v. 13).

Obviously, we could go on and on about the consequences of being the determiners of Truth. Suffice it to say, only God has that privilege and responsibility. It is God who tells us we are naked and not someone else. That does not mean that we cannot admonish one another or correct one another. However, the proper use of the truth comes only through one who is "rooted and grounded in love" (Eph. 3:17), and who has the core values of the tree of life, not the tree of the knowledge of good and evil.

As we all know, the fruit of the tree of the knowledge of good and evil has been passed on through the generations ever since the fall of Adam and Eve. The right-or-wrong core value always looks good and opens one's eyes and seems to make one wise. It seems delightful and makes one look good in front of his or her peers.

The Bible says, "In the day you eat from it, *you will be like God, knowing good from evil*" (Gen 3:5). Isn't that amazing—you will be like *God*? In other words, you will be omniscient. You will be all-knowing. You will be wise, the judge and determiner of all things. Your judgment will come through your knowledge. As we all know, when you have knowledge, you have power. Knowledge is power. So not only will you be omniscient or all-knowing, you will become omnipotent or all-powerful. You will be like God. You will be in control. You become a fruit eater or a fruit inspector rather than a fruit bearer. The world becomes a means to your own end. That is scary to me—a limited, finite person, theologian, or denomination who think they are all knowing and all powerful.

In my experience, the battle is over control. Whether we are Ford or Chevrolet, Baptist or Charismatic, a man or woman, secular or sacred, the right-or-wrong core value drives our behavior and manifests itself in competition and judgment. The fruit of this core value is "I am right, you are wrong, so I am in control."

This core value drives us to build ourselves up by tearing others down. It measures itself by itself and compares itself with itself and is without understanding. (See 2 Corinthians 10:12.) It drives us to put fig leaves on ourselves to cover our weaknesses. It causes blame-shifting and a victim attitude coming from a fear of failure or the perceived guilt of failure. Ultimately, it says, "You are naked; cover up now." It is a false righteousness that makes mountains out of molehills and causes us to focus on the XYZs rather than the ABCs. It creates a fear-based Christianity that has a holier-than-thou attitude toward other Christians as well as the community.

Who told us we were naked? Who told Jonah the Ninevites were naked? Who told us our communities were naked? Mercy triumphs over judgment, especially in our communities. Let's eat of the right fruit from the right fruit tree for the sake of one another, our churches, and our communities. Let's become fruit bearers rather than fruit eaters or fruit inspectors.

Not So, Lord!

We earthlings, whether "saints" or "ain'ts," are so used to living by the right-or-wrong core value that the abnormal seems normal. Living by grace and unconditional love is considered compromise. Rules and regulations are the norm. Comparison and one-upmanship are normal. In the church world, we keep the law rather than keep the grace. It is natural, it is normal, it is automatic, and it is fallen. If we throw in the life-and-death core value, everything gets a little strange. Life is not simple anymore, it requires God and the leading of the Holy Spirit in applying the "truth" and right-or-wrong issues in a life-giving way. What does this look like? How did the early church make the transition from the right-or-wrong core value to the life-and-death core value? Let's look at several examples:

> And on the next day, as they were on their way, and approaching the city, Peter went up on the housetop about the sixth hour to pray. And he became hungry, and was desiring to eat; but while they were making preparations, he fell into a trance; and he beheld the sky opened up, and a certain object like a great sheet coming down, lowered by four corners to the ground, and there were in it all kinds of four-footed animals and crawling creatures of the earth and birds of the air. A voice came to him, "Arise, Peter, kill and eat!" But Peter said, "By no means, Lord, for I have never

> eaten anything unholy and unclean." And again a voice came to him a second time, "What God has cleansed, no longer consider unholy." And this happened three times; and immediately the object was taken up into the sky.
>
> —Acts 10:9–16

What a story! Can you imagine God asking Peter to "kill and eat?" Actually, the word used for kill means to sacrifice. Peter's right-or-wrong core value put him in a major spiritual tilt! He knew from his religious upbringing, you do not eat unclean animals. He had never eaten anything unclean or unholy. I enjoy his response in the King James Bible, "Not so, Lord." Now there is an oxymoron. How can you say "not so" and "Lord" in the same sentence? Of course, God was trying to move him from the tree of the knowledge of good and evil to the tree of life. The law was only a tutor to get him to life. God was moving him from church-centric to community-centric, and from kindergarten to college. God had to show Peter three times because Peter was so right-or-wrong oriented. The "normal" that God had established seemed so "abnormal," Peter's only response was "Not so, Lord." Peter was afraid of being contaminated if he had contact with unholy things. God had to be patient with Peter. God had to help Peter understand that what was "normal" to Peter is really "abnormal." Peter finally understood in Acts 10:45–48:

> And all the circumcised believers who came with Peter were amazed, because the gift of the Holy Spirit had been poured out on the Gentiles also. For they were hearing them speaking with tongues and exalting God. Then Peter answered, "Surely no one can refuse the water for these to be baptized who have received the Holy Spirit just as we did, can he?" And he ordered them to be baptized in the name of Jesus Christ. Then they asked him to stay on for a few days.
>
> —Acts 10:45–48

God was moving Peter from the concept of right-or-wrong-first to the concept of life-and-death first. Peter was learning how to become all things to all men that some might be saved (1 Corinthians 9:22).

God was more concerned with the salvation of the Gentiles (their eternal life) than their fallen status. Peter learned the lesson that God wanted Jonah to learn, but Jonah did not.

THE JERUSALEM COUNCIL

> And some men came down from Judea and began teaching the brethren, "Unless you are circumcised according to the custom of Moses, you cannot be saved." And when Paul and Barnabas had great dissension and debate with them, the brethren determined that Paul and Barnabas and certain others of them should go up to Jerusalem to the apostles and elders concerning this issue.
>
> —ACTS 15:1–2

> And God, who knows the heart, bore witness to them, giving them the Holy Spirit, just as He also did to us; and He made no distinction between us and them, cleansing their hearts by faith. Now therefore why do you put God to the test by placing upon the neck of the disciples a yoke which neither our fathers nor we have been able to bear? But we believe that we are saved through the grace of the Lord Jesus, in the same way as they also are.
>
> — ACTS 15:8–11

The key to this example is to look at the first verse. Like Jonah, these men from Judea had a right-or-wrong core value resulting in a disturbance within the church. Those who go by right-or-wrong-first core values seem to always end up disturbing the church and its mission to the community. Peter addresses the situation and takes them back to the tree of life. In fact, James, Peter, and the apostles reinforce the life-and-death-first core value to the brethren. They say, in effect, "Look, do whatever you want, eat whatever you want, except keep out of idolatry and food sacrificed to idols and do not fornicate. If you keep yourself free from these things, you will do well."

That is quite a statement. Its effect was to keep evangelism flourishing among the Gentiles. The disciples had faith in the Holy Spirit and knew that He, not the Judaizers, convicts sin, righteousness, and judgment. The apostles knew that it is God who transforms men from the inside out, not the outside in. God's way is not man's condemnation, but the Holy Spirit is conviction.

David's Moment of Knead

> And it came about that He was passing through the grainfields on the Sabbath, and His disciples began to make their way along while picking the heads of grain. And the Pharisees were saying to Him, "See here, why are they doing what is not lawful on the Sabbath?" And He said to them, "Have you never read what David did when he was in need and became hungry; he and his companions: how he entered the house of God in the time of Abiathar the high priest, and ate the consecrated bread, which is not lawful for anyone to eat except the priests, and he also gave it also to those who were with him?" And He was saying to them, "The Sabbath was made for man, and not man for the Sabbath. Consequently, the Son of Man is Lord even of the Sabbath."
>
> —Mark 2:23–28

Here again we see the fruit of the tree of the knowledge of good and evil. Here again we see godship demonstrated through the Pharisees. Here again we see the right-or-wrong core value driving the Pharisees' behavior. Evidently, Jesus and his disciples were hungry on the Sabbath. That was a bad day to be hungry. The ever-judging eye of the Pharisees (I call them the fruit inspectors) was on them. Low and behold, they caught Jesus on a technicality. Jesus missed the mark and they caught him. Jesus responded with an amazing statement: *the Sabbath was made for man, and not man for the Sabbath.* In other words, the Sabbath was put in place by God for the benefit of man, not the judgment of man. The Sabbath was a life-giving concept, not a law-giving concept. The Sabbath is not the master, it is the servant of the master. Life-and-death was the essence of the Sabbath, not right-or-wrong. Which tree we choose determines our destiny.

There are many other examples, such as Jesus healing on the Sabbath (Mark 3:1–6). Remember the disciples of Jesus complaining about the "someones" who cast out demons in Jesus' name. The disciples even tried to stop them (Mark 9:38–50). What about the power play by some to preach Christ even from envy and strife and out of selfish motives, thinking to cause Paul distress? Paul's answer is It does not matter, "whether in pretense or in truth, Christ is proclaimed" (Phil. 1:14–18). With all of these examples and hundreds more, the key is to realize God is in control, not us. His primary core value is life-and-death-first, right-or-wrong second. The question is, what are our core values and what order are they in?

PHARISAIC ACADEMIA

What happens to you when your life's behavior toward the church and community is driven by the right-or-wrong core value? What happens when the right-or-wrong core value is the master in your life and not the servant in your life? One of the best examples we have of this is Paul's experience with the Sanhedrin in Acts 23:6–10:

> But perceiving that one part were Sadducees and the other Pharisees, Paul began crying out in the Council, "Brethren, I am a Pharisee, a son of Pharisees; I am on trial for the hope and resurrection of the dead!" And as he said this, there arose a dissension between the Pharisees and Sadducees; and the assembly was divided. For the Sadducees say that there is no resurrection, nor an angel, nor a spirit; but the Pharisees acknowledge them all. And there arose a great uproar; and some of the scribes of the Pharisaic party stood up and began to argue heatedly, saying, "We find nothing wrong with this man; suppose a spirit or an angel has spoken to him?" And as a great dissension was developing, the commander was afraid Paul would be torn to pieces by them and ordered the troops to go down and take him away from them by force, and bring him into the barracks.

Isn't that story amazing? All Paul had to do to get himself out of a difficult situation was make one statement and it threw the whole council into confusion. Notice the descriptive words like "great dissention," "divided," "great uproar," "argue heatedly," and "afraid Paul would be torn to pieces." I have seen some church board meetings like that. Where does that behavior originate? Each group, the Pharisees and the Sadducees, knew they were right. In the name of rightly dividing the Word, they wrongly divided the Sanhedrin council. The two factions had no regard for each other, the Romans watching this whole fiasco, or God. In the end, nobody changed anybody's mind, the Jewish testimony to the Romans only got worse, and Paul got a life insurance policy and an all-expense paid trip to Rome.

I call this the Doberman pinscher strategy. Someone has two Doberman pinschers guarding his house from robbers. If you are the robber, all you have to do is throw a piece of steak into the yard, let the Dobermans fight over it, walk into the house, and rob it. (Of course, you had better have another steak for your way back out of the house!) That is what happened here. Paul threw in the steak and the dogs fought. Why? You know the answer—both sides were driven by the right-or-wrong core value.

Do you see the strategy here? When the church is right-or-wrong driven, we lose. Frankly, the enemy knows this also. All the enemy has to do is throw in a doctrinal steak, and all hell breaks loose. From the beginning of history and the fall of man, the two different trees represent two different destinies. After the Fall, the first thing Adam did was justify himself. He had to be right, not God. Then Eve justified herself, she had to be right, not God. Ever since, all of mankind, including the Church, has lived with the consequences.

Academia, Knowledge, and the Church

> But beyond this, my son, be warned: the writing of many books is endless, and excessive devotion to books is wearying to the body.
>
> —Ecclesiastes 12:12

> Do not be excessively righteous, and do not be overly wise. Why should you ruin yourself?
>
> —Ecclesiastes 7:16

> Now concerning things sacrificed to idols, we know that we all have knowledge. Knowledge makes arrogant, but love edifies. If anyone supposes that he knows anything, he has not yet known as he ought to know.
>
> —1 Corinthians 8:1–2

At the beginning of this chapter I mentioned a statement I made to Cheryl Saks. I said, "If nine out of ten churches reflect in their actions the value of right-or-wrong rather than life-and-death, why would God ever send us revival?" I was serious. Of course, most Christians and churches are not as extreme as the Pharisees or Sadducees. However, churches and church culture have a strong tendency to be right-or-wrong oriented.

As with any culture, churches quickly adopt a culture of do's and don'ts and what is acceptable, and very quickly tend to become islands of self-culture. These cultures, if not constantly policed by the community and apostolically-oriented leaders, will individualize, creating a disconnect from the community. In these cases, the mission of the church to the community is jeopardized. I once heard a speaker say, in effect, that any local church without consistent apostolic input will quickly revert to the law. He was saying that apostolic input kept local churches in grace and out of the law. In other words, he was talking about local churches maintaining the life-and-death core value, which keeps them healthy, outward, and community-centric. In a very real sense, you cannot have real, tangible, and lasting community transformation and the right-or-wrong core value at the same time. The right-or-wrong core value first cancels out the vision of community transformation. Remember the man from Kenya.

Why do many churches become right-or-wrong oriented in their core values? As I stated previously, it is part of our nature to use knowledge to maintain control. We like to be like God. We want to be in control. We are afraid of not being in control. We use God's Word or our opinion on God's Word to judge and justify. Many people do not do this intentionally. In fact, most church leaders and churches would not even be aware of this.

Teacher-driven, Right-or-Wrong Church Ethos

Another reason that a church might tend to operate from a right-or-wrong core value is because of the office gifts that are determining that church's culture. In Ephesians 4:11, we see that Jesus has given the Church five basic leadership or office gifts. I realize some people would say that apostles and prophets are not for today and the teacher alone is not a valid office gift because pastors and teachers are connected. But for the sake of illustration, let's list their gifts in a particular order to show why the Church's tends toward the law a more law-giving ethos.

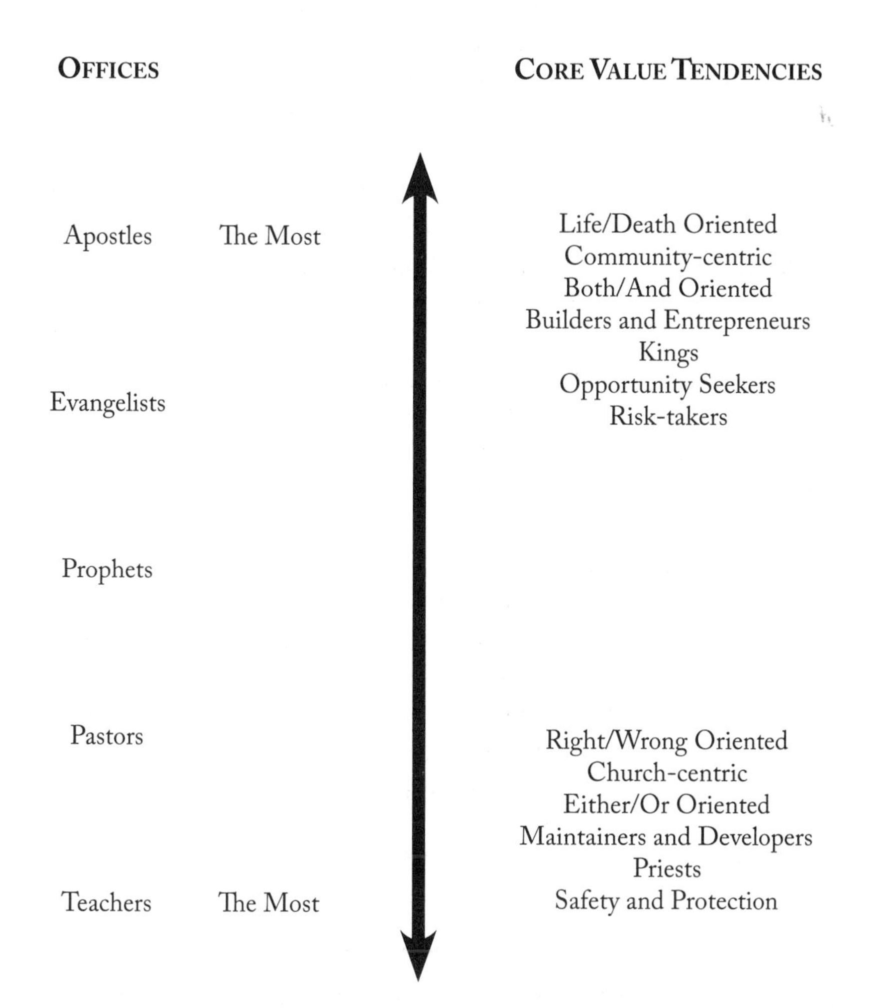

We need to look at the tendencies of most apostles, evangelists, prophets, pastor/teachers, and teachers. Did you notice I said "tendencies"? That means that the observations I make will not be true in every case, but in most cases. Remember also, I am talking about values (what we do and how we behave) not beliefs (what we mentally agree with). Most apostolic ministry and evangelistic ministry would strongly tend toward the values of life-and-death-first, community-centric, both/and, and building or being entrepreneurial minded. I think it is interesting that a prophet can go either way, to the community or to the church. Pastor/teachers and teachers strongly tend to value right-or-wrong-first, their opinion of the truth, church-centric, either/or and a maintaining or developing ministry minded.

Now, I will ask you a question: until a few years ago, if you wanted to be a pastor or leader in a church, where did you go to get your training and education? Most church leaders went to a seminary or Bible school. Now, which office of the five usually leads and teaches in seminaries or Bible schools? The answer is teachers, especially if the institution is a seminary. In other words, the most right-or-wrong oriented, church-centric, either/or oriented, and maintainer/developer oriented office has determined much of church culture or ethos.

Jesus said that the pupil, after he has been fully trained, will be like his teacher (Luke 6:40). So we have pastors who have become teacher-oriented with a teacher ethos who train their people in their churches to be teacher-oriented to be just like them.

I am not saying that education is wrong or seminary is wrong. What I am saying is that, through the vehicle of seminaries and Bible schools, many teachers and many pastor/teachers have determined the culture and core values of the whole church. By their gifting, teachers tend to be "an inch wide and a mile deep." The culture of academia, whether secular or sacred, encourages determining what you believe to be truth and defending it at all costs. The culture or ethos of church academia often creates an adversarial culture using head-knowledge as a weapon against other Christians and the community, which produces an us-against-them mentality. Many times, the end has justified the means and, as a result, many have wrongly divided the Church in the name of rightly dividing the Word.

FRUIT EATERS OR FRUIT BEARERS?

Teachers tend to value the intellectual rather than the practical. Many teachers and pastor/teachers tend to speak "at" their audience, not "to" them. Their style is mainly directive and non-participatory. In extreme cases, knowledge and doctrine become the end rather than a means to an end. The culture of academia tends to be more about information than formation or transformation. Teachers tend to produce a church culture of speculating rather than participating. Their perspective is more idealistic than pragmatic. They tend to focus on the way things ought to be rather than the way they are. Greek, Latin, and systematic theology may take the place of being conformed to Jesus, knowing God, and reaching the community. In a teacher-led culture, life revolves around the church, Christians, and doctrine. What they would call a Bible study is, in reality, a doctrine study. The net result is that church culture for 1,700 years—and especially since the Reformation—has been determined mainly by the office of the teacher. The result is a fruit-eating or fruit inspecting church culture *with very little community awareness* that reflects the ethos of the teacher. People tend to sit in church "getting fed" or judging everything and everyone else rather than bearing the fruit of the word of God.

While the teacher has a wonderful gifting, his world of teaching limits the potential of the church. In order to be community-centric, local churches need the input and leadership of the other four offices also. Pastor/teachers and teachers desperately need the more community-centric offices in order to maintain a good witness to the community. Traditional pastors and teachers need the entrepreneurial abilities and life-giving core values that apostolic outlook and input can bring. The office of the teacher is 20 percent of the office gifts on a good day. The teacher by himself cannot bring the church to its full potential.

If we are going to see communities transformed, each office's perspective and gifting are needed. All of the offices working together create winning wineskins, not whining wineskins. The community and kingdom of God require churches that win the lost, disciple the found, and release the ready into the community. We need these life-giving offices to reinstate the life-and-death core value as the primary core value of the Church. Our friends, our relatives, our neighbors, our business associates, and our communities are waiting for us. In fact, community transformation is very improbable without this shift in core values. That is what I was trying to say to Cheryl at the beginning of this chapter. Real, tangible, and lasting community transformation requires a core value transformation.

WHY CHURCHES MISBEHAVE

The fruit of the right-or-wrong core value coming from the tree of the knowledge of good and evil pervades the Church. After all, knowledge and rightness make us look good to ourselves and others in the Church. We want to be wise. We want to be right. We want to be spiritual.

Let me ask you a few questions. How can we have unity with each other or other churches if our core value is right-or-wrong? How can we humble ourselves if we have to be right? How can we even ask forgiveness from God or each other if we cannot admit we are wrong? Adam could not do it and neither could Eve. The Pharisees and Sadducees preferred to be right than to switch.

How can we reach the community if we think we are too holy to be bothered by them? How could we even help the Samaritan man if our primary core value is right-or-wrong? Why is it so hard for the Baptist to tolerate the charismatic or vice versa? If you were to ask him, what would he say? That charismatic is wrong! That Baptist is wrong!

We have "Christian" radio programs that hack leaders in today's churches rather than attack extreme cults. Why is that? Where does this type of behavior begin? From the right-or-wrong core value embedded in the body of Christ through well-meaning, but judgment-driven church-centric teachers. These people are better at contending *in* the faith than *for* the faith.

I remember an example of this right-or-wrong core value at work in our church in 1994. I had just completed a community-centric series entitled *When the Saints Go Marching Out*. One of the people in our church came up to me in a huff. His statement was "We do not want any unbelievers here, and we do not even want new Christians here."

He went on to say, "If they came here, this church would not be holy. And if we are not holy, then Jesus will not return because He wants a spotless bride."

I was shocked. I thought about his statement. In essence, he was saying that one church in Phoenix, Arizona, was going to get so holy it would bring Jesus back. Where does that type of behavior come from? The right-or-wrong core value! Once again, *wrong tree.* His heart for God was wonderful, but his theology was completely wrong. He was judging both new believers and the unchurched before they even came into the door of the church.

Let's look at John 3:16–17:

> For God so loved the world, that He gave His only begotten Son, that whoever believes in Him shall not perish, but have eternal life. For God did not send the Son into the world to judge the world, but that the world should be saved through Him.

Notice that God did not send the Son into the world to judge the world (v. 17). If Jesus does not judge the unchurched, neither should we. The key to understanding John 3:16 is understanding John 3:17. How quickly we forget! Here is the life-and-death-first principle in action. There is no John 3:16 without John 3:17.

A few years later, this wonderful person, made in the image of God, had to be shown his own inadequacies and limitations by God. Today he is a life-giving leader and a great fruit-bearer for the church and community. He understands Church@Community now.

What Teachers Teach . . . Not the Teacher . . . Is the Issue

It is important at this time to separate the teacher from what he or she teaches. The office of the teacher is important, necessary, and essential to the well being of the church and the community. Bible knowledge, theology, and the essential doctrines of the church are very important. However, when an influential teacher teaches from a right-or-wrong tree of knowledge perspective, the church takes on an adversarial nature. The sheep begin biting. The ministry of Jesus is reduced to knowledge in the church rather than wisdom in the community.

As I have said before, teachers taught by western seminaries and bible schools tend strongly to propagate a right/wrong, church-centric perspective that creates a disconnect from the community. It projects, whether unintentional or real, an attitude of elitism and one-upsmanship toward the community and other churches. The results are disastrous in the context of community transformation.

In order to reach our communities, we need the teachers to teach the church about being entrepreneurial, proactive, community aware, and how to be community-centric. The church and those in church need to be taught how to be "both/and" Christians. The teachers need to equip the saints be effective leaders and Christian outside of the church, not just inside of the church. Let me say it another way. The teachers need to teach today's leaders and influencers inside of the church to be tomorrow's leaders and influencers outside of the church. The teachers need to teach Christians and the "churched" how to relate to the community and other spheres of influence in the community. The church needs life-giving teachers, not law-giving teachers. Twenty-first century church teachers need to learn how to teach strategically as well as academically. Teachers need the apostolic input and an apostolic world-view to help them be more community aware, thus enabling community transformation. Today's effective churches will have a healthy perspective given to them by all of the offices in Ephesians 4. They will have, like Jesus did, favor with God and man.

GRACE, THEN TRUTH

> And the Word became flesh, and dwelt among us, and we beheld His glory, glory as of the only begotten from the Father, full of grace and truth.
>
> —JOHN 1:14

> For the Law was given through Moses; grace and truth were realized through Jesus Christ.
>
> —JOHN 1:17

I want to finish this chapter by pointing you to the above verses. Notice the order of grace and truth. Jesus comes with grace first and then truth. John says it two times in the same order just so we will not miss it. Grace, then truth!

Jesus used that strategy with both the woman at the well and the woman caught in adultery. His statement now is the same as it was then. Let he who is without sin cast the first stone...now go...and sin no more. He always created a context for truth first before he said the truth. As Paul says, "speak the truth in love" (Eph. 4:15).

Truth without a context is trouble. Truth is never the end in itself, it is the means to an end. Any other view of truth will give you "truth decay." Truth is the vehicle, never the driver of the vehicle. The end is salvation and the means is truth. Jesus said, "You shall know the truth, and the truth shall make you free" (John 8:32). Salvation is the master, truth is the servant. The same is true for teachers. Teachers alone should never determine the culture of a church. Teachers were created to determine part of the culture of a church jut like any other office gift. Jesus did not say, "I am the truth, no man comes to the Father except by me." Jesus said He was "the way and the truth and the life!" The *way* to *truth* is through *life*. Truth serves life, not vice versa.

Do you understand the importance of these two core values? Every behavior we have, individually and corporately, emanates from one of these two primary core values. It is time for strategic teaching, not academic teaching alone. It is time for purpose-driven theology whose end is to help people know God, not just to have knowledge about God. It is time for real, tangible, and lasting community transformation, empowered and enabled through the same core values Jesus and the early church used. It is time to shift our perspective from right-or-wrong first to life-and-death first. Community transformation requires it.

LIFE AND DEATH FIRST... RIGHT OR WRONG SECOND

Life-and-death first is the primary core value or "government" that enables the vision of community transformation. When you adopt this core value it changes the way you see people and the community. We shift from being fear-based to being faith-based allowing the Holy Spirit to work in people and the community. We become life-giving not law-giving. We open the doors to the community so we can have contact redemptively so that some may be saved. We live life from a higher level. We approach rather than avoid. We become pro-active rather than reactive. We enable community transformation. We become like Jesus demonstrating life-and-death first core value.

Adopting a life-and-death first core value changes entire continents. Many have asked, why is there community transformation and revival in Africa or Latin America? The answer is simple. Most Christians in those places live by the life-and-death core value. The message they have is simple. Their perspective is *receive Jesus now*. They understand the importance of salvation. I find most Westerners are more concerned with holiness or discipleship. Which core values do you see at work here in both groups? One enables community transformation while the other, while very necessary, disables community transformation. As we said before, you catch the fish first, then you clean it. The Africans and Latin Americans are more naturally evangelistic and community aware because they have not be as influenced by the Western right-or-wrong, teacher driven ethos of the West. They do not theorize evangelism, they live evangelism. In my opinion , the spiritual air is not more open in these countries than the West. The harvest is always ripe for harvest. My belief is that the spiritual air is more open in their minds. They live by the life-and-death core value first enabling community impact. As one who has traveled in twenty countries of Africa and most of South America, I have another observation to make. These churches are not as inept at discipleship as some would suggest. The reason most Westerners are critical of the discipleship efforts of these countries is the fruit inspecting, right-or-wrong ethos of those doing the inspecting. They end up projecting their "the way it ought to be" standards on those in other places of the world. In most cases, they have little awareness of the culture and how hard it is to disciple someone who has spent their whole life in a survival mode. It takes a while to clean those types of fish! Perhaps the Western church world could learn something from the leaders of many developing world churches. The life-and-death core value moves you from the possibility of community transformation to the probability of community transformation. It is amazing to see how one little core value change can change everything. Incidentally, that was Jesus' mission to the Jews in His day. Just change one little core value.

Are you ready for the next Intelligent Fire core value? In the next chapter we will explore the both/and core value that really is a result of living by the life-and-death core value. We will learn how to get out of the trap of being...an inch wide and a mile deep.

Chapter 8

A Mile Deep and an Inch Wide:
The Principle of Both / And

Every morning in Africa a gazelle awakes. It knows that it must run faster than the fastest cheetah or it will be killed. Every morning a cheetah awakes. It knows that it must outrun the slowest gazelle or it will starve to death. It does not matter whether you are a cheetah or a gazelle—when the sun comes up, you had better be running.

This illustration makes us aware of two worlds—the cheetah's and the gazelle's. Both worlds are equally valid, yet come from completely different perspectives. The two worlds are not "either/or" but "both/and." It would be unwise for the gazelle to live by the my-world-is-the-only-real-world philosophy. The gazelle who ignores the reality of the cheetah's world is just what the cheetah wants. The result? Gazelleburgers. The theory may be something like "Gazelles are from Venus; cheetahs are from Mars," but the reality is both cheetahs and gazelles are from Earth and they had better learn to deal with it. As the story says, each must wake up running with awareness of the other's world. After all, their worlds do intersect.

Me Tarzan, You Jane

One of the most destructive consequences of the right-or-wrong core value is a disconnect from the community. The Church's pursuit of rightness at all costs creates a win/lose, us/them, sacred/secular scenario that disables the process of real, tangible, and lasting community transformation. We will never achieve the goal of transformed communities with a "Me Tarzan, You Jane" type of mindset or attitude. This attitude is called dualism and thrives on absolutes and extremes. The we-are-right-and-everybody-else-is-wrong attitude the Church has tended to exhibit for hundreds of years has disconnected the Church from itself and the community.

The problem with this attitude is for every action there is an equal and opposite reaction. In today's world, which is not Tarzan's world, it is "Me Jane, You Tarzan." The consequence of this superior/inferior attitude toward the community is that it contributes to an equal and opposite reaction from the community toward the Church. The adversarial nature of this attitude undermines the Church's essential contribution to and role in the community. The right-or-wrong core value creates an either/or ethos or culture in our churches that renders community transformation improbable if not impossible.

In my opinion, no amount of prayer for revival, binding, or loosing can overcome the consequences of the attitude that comes across through a great majority of churches to the community. The superior attitude of many pastors and churches toward businessmen and women, government officials, educators, and education and the media has to decrease in order that Christ's influence in the community may increase. What we need to be praying is that there will be a core-value shift in the ethos of the Church from either/or to both/and. In order to create that shift, we need to pray also for a core value shift from right-or-wrong to life-and-death. Adopting the life-and-death core value activates the both/and core value to operate within the Church and the community.

The High Cost of Dualism

The consequences of the right-and-wrong core value adopted by much of the Church creates what is called dualism. This thought paradigm creates the following worldview:

- Either/Or
- Good/Evil
- Win/Lose
- Black/White
- God/Not God
- Successful/Unsuccessful
- Us/Them
- Tarzan/Jane
- Cheetah/Gazelle

In his book *Built to Last*, author Jim Collins calls this the "tyranny of the or." [1] Studying the most successful and visionary businesses in the United States, Collins found that they learned how to "embrace paradox" rather than be limited by the world-view of either/or. "The 'tyranny of the or,'" he says, "pushes people to believe that things must be either A or B, but not both." He then cites some examples of this:

- You can have change *or* stability.
- You can be conservative *or* bold.
- You can have low cost *or* high quality.
- You can have creative autonomy *or* consistency and control.
- You can invest for the future *or* do well in the short-term.
- You can create wealth for your shareholders *or* do good for the world.
- You can be idealistic (values-driven) *or* pragmatic (profit-driven).

Collins notes that most unsuccessful companies adopted the "either/or, right/wrong"-way of interpreting life and business. These companies limited themselves, oppressed themselves, and then lost themselves.

He goes on to say that these highly successful, visionary companies "liberated themselves with the 'genius of the AND—the ability to embrace both extremes of the number of dimensions at the same time. Instead of choosing between A *OR* B, they figure out a way to have both A *AND* B." (Ibid, p. 44.) For example:

ON THE ONE HAND:		**YET, ON THE OTHER HAND:**
Purpose beyond profit	AND	Pragmatic pursuit of profit
A relatively fixed core ideology	AND	Vigorous change and movement
Conservatism around the core	AND	Bold, committing, risky moves
Clear vision and sense of direction	AND	Opportunistic groping and experimentation

THE MIND OF CHRIST

Isn't this the way Christ thought? Didn't Christ exemplify first-rate intelligence? Yes, Christ had absolutes, but there was great flexibility around those absolutes. He was able to see all the sides—the extremes, the middles—both secular and sacred. Do you realize God is so—*big* that He is everywhere? He is in the extremes *and* in the middle. God is a paradox. He is Spirit (John 4:24). He is Light (1 John 1:5). He is Love (1 John 4:16). God is *Elohim*—Three in One. Friends, that is paradox. God is multi-faceted, "like the sound of many waters" (Rev. 1:15). God uses seemingly opposite persons and circumstances to sharpen us (Proverbs 27:17). God is able to integrate seemingly opposite themes and make them precious, amazing, and productive.

Christ's world and ours includes seven continents, not one. There are seven days in a week and seven colors in the rainbow. There were twelve tribes, not one tribe that made the nation of Israel. Joseph and Judah were about as opposite as you can get, but the mind of Christ integrates them perfectly. Christ lived the genius of the both/and principle. The overly religious Jews lived the tyranny of the either/or principle. The Jews' world marginalized, demonized, and despised a whole people group called the Gentiles. The genius of the mind of Christ was to include both of these very opposite people groups.

The mind of Christ integrates:

- Jews and Gentiles (Romans 1:16)
- Men and women (Galatians 3:28)
- Fathers and mothers (Ephesians 6:2)
- Young and old (Acts 2:17)
- Rich and poor (Ephesians 6:5–9)
- Slave and free (Acts 2:18)
- Apostles and prophets (Ephesians 2:20)
- Grace and truth (John 1:14)
- Grace and knowledge (2 Peter 3:18)
- Spirit and truth (John 4:24)
- Kings and priests (Revelation 1:6)
- Natural and spiritual (1 Corinthians 15:46)
- Old Testament and New Testament (1 Corinthians 10:11)
- Bride and groom (Revelation 21:2)
- Praise and worship (Psalm 34:1–3)
- Alpha and Omega (Revelation 22:13)

- Joseph and Judah (Ezekiel 37:19)
- Light and truth (Psalm 43:3)
- The lost and the found (Luke 15)
- Seedtime and harvest (Genesis 8:22)
- Kingdom and church (Matthew 16:18–19)
- Martha and Mary—worker and worshipper (Luke 10:38–42)
- Fruit and gifts of the Holy Spirit (1 Corinthians 12:1–11; Galatians 5:22–23)
- Heaven and earth (1 Corinthians 15:40)
- Mortal and immortal (1 Corinthians 15:53)
- Perishable and imperishable (1 Corinthians 15:54)
- Power and authority (Luke 9:1)
- Power of His resurrection *and* fellowship of His suffering (Philippians 3:10)

To proclaim the favorable year of the Lord, *and* the day of vengeance of our God.

—Isaiah 61:2

For he causes His sun to rise on the evil *and* the good, *and* sends rain on the righteous and the unrighteous.

—Matthew 5:45

Morning comes, but also night.

—Isaiah 21:12

Faith, hope, and love.

—1 Corinthians 13:13

That is paradox, yet integration. The diversity of the seemingly opposite gives us the manifold wisdom of God needed for the fullness of Christ to be expressed on earth as it is in heaven.

The Second Peter Principle

The apostle Peter in his later life began to realize the power of both/and. Peter was transformed by the concept of growing up in all aspects into Christ. Look at the following verse penned by the apostle Paul:

> But speaking the truth in love, we are to *grow up in all aspects into Him*, who is the head, even Christ.
>
> —Ephesians 4:15

Peter put this principle about which Paul wrote into his own words (from God) in 2 Peter 1:5–8 (KJV):

> And beside this, giving all diligence, *add* to your faith virtue; and to virtue knowledge; and to knowledge temperance; and to temperance patience; and to patience godliness; and to godliness brotherly kindness; and to brotherly kindness charity. For if these things be in you, and abound, they make you that ye shall neither be barren nor unfruitful in the knowledge of our Lord Jesus Christ.

Please notice that Peter wrote the word "add." In other words, he was saying, now that you have faith, *add* virtue, then *add* knowledge, then *add* temperance, then *add* patience, then *add* godliness, then *add* brotherly kindness, and then *add* charity. It was not a matter of balance, it was a matter of fullness. You do not subtract faith to bring in virtue. Peter said, keep your faith, but add virtue. Bring virtue up to your high level of faith. The same is true for all the other qualities Peter was writing about. Peter was writing, in effect, that we need it all; do not take away—"*add*."

If we were to use the 2 Peter principle in today's right-or-wrong-oriented church, we would ruffle a few feathers. Here are some examples:

- Now, Charismatics, *add* to your gifts the fruit of the Spirit.
- Now, fundamentalists, *add* to your fruit the gifts of the Spirit.

- Now, worshippers, *add* praise to your meetings.
- Now, praisers, *add* worship to your meetings.
- Now, teachers of the Word, *add* meaningful praise and worship (other than hymns) to your service (and for more than five minutes).
- Now, Mary, there is a time to cook dinner.
- Now, Church, it is good that you are upward and inward, but now let's *add* outward (that is, missions and evangelism).
- Now, Holy Spirit people, let's *add* the Father and the Son to the Trinity.
- Now Father, Son, and Holy Scriptures people, let's *add* the Holy Spirit to the Trinity in our practice.
- Now, Church, we are not just a "found" department, we are a "lost and found" department. Let's add the unchurched to our churched people.

The examples go on and on.

Do you see where the right-or-wrong, either/or core values take us? How can the fullness of Christ be expressed through Christians and churches if we are driven by the either/or core value? In order to have real, tangible, and lasting community transformation, we must have a leadershift from the either/or to the both/and.

The Roman/Greek way of thinking is a wonderful servant but a terrible master. The Roman/Greek way of thinking limited the Greeks, and it will limit us. (See 1 Corinthians 1:23.) What we need to do is to think Hebrew also. Hebrew is not limited to rational and logical thought only. Both systems by themselves are incomplete in discerning the mind of Christ. Remember, God honors both Jews and Gentiles. Therefore, He honors both of their ways of thinking and would be inclusive of both. Unfortunately, most of our seminaries and Bible schools taught by teachers and educators are extremely

Roman/Greek in their way of thinking. This has created a culture of right-or-wrong-, either/or-oriented churches operating in the "tyranny of the or." The result has been spiritual prejudice, dualism, and one-upsmanship from one seminary to another and from one church to another leading to a dysfunctional culture in the Church and an adversarial culture toward those outside the Church.

Precious Meddles

I thought long and hard about including this section in the book. I need to address the extreme either/or groups imbedded in the church world. These groups have an *opinion* of the truth that they project into both the Church and the community. They do not contend earnestly *for* the faith as Jude says (v. 3); they contend *in* the faith. They have doctrines or beliefs that are "precious" to them, and if anyone believes anything different from their beliefs, they attack, they meddle, they undermine. Their either/or world will not allow them to do anything else.

I can imagine what some of them are thinking right now. The both/and world view I am writing about is absolutely essential to community transformation. It is also biblical. Yet some would consider it compromise. They would say, "What about the absolutes? What about truth? The both/and view is a license to do anything! Put him on our Web site as the next anti-Christ (along with many other of my friends). We are the Bible answer men and only we have the truth!" If you have been in the church world for even a short time, you have heard this mantra on the radio or read it on the Internet.

I can only say I believe in orthodoxy. I believe in the Apostle's Creed. I believe in One Savior, Jesus. I believe in the Trinity. I believe in the very essential core values of Christianity. I also believe, like Paul, that there is great flexibility outside of the core values and pillars of the faith. I believe there are other issues such as growing up into all aspects of Christ. I believe we should hold the apostolic value of becoming all things to all men that some may be saved (1 Cor. 9:22). I believe reaching and transforming our needy communities is a higher priority than theologically micromanaging the Bible. I believe when we eat of the wrong tree the result is living Christianity from the wrong place.

I do not believe in five hundred-page documents defining what a Christian is. I do not believe you have to conduct a church service like those in the times of the Reformation to have a "truly biblical" church service. I do not believe you have to speak in tongues to be a Christian. I do not believe someone who speaks in tongues is of the devil. I do not believe that education is of the devil. I do not believe that most citywide movements of churches proactively seeking unity are the one-world church. I do not believe someone who has the gift of healing is a New Age psychic. I do not believe that the King James Bible is the "only" true Bible. These are all church-centric issues and transport us away from community transformation.

Truthfully Speaking

The great news is that there are more and more Christians who believe and think in a more both/and way. These people are inclusive, pro-active, Bible-educated, and aware of the core values and non-negotiables of Christianity. They realize that a river without borders is a swamp! Without borders there would be no river. They honor the borders.

They understand that God has absolutes. They honor and obey those absolutes. They also understand, however, that theological micromanaging undermines the mission of Christ. They understand that many have wrongly divided the church in the name of rightly dividing the Word. They understand this is counterproductive and undermines community transformation. They understand that when the brothers (Christians) dwell together in unity, there is a blessing with the power of government behind it. They understand that a community reached is just as important as a message preached.

They understand that you cannot be Christ-centered without being community-centered. Their world is bigger than their church, their theological emphasis or "right" doctrine. They are world-class Christians growing up into *all aspects* of Christ, not just a few aspects of Christ. They can spot "religi-holics" a mile away.

They are not just from the new types of churches, they are from all denominations, cultures, streams, and nations. They are being conformed to Christ in character, ministry, and mission. They are multi-dimensional, seeing the big picture, and majoring on the majors. They have the life-and-death core value first and the right-or-wrong core value second. They are both/and people with crisp awareness of the absolutes of Christianity.

They are not fruit inspectors or fruit eaters, they are fruit bearers like the Church in the book of Acts. They do not go to church, they *are* the Church in their spheres of influence. They do not argue, they enhance. They are empowered evangelicals living intelligent fire core values out loud. They are orthodox, empowered, focused, yet very aware of the need for the fullness of Christ incarnated in the community.

They are not a mile wide and an inch deep. However, they have been liberated from the tyranny of a mile deep and an inch wide. They are both deep and wide. They are rooted, shooted, and fruited for the sake of the community.

All the Tools in the Toolbox

Let's look at a world-class, welcome-to-a-bigger-world Christian:

> That the man of God may be adequate, equipped for every good work.
>
> —2 Timothy 3:17

Do you realize that God wants the "man of God" to be "adequate, equipped for every good work"? The either/or viewpoint trains us to say, "I am not called to do that, I only do this." The problem with this view is the Christian becomes a one-dimensional person in a multi-dimensional context. Timothy tried that strategy with the apostle Paul in 2 Timothy 4:1–5. I can almost hear Timothy saying, "I am a pastor; I only do church!"

Paul retorts (and I am paraphrasing), "Timothy, your church needs new converts; get out there, get in the streets, do the work of an evangelist." Perhaps evangelism was not Timothy's calling, but he still could "do the work of an evangelist." Paul wanted Timothy to "grow into all aspects of Christ," not just one aspect of Christ.

Paul wanted Timothy to grow up before he grew old! Paul knew that Timothy needed to be the man of God who was adequate and equipped for *every good work*. Paul wanted Timothy to have all the "tools" in the "toolbox," not just one. If Timothy were a carpenter, his "gift" might be using the screwdriver but he would still need to have and know how to use a hammer.

God wants you and me to be able to show up on any job and at least perform it adequately. That is maturity and it takes a both/and core value to embrace the "hammer" and use it. To be honest, many in the church today with the either/or core value would say, "The screwdriver is of God, the hammer is not of God." I would say they are right—partially. I also would say they are wrong—partially. Both the screwdriver and the hammer are of God! The issue is not right-or-wrong; the issue is that neither is complete. It is a partial truth.

The man who describes what an elephant looks like by feeling the elephant's trunk is right, partially. However, he does not have a complete or full picture of the elephant. In one sense he is not wrong, just very incomplete. That is what the tyranny of the either/or does to the Church. God wants fullness, completeness, and adequateness.

> For it was the Father's good pleasure for *all the fullness* to dwell in Him.
>
> —Colossians 1:19

> Until we all attain to the unity of the faith, and of the knowledge of the Son of God, to a mature man, to the measure of the stature which belongs to the *fullness* of Christ.
>
> —Ephesians 4:13

There is that word "fullness" again. Jesus' desire was that you and I not operate by an either/or way of life. Yes, there are absolutes, but there is no way you or I may be adequate, equipped for every good work without a larger way of looking at life than either/or. Our community requires it. In order to have real, tangible, and lasting community transformation, we must have the enabling core value of both/and. The both/and is a vehicle to the vision of community transformation and enhancement.

The Implications of Application

I will wrap up this chapter with some practical applications of this core value.

1. Both doctors and divine healing are OK.

I have had people in both charismatic and fundamental camps walk out on me when I have made the above statement. Why? They are right-or-wrong, either/or-core value driven.

Might I suggest that God's world includes both of these ways of healing? The important thing to God is *to get well.*

2. Both God and government are OK.

Jesus rendered unto Caesar the things that were Caesar's. Jesus respected the government's boundary. Romans 13:1 and 13:4 say that government is of God. Government's assignment from God is to serve vision, protect vision, and collect the tithe or tax to do the vision.

Meeting both spiritual and physical needs of people, communities, and nations is okay. Some people think only in terms of spiritual. Some think only in terms of physical. Both are needed, and both have different roles. Both are necessary and of God.

3. Business and church are OK.

The either/or world of church is only creating a huge separation in the strategic alliance of kings and priests. Both worlds are okay. One world is not more spiritual than the other.

4. Public education and Bible are OK.

These are fighting words among many in the church. However, wherever the church has marginalized education, the community underachieves. Daniel went to the University of Babylon and led that nation back to God.

5. Organizational, financial, and spiritual issues are biblical.

You cannot solve a spiritual problem with an organizational solution, *and* you cannot solve an organizational problem with a spiritual solution. Many in the church spiritualize everything, much to their own hurt and detriment.

6. Jesus is the way, and the truth, and the life.

Jesus never said, "I am the truth, no man comes to the Father but through me." This statement is only one-third of the equation in John 14:16. Actually, I would say it like this: "The way to truth is through life!"

7. The church is upward . . . and inward . . . and outward.

The either/or value in the church has many of the worship people and intercessors in the church (upward) judging the evangelistic-oriented and fellowship-oriented people. Meanwhile, these other groups (outward and inward) judge the worship and intercessor people. It is all the tools in the toolbox—upward, inward, and outward.

8. Love the Lord thy God with all your heart, soul, mind, and strength (Mark 12:30).

The right-or-wrong group tends to love the Lord with their mind only. They need the heart also. Others love the Lord with their heart, but they checked-in their minds at the door. Think fullness!

I am sure you can think of additional examples, but I wanted to illustrate how the both/and core value enables the community to see a more complete picture of Christians *and* churches. The either/or core value cuts us off from each other as well as from business, education, government, and media/entertainment. People within these spheres of influence sense the us/them, win/lose, good/evil attitude of the church, and withdraw. They define us by our attitude toward them and, frankly, why wouldn't they? The real loser is the whole community.

The Lion and the Lamb

That is a paradox, isn't it? How can Jesus be both the Lion and the Lamb? This is the both/and core value in action.

Real, tangible, and lasting community transformation requires a deeply held belief that sees the world more in a both/and way than in an either/or way. Yes, there are absolutes, but God is more concerned about fullness than about fragmentation. If the Church sees everything from an us/them perspective, then how can we transform our communities? How can we work with business, government, educational, or in media spheres for the sake of the community? How can we form strategic alliances or mutual collaborations for the sake of the city with others? The answer is we cannot and we will not. We cannot even have unity or multi-church projects with a primarily either/or core value. In the end, the Church will underachieve and create a disconnect from the community it was called to serve. The Church needs the both/and core value to be all that it can be in the context of the community.

Chapter 9

Sacred Cows Make the Best Hamburger: *The Principle of Wonderful Servants, Terrible Masters*

What God blesses as a supplement
He curses as a substitute.

By now, I hope you see that you cannot hold to a right-or-wrong core value and accomplish real, tangible, and lasting community transformation at the same time. The same is true of the either/or core value. The vehicles of right-or-wrong and either/or are incapable of driving you to the distinction of community transformation. These disabling values render community transformation impossible 99 percent of the time. I realize there are always exceptions when we work with God, but frankly I prefer to follow God's preexisting pattern rather than the anomaly.

Intelligent fire helps us to see how correct core values along with a burden for the city and prayer increase the probability of community transformation. We move toward the idea of the Kenyan man who practices, eats correctly, and gets properly coached to win the Olympic marathon. The vision and values are compatible and symbiotic. They work together toward the vision rather than away from the vision. Therefore, as I stated earlier, the church needs to shift away from right-or-wrong first to life-and-death core values first. As that shift occurs, we begin to energize the both/and core value which enables us to embrace the other spheres of influence in the community. It also enables us to embrace other churches, other emphases in the church, other Christians and the community. It allows for what I called in the preceding chapter "fullness." The community needs to see the whole person of Christ presented in and to the community for tangible community transformation. That brings us to the third core value that is necessary for community transformation.

Churches That Shape the Community's Destiny

Remember that in the community transformation context, we must start with the question, "What does the community see when they go to church?" Is church understandable to my uncle or neighbor who has not been to church in years? Is church real or relevant *to them*? Have we connected the messenger with the audience? Was our service something that only Christians can understand? Could our church hold the new wine of community transformation or would our wineskin burst? Does our church demonstrate community transformation "on *our* terms" in an attitude and style that actually disable community transformation? Are we aware, or are we so focused on our theme or emphasis that a disconnect renders community transformation next to impossible?

Ultimately, it boils down to the following questions: what should the church look like to the community and in a community? Are our current forms of church disabling or enabling community transformation? Are our church-centric core values leading away from real, tangible, and lasting community transformation?

Let's discuss these questions and "consider our church ways" and the effect our ways have on the community.

The third core value necessary for community transformation is the need for the Church to look like Jesus in character, ministry, and mission and to the community. The community must see the whole picture *of* Jesus *in each church* as it was in the book of Acts. The church at Ephesus loved Paul because he "did not shrink back from declaring to [them] the whole purpose of God" (Acts 20:27). In the community transformation context, a half-truth is a whole lie. Since the foundation of the Galatian church, God has been patiently laboring to form Christ in us and in the church for the sake of the community (Gal. 4:19). We do not realize the power of our culture that has formed the Church in its own image. The concept I am referring to here is specialization. Specialization in the church is a wonderful servant but a terrible master. Specialization in many cases has disabled community transformation.

SPIRITUAL A. D. D.

Specialization is a unique characteristics of our culture. The advantage of specialization is the tremendous focus that it brings, allowing specialists to excel in their areas of concern. An eye doctor, for example, may specialize with excellence concerning the eye, yet be completely *unaware of the rest of the body*. His area is "eyes." You might say he has purpose or focus, yet is totally *unaware* of what to do if the heart is acting up. After a period of time, most specialists become so consumed with their specialty that it becomes their "world." They have *focus*, yet lack *awareness* that the eye is part of a much larger body.

Many churches today have become specialists. In the charismatic world, churches might be faith churches, spiritual warfare churches, prophetic churches, worship churches, prosperity churches, or cell churches. In the evangelical world, they might be Calvinist churches, Armenian churches, or "correct" theology churches. Then there is the sacramental world, the holiness world, the social justice world, and many more church emphases or themes. While all of these emphases are good, individually they do not present the full picture of Jesus Christ to the community. The community sees only a part of Jesus Christ and, as in the case of the eye specialist, what happens in these churches is so esoteric only the "eye doctors" know what is going on. They exist in what I call "the bubble."

There are churches where worship is the emphasis and specialty (not in word, but in deed). "Worshipers" enjoy attending these churches, but frankly, very few others in the community, if any, would want to. In my opinion, these churches are "conformed to worship," not to Jesus. Worship is part of Jesus, but not all of Jesus. They are being conformed to Jesus in ministry, but perhaps not in mission. They could become a "holy huddle" or the "deeper life club" and largely alien to the community. I realize that people may receive Jesus in a context like this, but that is by far the exception. These congregations really do not have church services every week—they have a worship conference every week. A conference is one-dimensional; a church is multi-dimensional. Conferences are wonderful places to build your knowledge and experience on a particular emphasis—worship, spiritual warfare, faith, prayer, the prophetic, cell groups, Bible knowledge, church history, Greek, Hebrew, and so on. However, these emphases are all part of Jesus, not the *whole* person of Jesus.

IT IS THE WHOLE BODY OR NOBODY

One might say, "In our city, we have different churches with different emphases. We are like the lungs, another church is like the hands, another church is like the eyes, etc. That is wonderful justification for being emphasis-driven, yet not very realistic. As one prophetic leader has said, "the problem is not the parts, it is the joints." Using this thought paradigm, it is like dissecting our bodies into their individual organs. The community does not experience the body, only the "lungs." The community experiences an emphasis, a theme, or a part of Jesus, not Jesus.

The early apostles initiated the joining of all these parts together—Christians who look like Jesus, churches that look like Jesus, cities and countries with churches that look like Jesus! In other words, Jesus wants churches that look and live like Him, "the fullness of the Godhead in bodily form."

Look at the following Scripture:

> And we know that God causes all things to work together for good to those who love God, to those who are called according to His purpose. For whom He foreknew, He also *predestined to become conformed to the image of His Son,* that He might be the first-born among many brethren; *and whom He predestined, these He also called*; and whom He called, these He also justified; and whom He justified, these He also glorified.
>
> —ROMANS 8:28–30

Our primary purpose as Christians and churches is to be conformed to the image of Jesus (it is predestined), and *secondly* to fulfill calling. If your calling comes before being conformed to Jesus, you are in danger of becoming sectarian, judgmental, and one-dimensional. *Emphases are wonderful servants, but terrible masters.* Your calling is never the standard, Jesus is! Every emphasis needs a context. You are a Christian first, a prayer warrior second. You are a Christian first, a theologian or church historian second. You are a Christian first, a pastor second. You are a Christian first, a Calvinist second.

God has designed the church to first be conformed to Jesus in character, ministry, and mission. Your specialty and emphasis are secondary. Every emphasis has a *measure of grace* (Romans 12:3, 6). When all the emphases come together, your church turns *into grace without measure*—the character, ministry, and mission of Jesus Christ. Your community will then be aware or have knowledge of the glory.

The Church is built by Jesus and on the rock of revelation of Jesus—nothing more and nothing less. To be emphasis-driven may keep life simple, but it lacks in fulfilling the vision statement of God: and the earth shall be filled with the knowledge of the glory (the fullness of Christ).

In the months and years to come, more and more churches will depart from the emphasis-driven mentality and move towards being conformed to Jesus in character, ministry, and mission. They will become less church-centric and more community-centric. There may be "seasons" of an emphasis, but it is crucial that we understand that these emphases are aspects of Jesus' character, ministry, or mission which God may want to recover, yet they must ultimately be integrated into a larger wineskin. *All* of the "wisdom of God" will be demonstrated "*through the church to the rulers*" (Eph. 3:10). Community transformation leaders and facilitators exist to bring awareness and to make sure that the local church is conformed to Jesus Christ in character, ministry, and mission. Community transformation leaders understand the *genius of both/and*, and seldom use the *tyranny of either/or*.

APOSTOLIC DAYS REQUIRE APOSTOLIC WAYS

One of the most amazing ministries in the Bible is that of the apostle. It is not coincidental that such words as apostle, bishop, and apostolic ministry are being used more and more in today's church all over the world. My good friend, Pastor David Cannistraci, wrote one of the most current of the apostolic books that have been published in the last few years. He called it *The Gift of Apostle: A Biblical Look at Apostleship and How God is Using It to Bless His Church Today*. When David gave me the original manuscript of this book, I immediately thought it should be published by a major publisher. I gave the manuscript to Dr. C. Peter Wagner, who took it from there to Regal Books, and the rest is history. Since then, many more books have been written on apostolic ministry by a whole new wave of authors.

In my book *Making Sense of Apostolic Ministry*, I address the fact that apostolic ministry is not a status, but a task. We should expect that as the urgency and efficiency of real, tangible, and lasting community transformation occurs, the essential core values that apostolic ministry brings will become necessary also. One will not happen without the other.

While many would want to argue about the term "apostle," I think we can all agree with the necessity of apostolic ministry or apostolic ways in today's church for the sake of the community. We need a "wineskin" that can hold the "wine" of community transformation. Apostolic leaders are the groom's servants and the bride's attendants who ensure that the church can be a wineskin to accommodate both the lost and the found. The early church was a both/and, not an either/or community of believers.

Apostolic Leaders—the Groom's Servants, the Bride's Attendants

The role of the apostolic gift in a local church or church movement is to ensure that the local church or church movement is conformed to the image of Jesus in character, ministry, and mission.

If the local church (bride) is not conformed to Jesus (groom), then the apostolic leader brings in that which is lacking, wanting, or in need of building up to conform the church to the image of Jesus Christ in character, ministry, and mission. Why? So the earth (both church and community) may be filled with the knowledge of the glory of the Lord as the waters cover the sea.

Apostolic ministry and leadership, whether inside or outside of the local church, exists to make sure that the local church is like Jesus in character, ministry, and mission. For example, if a local church is strong in the charismata and charismatic emphasis, but weak in evangelism, an apostolic leader can use his governmental influence to bring in that which is lacking, wanting, or in need of building up—that is, going and making disciples, evangelism. If a church excels in evangelism, but not in "teaching them to observe all that Jesus commanded," the leader can help the church to bring in true discipleship building.

If a church puts too much emphasis on holiness, rules, and regulations with no witness or a bad witness of "religion" in its community, an apostolic leader can bring in that which is lacking, wanting, or in need of building up, such as grace and awareness. If a church is a "Holy Ghost party" but has significant flaws in the character of its people, an apostolic leader can work with its governing board to ensure that the local church is conformed to Jesus in character.

If a local church is not evangelizing, discipling, or producing a good witness for influence in the community, an apostolic leader can work with its existing leadership, to correct that which is lacking, wanting, or in need of building up. His ministry is to measure the local church against the plumb line of God—the Chief Cornerstone—the church being conformed to Jesus in character, ministry, and mission. An apostolic leader's "government" is *never* for autocratic reasons, to rule, to be the boss, to "lord it over," or to have an apostolic network. *Apostolic ministry is not a status, it is a task.* An apostolic leader's government or influence is used for the task of the local church becoming conformed to Jesus in character, ministry, and mission that the community may see Jesus and have knowledge and awareness of the glory of God.

THE APOSTOLIC MINISTRY OF PAUL

Look at what Paul says to the Corinthian church in 2 Corinthians 2:9–10 after he had to bring in governmental influence to address a character problem in the church that its own government did not correct (1 Corinthians 5:1–8):

> For to this end also I wrote that I might put you to the test, whether you are obedient in all things. But whom you forgive anything, I forgive also; for indeed what I have forgiven, if I have forgiven anything, *I did it* for your sakes in the presence of Christ.
>
> —2 CORINTHIANS 2:9–10

Notice that Paul brought government and correction "for their sakes," not because of his need to control. What was Paul after? That the church in Corinth would look like Jesus in character, ministry, and mission, which would in turn produce a strong jurisdictional presence in its area of influence. That was for the sake of the Corinthian church and the church's area of influence or witness to the city or community. Paul's agenda was that the local church would be self-governed. His "accountability and government" was only engaged if the local church started "laying a foundation other than the one which is laid, which is Christ Jesus" (1 Cor. 3:11). As the Corinthian church refused to deal with the character issue in their church, they were, in Peter's words, rejecting the Chief Cornerstone in the area of character. Remember, apostolic governmental influence is always for the sake of the witness of the local church to the community—it was never for profit or a self-serving agenda.

Apostolic leaders working alongside prophetic leaders are truly "the attendants of the bride," and the "servants of the groom." Apostolic leaders are friends of the community and friends of the church. The apostle Paul said it best in Galatians 4:19, "My children, with whom I am again in labor until Christ is formed in you."

Apostolic Sensitivity to Lack in the Church

We can get a truer picture of apostolic ministry by looking at the apostles' activities. Consider Barnabas. Barnabas visited the church in Antioch and sensed that something in the church was lacking, wanting, or in need of building up. He realized that the church in Antioch could not be truly conformed to Jesus and fulfill its destiny in God without an apostolic teacher and pioneer church planter to the nations. Where did he go? Who did he bring back with him? Who did he bring in? You know the story—Saul (Paul) of Tarsus!

A few years later, the leaders of the church at Antioch sensed that large areas of Asia had no knowledge of the glory of the Lord (Jesus). They responded by forming an apostolic missionary endeavor to "go, make disciples and teach them to observe." Asia was lacking, wanting, and in need of the Gospel, and the leadership and church at Antioch were "aware" of it.

The apostle Paul also was sensitive to that which was lacking, wanting and in need of building up to conform the church to the image of Jesus in character, ministry, and mission. When the church at Corinth had a serious moral problem, and the leaders refused to deal with it, Paul, as their spiritual father, wrote a letter and sent it by special envoy. At that point, the church was lacking in character. Paul also addressed the "emphasis-drivenness" (tongues) of the church in Corinth. His first few sentences in 1 Corinthians 12:1–3 basically said, "Tongues is not lord, Jesus is Lord!" They were making *an* emphasis—*the* emphasis. In another instance, Paul sensed a need in the area of ministry within the Roman churches, so he longed to come to Rome to "impart some spiritual gift" (Rom. 1:11). He wanted to make sure that the fullness of the ministry of Jesus, including spiritual gifts, was present in the Church in Rome.

You see, the churches that are required for community transformation are "whole counsel" churches. The problem is, every church would call itself a whole-counsel church. Calvinist churches would call themselves whole-counsel churches. Sacramental churches would call themselves whole-counsel churches.

Apostolic ministry says, "Let's measure your church against the Chief Cornerstone. Do you look like Jesus in character, ministry and mission? Does your church have all the tools in the toolbox? Are you and your church adequate, equipped for every good work?" The apostolic ministry would ask the most difficult questions of all, "What does the community see when they see you? Are you emphasis-driven or theme-driven? Are you relevant? Do you have Spiritual A. D. D.? Have you made a part of Jesus, all of Jesus? Have you made *an* emphasis, *the* emphasis?"

I believe that emphasis-based or theme-based churches limit the potential of community transformation because they do not present all of Jesus to the community.

Rawhide—Spiritualizing Incompleteness

I have entitled this chapter "Sacred Cows Make the Best Hamburger" for a reason. It was the American humorist Mark Twain who first made this statement. As I speak all over the world, many times I find myself in theme-based churches with essentially no witness to, or influence in the communities they were created to serve. Behaviors such as speaking in Latin or Greek, running around with banners and flags, or speaking in "Christianese" with words and phrases that only a ten-year-old Christian knows the meaning of reflect church-centric values.

I have been in churches that were prayer churches whose "calling" was to pray. I have been in worship churches with intercessors, Jewish prayer shawls and, frankly, weird behaviors. I have been in faith churches and had people walk out on me for saying (or confessing) the word "suffering." I have heard dogs barking, chickens clucking, and people laughing during the message. I have been in churches where people were judged for not wearing a suit or not having a King James Bible. I have seen people fight over pre-tribulation/post-tribulation raptures.

These church emphases and church themes drive the behavior and ethos of the church. They spiritualize the "cow" and call it their "calling."

They take ownership of their emphases, even forming networks and organizations out of them. They have *their* speakers who speak on *their* subjects with *their* language and *their* definitions, which alone are right. Please notice the us/them attitude. I have seen the spiritual smugness that single-emphasis churches can have. The spiritual inbreeding that occurs is destructive to themselves, to other churches in the community and, ultimately, to the whole community.

> For we are not bold to class or compare ourselves with some of those who *commend* themselves; but when they measure themselves by themselves, and compare themselves with themselves, they are without understanding.
>
> —2 Corinthians 10:12

Notice how Paul says (and I paraphrase), "We are not included with these 'commended' people. We are on the outside. We are the *them* in the us/them. They do not include us. Why are not we included? It is because they measure themselves by themselves and compare themselves with themselves and oh, what comparison. Boy, do they think they are good! They truly believe that what they are doing is what God is doing.

However, what is really happening? This "spiritual inbreeding" on their emphasis is causing the "positive DNA" in them to decrease and the "destructive DNA" to increase. They are like men and women within the same family having children through incestuous relationships over the course of several generations. As a result, they are losing their minds. They are without understanding and in danger of destroying themselves. Taken to extremes, the good things that were in them have become destructive things. Those good things are wonderful servants, but terrible masters. The inbreeding and over-breeding of any species will ultimately cause craziness or weakness. People need cross-pollination to remain healthy. The church needs cross-pollination to remain healthy.

Many times, emphasis-driven churches or movements unintentionally hurt their own people by feeding them what I call "pizza only." When my sons Matthew and Jonathan were young, the only food that existed for them was pizza. If they did not get pizza, they "did not get fed." When their mother gave them macaroni, steak, potatoes, fruit, chicken, vegetables, they felt as if they "did not get fed." Becky and I had to take them to Austria and Germany to broaden their taste for food groups. That experience convinced them that there actually was food beyond pizza!

Church-centric emphasis-driven Christians are like my pizza-only sons. If the pastor of a Calvinistic church does not speak on Calvinism, many will feel as if they "did not get fed." In a Spirit-filled church, if the pastor does not lay hands on everyone and all fall over, many will feel as if "they did not get fed." Enough said.

Here is my point: they did get fed, only it was not what they wanted. The problem is, in order for a body to be healthy for the sake of church people, churches, and the community, we need to have all seven food, not just one. A good shepherd moves his sheep from pasture to pasture. If the shepherd keeps his sheep in only one pasture, it will not take long before the sheep have nothing to eat but rocks. Why? The grass in that area has been all eaten. The same is true for churches. We are to be conformed to Jesus, not to an emphasis. We need the whole counsel of God for spiritual health.

Stewardship or Ownership

If you read the paragraphs above and heard me say I did not like faith, you heard a ghost. If you think that I do not like prayer or the Holy Spirit, you heard a ghost. If you heard me say I did not like spiritual gifts or good doctrine or whatever, you heard a ghost. If you think I do not like worship or Israel, you heard a ghost. I like all of these, but I like all of them as servants, not masters. All of them are an emphasis, not the emphasis. Nothing is sacred but God.

God wants us to be stewards of His manifold grace, not owners. (See 1 Peter 4:10.) The problem occurs when we start to *own* His emphases rather than be *stewards* of them. We draw our identity from them. We draw our acceptance from them. Our themes become a newfound source of significance and security. We deify them. We attack when our emphases are attacked. We believe our emphases are right; theirs are not as good as ours. If it moos it is a cow. If it moos when being challenged, it is a sacred cow.

That is usually when God starts roasting a few cows. (After all, He does own the cattle on a thousand hills!) That is when those in the river realize that their reality is stuck in an eddy and calling it the river. That is when the pastor who says miracles are not for today has someone in his church miraculously healed of cancer. That is when apostolic succession and speaking Latin do not draw people into the church anymore. That is when prosperity-driven individuals go bankrupt. God is saying, "You are taking ownership rather than stewardship. *Jesus* is your Master, not *one of the aspects of Jesus*."

I believe God wanted emphasis-based churches for a reason and a season. He wanted to legitimize all the emphases and He needed a context to do that. After all, He is after fullness. Remember, when fullness is achieved, we have balance. However, these are apostolic days that require apostolic ways. There is "such a time as this" like in the book of Esther, but there is also such a time as that. God formed the streams first and now He is merging the streams into a river. He is bringing the Church into the fullness of all in all whether they are contemplative, holiness, charismatic, social justice, evangelical, or sacramental. As author Richard Foster suggests in his Renovaré ministry, "God is bringing the Church to the churches."[1] Remember, it's the whole body or nobody!

Remember, the prophetic ministry of the Church is about *activating* gifts, emphases and ministries. The days of Martin Luther and the Reformation were a prophetic time. The activating of missionaries from the evangelical church was prophetic during The Great Awakening. The current prophetic time, since the 1950s, has been about the activating of gifts, themes, and ministries. Understand, however, that the apostolic ministry is about *integrating* gifts, themes, and ministries. Now is the time when all of these activated gifts need to integrate into the "fullness of all in all." Now is the time for the *celebration* of differences, not the toleration of differences. Now is the time when the parts of the body that are least esteemed by whatever movement you embrace need to be most esteemed (1 Cor. 12:22–24). It is time for the formation of churches that are conformed to Jesus in character, ministry and mission to rise up in the community.

I am not talking about a "one world," do-whatever-you-feel-like church. I am talking about all the tribes becoming a nation. I am talking about the church getting sufficient mass and momentum. I am talking about the church, due to its size and good reputation in the community, becoming a significant player in the community. I am talking about Christ—through the church—to the community. I am talking about a wineskin that is effective and meaningful to both the presently churched and the future-churched—a church that is balanced, blended, and blessed. It is about all the "stewards" of the manifold grace behaving as stewards and not owners.

"Equiliberated" to Equilibrium

On the road to fullness, the church, leaders of the church and the people of the church have gone through many toils, trials and snares. I liken it to five waves of recovery and restoration. All are equally important aspects of Jesus' life and ministry. All of them together offer a complete picture of Christ to the community. It is the *activation* of these waves and then the *integration* of these waves that present the Church to the community in such a way as to enable community transformation. The Church has to be *equiliberated* to achieve equilibrium.

At this point, I must note that I am not talking about *balance*, but about *fullness*. When The Church comes to the church, that is what the apostle Paul calls the fullness of all in all. That means individual churches are growing up in all aspects into Christ (Eph. 4:15), exhibiting Christ through the Church to the community. Individual churches that look like Christ create the Church in a community that looks like Christ.

My good friend, author John Noble, works with Pastor Gerald Coates, the founder of the Pioneer Church network in England. John recently wrote a book called *The Shaking*, in which he clearly identifies five waves of recovering and restoration that the Church has gone through in its history.[2] I want to explore his explanation of how all these waves work with and build upon each other.

The First Wave

First, the sacramental tradition expressed primarily through the Catholic Church has the Eucharist as its focus with its strengths in devotion, worship, and holiness. The altar is a central feature, and the pastor or priest plays the key role. The worst extreme of this tradition results in "ecclesiolatry" and abuse of the sacrament. The church actually comes between the people and a direct relationship to Jesus, producing passivity and bolstering the dependence on an up-front, one-man (with the emphasis on one-man) ministry.

The Second Wave

Second, the reformed tradition, which was the outcome of the first major shaking the church had experienced for centuries, refocused attention on the Bible. The strengths of the Reformation were preaching, exposition, and a quest for truth. The pulpit was the central feature, and the teacher played the key role. The weaknesses of this tradition were an overemphasis on the intellect and "bibliolatry" or Bible worship. The Trinity became Father, Son, and Holy Scripture, which led to pride, legalism, and empty worship. This left much of the church and her practices irrelevant to the people she was seeking to reach

The Third Wave

Third, the missionary tradition was a natural progression beyond the Reformation, as truth understood had to be proclaimed. Heralded as the "Great Awakening," this tradition focused on the task of fulfilling the great commission. Its strengths were evangelistic zeal and a willingness to sacrifice all in the cause of preaching the gospel to every people. The field was the central feature, the evangelist was the key player, and under this ministry the Church grew by leaps and bounds. The weaknesses were seen later, as the gospel message was unwittingly mixed with culture in its application and was imposed through paternalism and Western imperialism. The evangelistic ministries of the day were largely marginalized by the Church, which gave rise to missionary societies and a welter of new denominations. However, another giant step in restoration had been taken, and Christ's new building continued to rise from the rubble of previous demolition.

The Fourth Wave

Fourth, is the Charismatic tradition that began with Pentecostal outpourings at the beginning of the twentieth century and was advanced through renewal movements during the sixties to the present time. The main focus became the Holy Spirit and his supernatural manifestations. The restoration of prophecy and healing together with other gifts of the Spirit were the strengths that brought the Christian faith into public view. This at a time when humanism, the Enlightenment, and rationalism had done serious damage to religious belief. The tide of doubt and skepticism began to turn, and today there is more openness to the gospel than at any time in history.

The central feature of this tradition has been the "tarrying" or "renewal" meeting when the Holy Spirit is given room to move.

The prophet has played a key role, although all-member "body ministry" has also been encouraged. The weaknesses were seen in an over-emphasis on experience and a neglect of Bible teaching. The movement has also produced the personality cult and the extremes of some prosperity doctrines. Nevertheless, the effects of Pentecostal/ Charismatic Renewal have seriously reshaped the church. By the mid to late-nineties some nations that had had virtually no Christian presence, such as Korea, had experienced a rise in their Christian populace to 30 percent of their total population, while some south American countries had seen even greater Christian growth. The momentum of restoration is quickening and there is a sense of urgency as the harvests of good and evil ripen before our eyes.

The Fifth Wave

Now the time is right for a full-blooded apostolic tradition to appear, which will take the best elements of the other four and bind them together to make a final, strong witness to Christ's character and power in all the Earth. The focus will be on solid foundations based on right relationships with God and one another. In other words, Jesus will once more occupy pride of place. The unique feature of the apostolic tradition will be flexible, mobile teams which will serve the church at large and prepare her for ministry. The primary role will belong to the apostle who, together with the other ministries, will be able to handle unity with diversity, bridging strong personalities, different cultures, and diverse church traditions.

WAVES OF TRADITIONS	FOCUS	MINISTRY	BEST FEATURE	WORST FEATURE
1. Sacramental	Sacraments and the priest	Pastor	Devotion to Jesus and the church	"Ecclesiolatry" —worship of the church; passivity
2. Reformed	The Bible and the pulpit	Teacher	Knowledge of the Scriptures	"Bibliolatry" —worship of the Bible; theoretical
3. Evangelical	The Great Commission and the missionary	Evangelist	Reaching the unreached	Export and imposition of culture
4. Charismatic	Baptism and gifts of the Holy Spirit	Prophet	Body ministry	Personality and theme churches possible
5. Apostolic/ Fullness	Church foundations, right relation-ships, and the End Times	Apostolic team	Local and extra-local team ministry	Authority abuse; misdirected discipleship

Notice how each of these waves of tradition has an important contribution to make, yet each has an inherent potential weakness. That is why all of these are needed. Each one of the waves is incomplete in itself. Each one needs the others' contribution to guard against its inherent weaknesses and limitations. It is a "both/and," not an "either/or." Of course, as I stated earlier, each of these traditions tends to individualize from the other because of the right-or-wrong ethos of the church. The problem is that these different yet necessary waves have become the end rather than the means to an end. They have become masters, rather than servants that enable Christ to be demonstrated through the Church to the community. While we are aware of and honor the call of God on each of these traditions, we also need to be aware that they are meant to be "wonderful servants," not "terrible masters."

ACTIVATED AND INTEGRATED

I love the cause of community transformation because real community transformation is a higher cause than the "borders and boundaries" of the sacramental, reformed, evangelical, charismatic, and apostolic traditions. As I have said, the church in its fullness and maturity is a community with a cause, which is the community. It is the manifold wisdom of God demonstrated in churches that look like Jesus in character, ministry (tradition), and mission. The character and ministries are for the mission.

Just think of the possibilities of brothers dwelling together in unity. I said brothers, not "others." The result is the commanded blessing of God (Ps. 133). That is a blessing with the power of government and God's jurisdiction behind it. That is a corporate blessing. Corporate blessing is the highest form of blessing in the Bible. It is where two or three agree. It is powerful; it shifts communities; it impacts nations.

Let me show you another chart that John Noble includes in *The Shaking*. It is what he calls "Apostolic: The Completion of Evangelicals, Social Activists, and Charismatics."

STREAM	Evangelical	Social activist	Charismatic	Apostolic Fullness
REALM	Hell	Earth	Heaven	Hell Earth Heaven
FOCUS	Soul	Body	Spirit	Soul Body Spirit
PRIMARY EMPHASIS	Salvation	Justice	Healing	Salvation Justice Healing
DISTINCTIVES	Proclamation	Care	Miracles	Proclamation Care Miracles
MAIN CONCERN	Truth	Practical help	Spiritual gifts	Truth Practical help Spiritual gifts
DESIRED	Word	Works	Wonders	Word Works Wonders

John and I put our heads together and came up with the combining of all these "worlds," which moves us from a tribe to a nation. In the next chapter, you will read about "The Principle of Dual Citizenship—Both Tribe and Nation." I believe this principle, if applied, may enable the church to combine the traditions for the sake of the community. The principle will give us a mental "wineskin" to hold the fullness of all in all.

THE THIRTY-ONE-FLAVORS CHURCH

Let's apply this concept in the context of a local church in the community. I have posed the questions:

- Why be a Christian fellowship when you can be a church for the community?

- Why be church-centric when you can be community-centric?
- Why be one-dimensional and emphasis-driven when you can be multi-dimensional?
- Why be conformed to an emphasis or tradition when you can be conformed to Jesus?

The community wants to see Jesus, not part of Jesus! Real, tangible, and lasting community transformation requires churches that are Christ-centric, not emphasis-centric. It is both biblical and powerful to have all of the emphases working together to bring the Church up to the fullness of all in all. Even small churches can move toward the integration of the "specialists" God has given them to present Christ to the community. Remember, with God it is not the exaltation of an emphasis, neither is it the disintegration of an emphasis. Rather it is the integration of the emphasis.

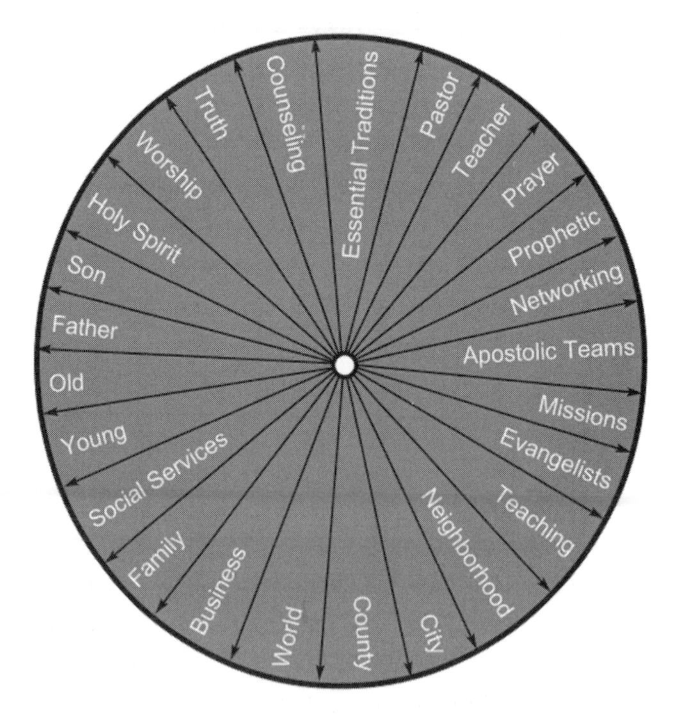

A good example of this is the Baskin-Robbins chain of ice cream stores. It is thirty-one flavors that make the ice-cream store, not "vanilla only." Most "vanilla only" stores went out of business a long time ago. To use the church right-or-wrong mentality, one would say, "Vanilla's right; chocolate's wrong. We are the First Church of the Vanilla!" This type of thinking will limit you and eventually put you out of business. God's Church has always been the wineskin that was meant to hold "thirty-one flavors," not just one flavor. It is time for each individual church to grow up into all aspects of Christ, not just one (Eph. 4:15).

Look at this chart on what I feel would be a thirty-one flavors church in a community:

Of course, this does not present all the aspects of Christ's ministry, but please catch the concept. This type of church is a community church. Community-centric churches and people initiate transformed communities. The power is in the sum of the parts, not in the parts themselves. Waves of doctrine and emphasis are wonderful servants, but terrible masters.

The Language God Speaks Is Jesus

While ministering in London, England, I heard Rod Anderson of the Prayer for the Nations ministry speak on a biblical concept that changed my life. He said, "The language God speaks is Jesus." Let's examine this concept. Look at the following verses:

> God...in these last *days has spoken to us in His Son*, whom He appointed heir of all things, through whom also He made the world. And He (Jesus) is the radiance of His glory and the exact representation of His nature, and upholds all things by the word of His power.
>
> —Hebrews 1:1–3

The first part of these verses say this: God speaks the language of Jesus. The French speak French, the Spanish speak Spanish, the Russians speak Russian, but God speaks Jesus! Why? Jesus is the exact representation of God. God makes Himself known through Jesus; Jesus makes Himself known through the Church to the community.

The community knows what God is like through the Church conformed to Jesus in character, ministry, and mission. That is why apostolic ministry works to bring the full picture of Jesus (the fullness of all in all) into each church, network, or ministry.

God speaks Jesus, and apostolic ministry should speak Jesus. That is why Paul lamented to the Galatians:

> My children, with whom I am again in labor until Christ is formed in you.
>
> —Galatians 4:19

Paul knew the formula for success in the church was a language called Jesus!

Jesus said in John 12:31–32, "Now judgment is upon this world; now the ruler of this world will be cast out. And I, if I am lifted up from the earth, will draw all men to Myself."

Jesus was referring to the bronze serpent of Moses in the wilderness:

> Then the Lord said to Moses, "Make a fiery serpent, and set it on a standard; and it shall come about, that everyone who is bitten, when he looks at it, he will live." And Moses made a bronze serpent and set it on the standard; and it came about, that if a serpent bit any man, when he looked to the bronze serpent, he lived.
>
> —Numbers 21:8–9

When anyone was bitten by the serpents, if he looked at this bronze serpent, he would live. The same is true of Jesus. As Jesus is "lifted up" in the community and people in the community look to Him, he deals with the community's sin problem.

It is the Church's job to lift up the fullness of Jesus to the community. The community needs to see Jesus. As the song says, we are to "lift Jesus higher" for the world to see. When, instead, we lift up our specialty or emphasis to the community, we disable community transformation. We are to lift up Jesus. We are not to lift up church themes such as worship, prayer, doctrines, pre-tribulation rapture, social concerns, sacraments, and other church-based themes. Worship will not solve the basic problem of sin. Prayer will not solve the basic problem of sin. Pre-tribulation teaching will not solve the basic problem of sin.

The tendency of church culture to specialize and individualize has lifted up everything but Jesus. As a result, all men have not been drawn to Him. Just as the Greeks came to the disciples and said, "Sir, we want to see Jesus," so do our communities. Our mission *requires* it. We must have churches that look like Jesus in character, ministry, and mission to achieve real, tangible, and lasting community transformation. Anything less than churches and Christians conformed to Jesus ultimately takes the Church and the community to where neither wants to go, to each one's detriment.

Chapter 10

I'M OKAY, YOU'RE SO-SO:

The Principle of Dual Citizenship—Both Tribe and Nation

Politics is the art of making your selfish desires seem like the national interest.

Until we all attain to the unity of the faith, and of the knowledge of the Son of God, to a mature man, to the measure of the stature which belongs to the fullness of Christ.
—EPHESIANS 4:13

IT SEEMS LIKE everybody is talking unity these days. Everywhere I go all over the world the *talk* is unity—but how close are we to real and tangible unity? Pockets of unity in cities, or movements of pastors may spring up for a season, but most seem to die just as quickly. Notice these words: "until *we all* attain to the unity of the faith." What a quest! And it is the prayer of Jesus in John 17:23. To many pastors, leaders or denominations today, Ephesians 4:13 would realistically mean this: "When everybody believes our way, then we will have unity." That is a type of politicized unity that does not reflect a national unity.

Now, I know we would not say it that way, but our actions or lack of actions reveals our values. It reminds me of the license plate cover that says "I am OK...You are So-so." *Could it be that our value systems undermine the vision of unity in a real and tangible way?* Core values are the government that either enables or disables our getting to the vision. As I stated earlier, core values enable us to get to vision. If our core value systems undermine the vision of real and tangible unity, the results can lead us only to eventual failure.

If our "vision" is community transformation or revival (outside the church walls), we must have the core value or "government" of unity. *Unity is not a vision, it is a core value that enables us to get to the vision of community transformation. Unity is a pre-requisite to real and tangible community transformation.*

Without real and tangible unity, the church is like the man who has a vision to win the Olympic marathon, but never practices. His full potential will never be actualized. Unfortunately, this is the problem in the church world today—unfulfilled potential and frustration. Let's explore the issues and solutions together.

The Achievement Paradigm

As I travel the world, the conversation I hear among church leaders revolves around how many people are in your church, how many churches do you have, what is bringing you growth, or even, what books have you written? Of course, there are other subjects being discussed, but by and large, the conversation revolves around and reflects western cultural values. Our actions and values support the value of "Fame Equals Impact." I call it "The latest, the greatest, the biggest, the best!" It seems, *as indicated by our conversation and actions*, we do not consider ourselves family but rather competitors or unrelated institutions. This view creates a dualistic paradigm of us-them; right-wrong; win-lose; good-evil; either-or; successful-unsuccessful. Remember, I am not talking about what *we say or believe*. I am looking at *values*, or what we do—*the way we really think reflected by our actions.*

This dualistic paradigm comes from western culture and is based on the philosophy of achievement as a higher value than relationship. Much of this attitude has come from seminaries, Bible schools or churches where students have been taught "Our doctrine is the right doctrine; theirs is not." Also the our-emphasis-is-God, theirs-is not doctrine—we are OK...they are so-so—is problematic. Like Ford and Toyota, we compete with each other for the best automobiles and highest sales. The students after they have "been fully trained" by their teacher (Luke 6:40), reproduce this dualistic paradigm within their congregations, denominations, or movements. Competition and exclusiveness become core values of the churches and congregations they pastor.

The question is, does the achievement-over-relationship paradigm facilitate Jesus' vision of unity, or impede it? (See John 17:21, 23.) The truth is our competitive, success-oriented culture has moved most churches and church movements away from a very important and necessary core value of the church. In fact, the church can never be what she was designed to be without the core value of real and tangible unity.

Tribes and Nations

> From every tribe, language, people and nation.
>
> —Revelation 5:9

God has always viewed Israel as one big family with twelve sub-families. These sub-families were called "tribes" and all the extended tribal families were called a nation—the nation of Israel. When Jacob was approaching the end of his life, he gathered together his twelve sons and spoke to them of their unique destinies, distinctives, and callings—whether positive or negative. At that point, the brothers became the heads of their own *families* or *tribes*, yet they were still all part of the *nation* of Israel. Like twelve slices of a pie, each was a part of the whole pie. All twelve brothers *together* formed the "national" government—not one brother or tribe individually. Each brother was part of the "national" government, but none alone was the whole.

It is interesting to see that Israel's land inheritance (Canaan) was taken by the nation of Israel, yet divided up and settled by tribes. Genesis 49 tells us that each tribe's uniqueness, emphasis, and size was different yet totally necessary in the formation of the nation. For example, Judah was uniquely called to praise the Lord and be a protector of Jerusalem, while Joseph was a "fruitful bough" who was blessed to go to the nations. Joseph had the "crown" (v. 27) while Judah had the "scepter" (v. 10). They needed to cooperate so the crown and the scepter (authority and power) could work together. Also, some tribes had large populations and land ownership while others had small populations and land ownership, yet each tribe was just as important as the other because of their *family status*, not their size or emphasis.

Each tribe, whether large or small, also had an area of influence and was encouraged not to think of themselves more highly than they ought. The founding fathers of the United States captured this concept in forming the Senate as part of the legislative branch of the government. Each state, no matter what size or emphasis, has two votes. Each state is given equal status because of its "family" status. Yet, hopefully, each state realizes that it is part of the United States, not the whole nation—even Texas! The United States House of Representatives, on the other hand, represents the *institutional* value of "the bigger you are, the more influence you have." It is interesting to note that the Senate exists to preserve the "family" aspect of the United States no matter what "tribe" is dominant at any given time. United we stand, divided we fall.

Our Dual Citizenship

The tribes or families of Israel had to think in terms of two citizenships—a national citizenship (Israel) and a tribal citizenship (Joseph, Judah, Dan, etc.). Numbers 10:2–4 illustrates this:

> Make yourself two trumpets of silver, of hammered work you shall make them; and you shall use them for summoning the congregation and for having the camps set out. And when both are blown, all the congregation shall gather themselves to you at the doorway of the tent of meeting. Yet if only one is blown, then the leaders, the heads of the divisions of Israel, shall assemble before you.

One might say the trumpet symbolizes a prophetic call for a *reason* and a *season*. Verse 3 says when both trumpets were blown, all the leaders of the twelve tribes and their families assembled at the doorway of the tent. If only one trumpet was blown, just the heads of the tribes came to the doorway of the tent (v. 4). Verse 3 speaks of a "general conference" and verse 4 speaks of a "leadership conference."

Here is what I want to emphasize. When the trumpet was blown, they were to come together on a *national* basis with their *tribal* distinctions becoming secondary in importance. They did not have to give up their tribal identity, but joined together as a nation or extended family in a higher cause for a *reason* and a *season*. In effect, God was saying, "There are just some things that you *cannot do alone*, you have to do them *together*."

The four reasons for *all the tribes* to join together into a nation were:

- *For unity*—"summoning the congregation" (v. 2).
- *For transition or change*—"having the camps set out" (v. 2).
- *For war*—"when you go to war" (v. 9).
- *For feasts and celebrations*—"in the day of your gladness and in your appointed feasts" (v. 10).

Please note the order in which these four reasons are listed. First, they united *as a family*, then moved out *together*, then fought the common enemy *together* and all celebrated the victories and feasts *together*. Notice the value of *community*, *family*, *jointness*, *togetherness*, and *corporateness*. They got into unity *as a nation* before they went out to make war. They started at the first trumpet, not the third trumpet. How many "tribes" have tried to reach a city by themselves? How many churches, denominations, and church leaders have tried to live by themselves? *How many have called themselves independent fundamentalists or independent Charismatics? In my opinion, that is not a badge of honor, that is a recipe for failure.* You cannot live the Christian life independently; you live the Christian life corporately, especially when a big common enemy is confronting you! The truth is there are just some things in Kingdom living that cannot be done independently. They have to be done corporately. It is not good for man, a local church, a leader or a denomination to live alone.

It Takes a "Spiritual" Government to Transform a "Natural" Government

Let me make a statement here, and then I will explain. *Gad cannot drive out the Philistines, but Israel can!* You remember that Gad was one of the twelve tribes of Israel. One tribe alone could not conquer the Philistines. God knows that it takes a nation to conquer a nation. The same is true of the Church today. Each church or denomination is like a tribe. And it takes all the tribes of the nation to win its battles in the context of the community.

When all twelve of the tribes came together, they formed the nation or "government" of Israel. Twelve is the number of government. The Philistines were a governmental entity or force. Alone, Gad had a *measure of grace*, but when Gad joined together with the other eleven brothers (Israel) they corporately received *grace without measure*, or the government of God. A measure of grace, or grace without measure? Which do you think it will take to reach your city for Christ?

I believe it takes a "government" to transform a government. It takes a "nation" to transform a nation. For example, in considering reaching a city or nations for Christ, it is absolutely essential to get the family (churches, leaders, and denominations) together as a *nation*. The church of Buenos Aires has the potential to reach the city, but a church cannot. We start at the first trumpet, not the third trumpet.

When *a* church independently goes to war against a malevolent force in its city, that is like starting at the third trumpet stage. That church has only a measure of grace and, in most cases, will end up worse off than it was when it started. *A* tribe does not have the potential impact of *a* nation! Unfortunately, that church is operating under a "declaration of independence" whereas the nation of Israel or *the* church operates under the "declaration of interdependence" principle. They will never get to the fourth trumpet or "feast stage." It takes a functional community of churches to reach a community of people, even in small communities. Remember what Matthew 18:20 says, "For where two or three have gathered together in My name, there I am in their midst." That verse is referring to dealing with governmental issues. There must be "two or three to agree" for their community (Matt. 18:19). It takes a "spiritual" government to transform a "natural" government.

SPIRITUAL TRIBALISM

Returning to my original premise, does the church function best in the family paradigm, or the achievement-over-relationship paradigm? Which of these two paradigms enables us to get to a real and tangible unity, which is what the whole church emanates from (Ephesians 4)? Which paradigm enables us to start at the first trumpet? Which paradigm can bring us to a unity of the faith?

First of all, let me say it is biblical to be both a "tribe" and a "nation." It is not an "either/or," it is a "both/and." Your church, denomination or network, is really one of many "tribes" that make up a "nation." Pastors, denominational heads and leaders of apostolic networks need to think in terms of both "tribe" and "nation." The leaders of a "tribe" (Southern Baptist, Assembly of God, Calvary Chapel, Vineyard, Episcopal) need to think *vertically* as does the pastor or leader of a local church. He is like a general or shepherd who is concerned with his company, the condition of his flock or movement, and carrying out the day-to-day operations of that flock or movement. However, the leader also needs to think *horizontally* or *nationally*. He needs to see that he is part of a larger family or nation, and that he is not independent. He needs to be aware that he has *limitations* and, for his tribe's benefit, as well as the other tribe's benefit, *needs to relate to the other tribes as brothers and as a nation*. Sometimes the Father calls together a "family reunion" for a reason and for a season, and he needs to be there.

When a tribal leader does not consider the horizontal aspect of the church and becomes isolationist, the phenomenon of *spiritual tribalism* takes root. *Spiritual tribalism* occurs when a tribe thinks it is the nation. The church is interpreted through tribal eyes and that tribe tries to conform the nation to its calling, its distinctives, its doctrine, or its language. That tribe "sets the standard" for all other tribes—*We are OK, you are so-so.*

Spiritual tribalism has led to a multitude of doctrine-based denominations as well as emphasis or theme-based churches. When spiritual tribalism sets in, eventually isolationism and exclusiveness sets in. The tribe then sets the standards for what is right and wrong, correct and incorrect, important and unimportant, or relevant and not relevant. The end result is spiritual tribalism, the setting of endless standards, and isolation from the "nation." They begin, as Paul says in 2 Corinthians 10:12, to "measure themselves by themselves, and compare themselves with themselves, they are *without understanding*." They start thinking of themselves more highly than they ought, even leading to the negative effects of inbreeding. Paul describes them as "without understanding" as they micromanage themselves and the nation.

Someone recently sent me a poignant example of spiritual tribalism through the Internet. Unfortunately, this will be very real to both Christians and the future church. It is called *A Blessed Encounter*:

> I was walking across a bridge recently. I spied this guy who looked like he was ready to jump off. So I thought I'd try to stall him until the authorities showed up (or at least until I had time to put film in my camera).
>
> "Don't jump!" I said.
>
> "Why not?" he said. "Nobody loves me."
>
> "God loves you," I said. "You believe in God, do not you?"
>
> "Yes, I believe in God," he said.
>
> "Good," I said. "Are you Christian or Jewish?"
>
> "Christian," he said.
>
> "Me, too!" I said. "Protestant or Catholic?"
>
> "Protestant," he said.
>
> "Me, too!" I said. "What kind of Protestant?"
>
> "Baptist," he said.
>
> "Me, too!" I said. "Independent Baptist or Southern Baptist?"
>
> "Independent Baptist," he said.
>
> "Me, too!" I said. "New Evangelical/Moderate Independent Baptist or Conservative Independent Baptist?"
>
> "Conservative Independent Baptist," he said.
>
> "Me, too!" I said. "Calvinistic Conservative Independent Baptist or Lose-Your-Salvation Armenian Conservative Independent Baptist?"

"Calvinistic Conservative Independent Baptist," he said.

"Me, too!" I said. "Dispensational Premillennial Calvinistic Conservative Independent Baptist or Historical Premillennial Calvinistic Conservative Independent Baptist?"

"Dispensational Premillennial Calvinistic Conservative Independent Baptist," he said.

"Me, too!" I said. "Against-Women-in-Ministry Dispensational Premillennial Calvinistic Conservative Independent Baptist or For-Women-in-Ministry Dispensational Premillennial Calvinistic Conservative Independent Baptist?"

"Against-Women-in-Ministry Dispensational Premillennial Calvinistic Conservative Independent Baptist," he said.

"Me, too!" I said. "Unashamed-Fundamentalist Against-Women-in-Ministry Dispensational Premillennial Calvinistic Conservative Independent Baptist or Strict-Separation-of-Church-and-State Against-Women-in-Ministry Dispensational Premillennial Calvinistic Conservative Independent Baptist?"

"Unashamed-Fundamentalist Against-Women-in-Ministry Dispensational Premillennial Calvinistic Conservative Independent Baptist," he said.

"Me, too!" I said. "Pro-Disney-Boycott Pro-Life Unashamed-Fundamentalist-Against-Women-in-Ministry Dispensational Premillennial Calvinistic Conservative Independent Baptist or Anti-Disney-Boycott Pro-Choice Unashamed-Fundamentalist-Against-Women-in-Ministry Dispensational Premillennial Calvinistic Conservative Independent Baptist?"

"Pro-Disney-Boycott Pro-Life Unashamed-Fundamentalist Against-Women-in-Ministry Dispensational Premillennial Calvinistic Conservative Independent Baptist," he said.

"Me, too!" I said.

"*KJV-Only* Pro-Disney-Boycott Pro-Life Unashamed-Fundamentalist Against-Women-in-Ministry Dispensational Premillennial Calvinistic Conservative Independent Baptist or Modern-Versions Pro-Disney-Boycott Pro-Life Unashamed-Fundamentalist Against-Women-in-Ministry Dispensational Premillennial Calvinistic Conservative Independent Baptist?"

"*Modern-Versions* Pro-Disney-Boycott Pro-Life Unashamed-Fundamentalist Against-Women-in-Ministry Dispensational

> Premillennial Calvinistic Conservative Independent Baptist," he said.
>
> "Auugghh! You heretic!" I said. And I pushed him over.[1]

Here is what I want us to become aware of: spiritual tribalism leads to exclusiveism and away from the core value of the extended family or nation. Spiritual tribalism leads us to a *measure of grace* without the opportunity for the ministry of Jesus or *grace without measure*. Spiritual tribalism is a "declaration of independence" rather than a "declaration of interdependence" rendering Jesus' prayer of unity for the church unlikely if not impossible! As I mentioned earlier, unity is not a vision; unity is a core value. As Jesus said in Mark 3:25, "And if a house is divided against itself, that house will not be able to stand."

Incarnating Our Dual Citizenship

As we prepare to enter what I believe will be the best years of Christianity, here are some "practicals" on issues of "connecting the clans" that I think are prerequisites to the community transformation that all of us so desperately long for.

1. We need to act nationally for the sake of our communities

Do you realize the church has the largest public relations problem in the world? The community sees us as *divided* rather than diverse. That is to say, they see us in a negative way rather than a positive way. Perhaps it is time for the *nation* of Christianity to demonstrate unity to the community in a real and tangible way through service to the community. *We are here for the community, the community is not here for us.* Do we realize the community is watching us? We need good relationships for the sake of the community. We need to get along together for the sake of the community. We must not have church or denominational splits for the sake of the community. We love one another for the sake of the community. We must be non-religious and pro-Jesus for the sake of the community. Ephesians 3:10 says in effect that our job is to demonstrate Christ through the church to the community. We are here to give the church back to the community. We have been called to be a blessing to all the nations (Genesis 12:3). That is what Jesus prayed in

John 17:21, the ultimate verse on community transformation. It takes a *community of churches to reach a community of people!*

2. Our areas of influence/areas of interest

The United States military has a strategic concept in what they call "areas of influence" and "areas of interest." The Army's top general has direct influence over the Army, but not over the Navy or Air Force. However, the Navy and Air Force are areas of interest in that they are his partners in the "nation" of the military. To use tribes-and-nations vernacular, He is the tribal head of the Army, but not of the Navy or Air Force. His brothers (the Navy and Air Force) are areas of interest and part of the family. If He is wise, he will work with, cooperate with, and recognize the importance of his extended family. If He is not wise, his Army will likely suffer great loss through friendly fire or the Navy and Air Force mistakenly attacking his troops. That is quite a lesson for denominational heads, network leaders, and pastors in a community. We have areas of influence as well as areas of interest. It is called national awareness. Sometimes we get *too focused* on our tribe and become *unaware* of the big picture. Healthy living is a blend of *focus* and *awareness. Focus* without *awareness* is problematic to all.

3. Corporate cooperation is our friend, not our enemy

Do you realize God designed us to be a family? Our family structure is just like Jacob and his twelve sons. God is the head of the nations, and we (denominations, networks, and churches) are his "sons." *No one tribe could ever occupy the land of Israel—it is too big for one tribe. We all need each other to occupy the land.* We were created to be diverse, but never divided. In my opinion, our divisiveness has lead to the "collapse of our family" and as a result, unfulfilled potential.

4. Our relationship by national core values first, tribal distinctives second

Let's become aware of our "national" core values, as well as our "tribal" distinctives and callings. The early Christians captured this concept in the Apostles Creed and Nicene Creed. The core values and beliefs of Christianity are outlined in these creeds. We all realize there are no perfect creeds, but endless additions, subtractions, and redefinitions have led us to many different, long, and difficult documents defining what Christianity is. Most of these documents are really "tribal" views, not a "national" view. In other words, the nation has been defined by a particular tribe or thought paradigm.

I have said many times, *the Apostles Creed is a fairly accurate assessment (but not perfect) of our Christian "constitution."* In my opinion, nearly every statement of faith beyond the Apostles Creed has to do with tribal issues, not national issues. My goal here is not a mystical "ecumenical unity," but the kind of unity that is found when "brothers dwell together in unity" reflecting the corporateness of Christ and His church. I believe that in an attempt to be *correct*, many have gone way too far in defining a "brother" and an "other" leading us down a we are-okay-they are-so-so path. How about concentrating on what unifies us, not what divides us? It is time to connect the clans, not divide them in the name of "rightly dividing."

5. The need for a national protocol

In my opinion, our Bible schools, seminaries, and churches need to have classes on how "our tribe" relates to "our nation." Most pastors and church members have no idea how to relate to the church down the street from them. Are they the enemy? Is their doctrine right? Are we really related? Why would I want to spend my time meeting them? *Requiring that all participants take a well-thought-out class in this subject could be a major step forward in unity and in the understanding of the crucial paradigm of dual citizenship.*

In my travels all over the world, one of the biggest challenges I face is how to get one denomination to relate to another, one pastor to relate to another, or one church to relate to another. *We have been trained to act independently, not interdependently.* As I have said before, some things we just cannot do individually, we have to do them corporately. We need to develop a national protocol and national "manners" for us all to develop to our full potential.

The good news is that many churches are starting to see the need for a national protocol. The APCNZ (Associated Pentecostal Churches of New Zealand) has written a document on a protocol within its sphere of influence.[2] This document was written by pastor John Walton of the New Life Church in Palmerston North in New Zealand. He presented this document to the leaders of the largest and most influential Pentecostal churches in New Zealand in November of 2003. The purpose of this document is to bring peace, resolution and hopefully prevention of potential conflicts that could arise in church and pastor relationships. The document reads as follows:

INTERCHURCH ETHICS WITHIN APCNZ

In all attitude and action work toward harmony and good relations with other pastors and churches. "Making every effort to keep the unity of the spirit in the uniting bond of peace." Tensions will come from time to time, but we must have the grace to work through them.

Avoid judging another church or listening to a partial viewpoint when you do not have all the facts. We are not called on to judge every situation.

If breakdown comes in relations try to mend them, if this cannot be done, some matters we have to leave to God. Hudson Taylor said, "Move man by God through prayer alone."

Should you have concerns regarding the conduct of another pastor or church, if you have a good relationship with that church and its pastor, approach them with humility to share your concerns. Otherwise talk to that church's extra local oversight.

Avoid having a superior attitude to other churches even though they may be smaller or appear less effective than yours. Elitism is subtle and deceptive.

Contribute positively to build up rather than to pull down other pastors and churches. Genuine concern is allowable, but always work toward the positive.

Do not criticize other churches or ministers especially from the pulpit.

If another church wants to leave a movement to join yours, do not receive them without first talking it through with that movement's leaders. If a building is involved, make sure you do not acquire this without the approval of the movement of which it is a member.

If planting a church, seek to work harmoniously with other pastors in the area.

If another church is being planted in your area work toward its blessing. If concerned about the motive or wisdom of the plant, share this with the initiators and work toward an amicable outcome.

Remember a pastor's position of power can be used to sway a congregation into his desire of wanting to join another movement. This brings up an important ethical matter. If a movement has planted this church it should not ethically pull out without a harmonious decision with that movement. If it had been planted independently and chose to join a particular movement it has an ethical right to disengage; however, this should still be done with harmony.

When a pastor has been appointed by a movement to lead a church that is an established member of that movement, he or she would act unethically if he/she led that church out. The 'pull out' would require the wholehearted approval of the movement that planted it.

Pastors should not entice pastors from another movement to join their movement. Treat other pastors as you would a family member.

If a member of another church approaches you about becoming one of your staff, this should be discussed with his or her existing oversight in the early stages. Like-wise if you want a staff member from another church first get the approval of that church's oversight.

If a church member has been disciplined by his or her oversight for a serious proven sin, another church should not embrace that person without making thorough inquiry into the facts. They

> should respect the discipline imposed. If an injustice has been done in the disciplinary process, this would need to be thoroughly looked into by experienced leaders.
>
> If a minister is under discipline by a church or movement, another church should not allow that person to minister in their church. Neither should there be sympathy given that could undermine godly discipline.
>
> Respect for the autonomy of a local church should always be shown. Counsel can be given, but not command.
>
> While this document may not be perfect, it is a great starting place for better church-to-church relationships. Even better yet, it is a great start in church-to-community relationships.

6. The need for national ambassadors

God is raising up national ambassadors or what Dr. C. Peter Wagner calls "horizontal apostles" to facilitate in the connecting of the "clans" or "tribes." The church desperately needs these big-picture influencers and peacemakers to help the "tribes" in strategic events, tasks, or services that only the "nation" can do. They are a necessary and strategic component in community transformation. As the United States military learned in World War II, there needs to be coordination and cooperation among the armed forces or the result is chaos. The army, navy, and air corps needed the Joint Chiefs of Staff, or big-picture people to reduce the "tribalism" of each of these departments and to facilitate the big picture of "winning the war," not just "winning the battle." In the same way, the various church "tribes" need "joint chiefs of staff," or national ambassadors who lead and coordinate all the tribal leaders by influence, diplomacy, and ambassadorial skills in a national effort to reach the community or nation.

Recently I rented a fifteen-person van to take some junior high kids on a trip. As we were traveling, I looked in the back seat and all the junior-high kids had earphones on with their favorite CDs blasting in their ears. No one was talking! Each was on the bus and in the family, but listening to his or her tunes with eyes glazed over and heads straight forward.

Think about it: just like those junior high kids, we are all on the journey together and part of the family, but most of us are listening to our own themes, emphases, and doctrines without even a thought for each other. Like the man from Kenya, our living by tribal values without national awareness will forever keep us from achieving the vision of community transformation. Think of how much more the Lord could do for each of us if we worked together, and the potential unrealized until that happens. It would be fair to say that we all could use *more revelation, awareness, and maturity* in understanding and incarnating these very crucial principles. That is what Paul was talking about in the verse I opened with: "until we *all* attain to the unity of the faith, and the knowledge of the Son of God, to a mature man, to the measure of the stature which belongs to the fullness of Christ" (Eph. 4:13).

Unity is a core value or government, not a vision. Sufficient unity is an absolutely essential core value or intelligent fire component that is essential for community transformation. Real and tangible unity opens the door that the King of Glory may come in. This principle is also true for marriages, businesses, nations and especially communities! Without sufficient unity, we lower our number and potency of community transformation successes.

Chapter 11

Incarnationally Challenged:

The Principle of the Tiger's Head and the Mouse's Tail

There will be no transformation without incarnation, without becoming present among people. That is the way of the gospel. That was the way of Jesus who entered our frail humanity to save us—not from a distance, but from the position of a participant, a fellow human being.

—Pastor Alan Platt
Pretoria, South Africa

While I was speaking at a charismatic church in Phoenix, Arizona, a thought suddenly occurred to me. It was an on-stage revelation and I decided to test it on the congregation. I boldly said, "I can get the unchurched in this community to worship God better than you worship God." My statement startled them.

Following this pronouncement, the church grew extremely quiet. The pastor and leadership and especially the worship team were hushed. Everyone focused on what I was saying. Because of my great relationship with this church I could use some shock value. I could hear a cow mooing! I had just touched the untouchable.

"Do you want to know how?" I asked. "The Bible tells the church to 'let your light shine *before* men in such a way that they may *see your good works*, and *glorify* your Father who is in heaven'" (Matt. 5:16). After a few brief (but seemingly eternal) moments, the church erupted in agreement and applause. Their response, in so many words, was "Wow, you got us...you are right...we have the ability to get the unchurched worshipping...and we like worship...cool...let's demonstrate Christ's light by our good works to the community." I was glad to get out of that situation alive. I concluded by explaining that nonbelieving worshipping people were much easier to reach out to than nonworshipping unchurched people. The "light" of the church's good works opens the "eyes" of the community and causes them to glorify God.

Sight Needs Light

Jesus was saying in this verse that the community has to see real and tangible works of service in *such a way* that is meaningful to the community. These good works need to be strategic and performed in such a way as to catch people's attention and open their eyes to the reality of Jesus. They cannot be just any good works. The good works need to be the light that brings sight and opens the eyes of their hearts to the contribution of Christians and churches in the community.

Jesus was saying that these good works cannot be declared from the pulpit or in prayer only. These good works are not intended to remain only inside the church walls. These good works cannot be shouted with a voice of triumph or bound and loosed by faith only. These good works do not come from speaking Greek or having doctorates in theology. They are not "spiritual" only. These good works are strategic and incarnational. They become real and tangible and dwell among us and must be demonstrated in the community in such a way that there is no mistaking the Source. These works, as Pastor Tommy Barnett says, "find a need and meet it." These works activate unchurched people to "glorify God who is in heaven" because they know the Source is heavenly, hopeful and helpful.

There are three types of good works that have the potential to "catch the eye" of the community:

1. The church's good works in the community that are noticed by and that influence the community.

2. Good works among Christians that are noticed by and that influence the community.

3. Good works among Christians and churches that are noticed by and that influence the community.

There are also four reasons the Church is incarnationally challenged. By that, I mean we have trouble demonstrating good works in and to the community and to each other in a real and tangible way. These reasons are:

1. Theological issues and barriers in the church.
2. The culture of academia in the church.
3. Beliefs that have not become values.
4. Tendency of church culture to over-spiritualize.

Before explaining the issues and concepts listed above, I want to explore the concept of works in the Bible.

Calloused Hands and Good Works

Do you remember the fourth ingredient in Nehemiah's recipe for community transformation in Chapter 2? I called the ingredient Calloused Hands. Nehemiah 2:18 is my source for this concept:

> And I told them how the hand of my God had been favorable to me, and also about the king's words which he had spoken to me. Then they said, "Let us arise and build." *So they put their hands to the good work.*
>
> —Nehemiah 2:18

The process of arriving at good works "in such a way" is amazing to me. In Nehemiah's case it began with a "burdened heart" for the community. He understood the concept of "seek[ing] the welfare of the city where I have sent you into exile, and pray[ing] to the Lord on its behalf; for in its welfare you will have welfare" (Jer. 29:7). The word "peace" could be substituted for "welfare" in this passage.

After the burden and prayer, God gave Nehemiah a clear mind, or intelligent fire on the strategy to repair Jerusalem's walls. Ultimately the preceding three ingredients had to express themselves in action or the good work. All of these internal issues had to incarnate in the city in a real and tangible way. Impression without expression leads to depression. A burdened heart by itself is not enough. The bended knee by itself is not enough. The Word needs to become flesh and move into the neighborhood. The spiritual needs to manifest itself in the natural. God requires you to finish in the natural what you start in the spiritual. Ultimately Nehemiah and his friends had to "put their hands to the good work" (Neh. 2:18). The work was the expression of their faith and a real and tangible response to the problem of repairing the walls of the city.

Show and Tell

> But someone may well say, "You have faith, and I have works; show me your faith without the works, and I will show you my faith by my works."
>
> —James 2:18

From the beginning of time, God has required that man should work. In Genesis 2:27–28, God institutes three basic institutions that remain to this day. These institutions are marriage, family, and productive work. God knew that "filling the earth and subduing it" would require work expressed in a real and tangible way. Jesus did not stay up in heaven being "spiritual." He came from heaven to earth to *show* the way. The Word became flesh and dwelt (pitched a tent) in earth's neighborhood (John 1:14).

The apostle Paul's first question after being knocked to the ground by Jesus was "What shall I do Lord" (Acts 22:10). Churches and Christians were "created in Christ Jesus for good works, which God prepared beforehand, that we should walk in them" (Eph. 2:10). Real, pure, and undefiled religion is tangibly expressed in visiting orphans and widows in distress. In other words, pure religion is practical as well as spiritual.

Heaven comes to earth when orphanages are founded, built, and maintained by the church. Through works, we finish in the natural what we start in the spiritual. The apostle Paul was so serious about this principle, he said in 2 Thessalonians 3:10–11 that if a person has the opportunity to work and will not work, the church bears no responsibility to feed him. Women are called to adorn themselves with good works (1 Tim. 2:10). Jesus told his disciples, "Greater works than these shall he do; because I go to the Father" (John 14:12). James said, "Faith, if it has no works, is dead, being by itself" (James 2:17). It is faith and works—not faith or works! It is the Book of Acts of the Apostles, not the facts of the Apostles. Jesus makes this point very clearly in Matthew 7:24–26:

> Therefore everyone who hears these words of Mine, and acts on them, may be compared to a wise man, who built his house on the rock. And the rain descended, and the floods came, and the winds blew, and burst against that house; and yet it did not fall, for it had been founded on the rock. And everyone who hears these words of Mine, and *does not act on them*, will be like a foolish man, who built his house on the sand.

The principle I am illustrating here will change your life. It can propel you from dream to done. You cannot finish what you do not start, yet starting is not the same as finishing. The alpha is not the omega.

Moses had to lift his staff. Joshua had to step into the Jordan. Peter got out of the boat. He was not just walking on the water; he was walking in a real and tangible way on God's Word. Blind Bartimaeus had to call Jesus. The woman with the issue of blood had to press through the crowd. Abram had to leave Babylon. Esther had to address the king. David had to confront Goliath. Israel had to circle the city. Jesus had to die on the cross.

Impression is completed in expression. Word needs to be culminated in deed. Works are not the end in themselves, but the means to an end. The end is enlightening the community on the reality of Jesus and God. Good works in and through Christian churches and ministries to the community can open the gates so that the King of Glory can come in to the community.

Leading the Community in Worship

Works "in such a way" are how the community worships God without necessarily even knowing it. Just as churched people worship God through songs and hymns, the unchurched worship God by observing good works from Christians and churches for the betterment of the community. When Jesus says "in such a way," it implies that what people in the community observe when they see the church's good works is meaningful to them. It requires a response. Whether intentionally or unintentionally, they respond by glorifying God.

Every time the church demonstrates these good works, a positive public relations image in the community is achieved. The Word becomes flesh.

Do you realize that the church can lead the unchurched in worship? We just need to sing their songs, not ours. The chief end of man is to glorify God and enjoy Him forever. Let's help the community glorify God where they are, not our way yet. That is why it is important that we are aware of the culture and values of our community. We are to look for a way in, not a way out. While the church considers it spiritual to sing songs "to God," the community needs songs "about God" initially.

The culture of business, government, education, and media/entertainment is a culture validated by works. Jesus knew this. He was culturally aware and spiritually aware. He invented the pattern. The word has to become flesh—real and tangible—and move into the neighborhood and community.

As I said before, worshipping communities are easier to bring to salvation than non-worshipping communities. The church is saved by grace, but defined by works in the context of community transformation. Good works connect the message with the audience. Grace-based good works have the power to shift a community's opinion of the church and Christians. Grace-based good works redefine the church. So many times in the community the church has been defined by antagonistic people. Whether their arguments are valid or not, until we incarnate in the community, the definitions will not be changed. Why would we expect anything different?

The only way to redefine the church as a positive contributor to the community is to get into circulation in the community. The church defines itself through good works. As the lepers said in 2 Kings 7:3 in the midst of a famine, "Why do we sit here until we die?" Their response was action, an expressed "work" that sprang a miracle into action.

I will say it this way: "If we do not, He will not!" It is time to give the church back to the community. Let's cooperate with Jesus in leading the community in worship. "Worshipping non-believers," or the unchurched, are easier to lead to Christ than "non-worshipping non-believers."

It Is Alpha and Omega, Not Alpha or Omega

> I am the *Alpha* and the *Omega*, the first and the last, the beginning and the end.
>
> —Revelation 22:13

> And to the angel of the church in Laodicea write: The *Amen*, the faithful and true Witness, the *Beginning* of the creation of God.
>
> —Revelation 3:14

> Looking unto Jesus the *author* and *finisher* of our faith; who for the joy that was set before him endured the cross, despising the shame, and is set down at the right hand of the throne of God.
>
> —Hebrews 12:2, kjv

> For which one of you, when he wants to build a tower, does not first sit down and calculate the cost to see if he has enough to complete it? Otherwise, when he has laid a foundation, and is not able to finish, all who observe it begin to ridicule him, saying, "This man began to build and was not able to finish."
>
> —Luke 14:28–30

These verses instruct us that a strategic core value of Christianity and, therefore, community transformation is initiation and complication. The ethos or culture of the church should be described as a culture of completion. Initiation without completion undermines everything that Christianity is. The culture of Christianity is based upon the person of Jesus "who is and who was and who is to come" (Rev. 1:8). His name is Alpha and Omega. He is the Author and Finisher. He is the First and the Last. He is the Beginning and the Amen, or "so be it."

Did you notice that the both/and core value is right back with us again? Simply said, what He starts, He finishes. This principle is what gives Christ credibility. This is also what gives the Church and Christians credibility in the community. Community spheres of influence understand the law of completion. How long would a construction business last if it was known for starting houses but not finishing houses? How about the athlete who "talks the talk" but does not "walk the walk"?

The Chinese have an expression for this dysfunctional behavior. They call it "the tiger's head, the mouse's tail." It describes someone (or something) who starts or says something and then cannot back it up in a real and tangible way. His project starts big and then fades. It looks big but has no bite—the tiger's head, the mouse's tail.

God's way requires finishing in the natural realm what you start in the spiritual realm. It is not just learning and confessing but incarnating, working and completing the work to allow it to happen. It is faith, then works that gets believers to their goal. The alpha is where things start. It should never be where things get stuck.

In order to have real, tangible, and lasting community transformation, we need to move from the incredible to the credible. This is especially true in the Pentecostal/Charismatic part of the Church. In far too many cases, the ethos of this group emphasizes the incredible. People prophesy what is going to happen, what should happen, what God is going to do, or some great, huge change that will be totally unilateral on God's part. The ethos of this group seems to be that it is enough to say it, disclose it, or claim it. This is the alpha, but the alpha is not the omega.

The alpha is where it starts but not where it finishes. If we stay in the alpha, we will never arrive at the omega. The alpha is Christ in the cradle; the omega is Christ with the crown. The crown was begun by birthing in the cradle, but finished by good works at the cross.

Christ's credibility and influence were earned by His finishing what He started. Simply said, alpha is a means to an end, which is omega.

Winning Spiritual Lotteries

I was recently at a large conference in New Zealand, where a prophecy was made. Basically the prophecy said that God was going to move supernaturally and revival would come to New Zealand in a miraculous way. It was incredible! Soon afterwards, a pastor friend of mine happened to be hosting another conference. His guest speaker, a well-known, credible person whose name most of you would recognize, responded to this "incredible" prophecy with words that were prophetic in their own right. He said, "Oh boy, now we do not have to evangelize, reach people, help people, or share Jesus—we are off the hook. Let's just stay inside the four church walls. We do not have to let God work through us. Let's have a party."

Pause for a moment. I can feel emotions rising—it is the church ethos of right or wrong. While God may bring revival to New Zealand the way the prophetic person said, we need to realize this is the exception and not the rule of thumb.

Revival may come to a nation that way one out of one hundred times. That is the "all God, no man" theory. The speaker had a point here. *God works with and through men. He trains us to reign.* God's normal pattern is for the Church to be credible with some wonderful occasions of "incredible." To stay inside the church walls and call the people in from the north, south, east, and west through prayer is only the starting point.

There were probably instances where good success came when some churches prayed this prayer. That is good! That is wonderful! But that is the exception rather than God's normal pattern. We must also incarnate. We must become *harvesters that harvest a harvest.* What we start in prayer we finish in good works. Remember Nehemiah's recipe? To live your spiritual life depending upon winning spiritual lotteries is wonderful, if you are in the wilderness. Let's grow up before we grow old.

Manna Was Temporary; Corn Is Permanent

> And the manna ceased on the morrow after they had eaten of the old corn of the land; neither had the children of Israel manna any more; but they did eat of the fruit of the land of Canaan that year.
>
> —Joshua 5:12, KJV

This verse shows how God and man work together. It is not an either/or, but a both/and. God wants us to do our part of God's part. In the wilderness, God did everything for the Israelites. He provided a cloud by day and fire by night. Their shoes did not wear out. They were led everywhere. Food was provided, meat and bread, quail and manna. The manna was meant to show the Israelites a spiritual reality. The reality was that manna is from God and that manna is temporary (Exod. 16:13–21). In other words, this was a season in which Israel was coming out of slavery. They were not capable to taking care of themselves. God took care of them completely. He fought their enemies. He gave them daily miracles, daily feedings, daily *Shekinah* glory—it was incredible. They won spiritual lotteries everyday if they were open to it. God did everything for them.

After forty years (a generation), the season in which God did everything for them had to stop. They were moving from God giving to them to God living through them. God was going to give them a hand-up rather than a hand-out. God was going to give himself to the land of milk, honey, and giants *through* them.

Joshua 5:12 implies that on the day they "crossed the Jordan" the manna stopped. They learned to eat of the "corn" of the land. In other words, this land produced food and they had to work to get it. Crossing the Jordan means they were ready to enter into their purpose, calling and destiny. In essence, God was saying, "Grow up, you learn to work with me, you learn to be trained to reign, you move from slaves to kings, you fight the '-ites.'" Do not just incite the -ites, you smite the -ites; let's finish what we started."

I call this principle "My Cooperation with God's Operation Leads to a Community Revelation." Maturity is doing "my" part of God's part. Immaturity is expecting God to do everything all the time, while underachieving is trying to do everything yourself without God.

Joshua, Israel, and God finished what they started. It was a strategic partnership between heaven and earth. It was no longer an enmeshed, co-dependent-dependent, one-way relationship. It was a partnership between God and man, with God being the Senior Partner and man promoted to be the junior partner.

FOUR TOP REASONS WHY THE CHURCH STRUGGLES WITH INCARNATING

Incarnating is connecting the spiritual to the natural. It is connecting who we are and what we do. It is finishing what we start. It is letting theology become biography. It is being credible, not pretending. It is doing what we say we will do most of the time.

Earlier in this chapter, I stated four reasons why the church struggles with incarnating. Let's look at them:

1. Workaphobic or Workaholics?—Theological issues and barriers in the church.

2. Truth and Consequences—The culture of academics in the church.

3. Why I Eat French Fries—We have beliefs but those beliefs are not values yet.

4. From Bride to Wife—Church culture or ethos tends to over spiritualize.

1. Workaphobic or workaholic?

For ages, the church has debated the subject of works. The right-or-wrong, either/or crowd has divided into two camps on this topic. The arguments regarding this vital issue of Christianity have been like a continuous *Ground Hog Day*. That is to say, we keep going over these issues again and again. It is a current-day "Whose wife will she be in the resurrection?"— causing endless debate and dualism. The Calvinists are on one side, the Armenians on the other.

In defense of salvation by grace only, the Calvinists come across as "workaphobics." They shun works in order to defend their theological position. The Armenians, in defense of evidence of salvation, come across as workaholics, always striving to prove their salvation by works. This is one example of theological issues in the church that impede and distort the necessary component of "good works in such a way" that disable community transformation.

Another example regards the "Marys" and "Marthas" in church culture:

> Now as they were traveling along, He entered a village; and a woman named Martha welcomed Him into her home. And she had a sister called Mary, who moreover was listening to the Lord's word, seated at His feet. But Martha was distracted with all her preparations; and she came up to Him, and said, "Lord, do You not care that my sister has left me to do all the serving alone? Then tell her to help me." But the Lord answered and said to her, "Martha, Martha, you are worried and bothered about so many things; but only a few things are necessary, really only one, for Mary has chosen the good part, which shall not be taken away from her."
>
> —Luke 10:38–42

Here we have two wonderful women who represent the concept of relationship and task. Mary is "spiritual" and Martha is "natural." Mary would be the worshipper and Martha would be the worker. The obvious conclusion if we are "spiritual" would be that Mary is desirable and Martha is undesirable. After all, Mary chose the good part and therefore, Martha is less "spiritual" because she chose the "bad" part.

It is easy to walk down this path if this is the only story in the Bible you read. May I remind you that there are other stories in the Bible also? The point Jesus was making was that there are "Mary times" in our lives, and there are "Martha times" in our lives. We must learn to discern in our own walk with the Lord when it is a Mary time and when it is a Martha time. The Luke 10 story highlights a Mary time. Martha's timing was off.

However, there are Martha times also. It is not an either/or; it is a both/and. Both worshipping and working are necessary, especially in community transformation. In Nehemiah's recipe, the first two ingredients, a burdened heart and a bended knee, are the Mary times. The third and fourth ingredients, strategic mind and calloused hands, are the Martha times. Let's combine these two worlds in a chart and allow each of them to complete one another.

Warning! You will have trouble with this if you are still in the right-or-wrong, either/or core value crowd.

Spiritual Concepts Incarnated in Natural Concepts

Mary	and	Martha
Worshiper	and	Worker
Alpha	and	Omega
High value on relationship	and	High value on task
High value on who you are	and	High value on what you do
Being	and	Doing
Church	and	Community
Son of God	and	Son of Man
Faith	and	Works
Saved by grace (Ephesians 2:8)	and	Created for good works (Ephesians 2:10)
Prophetic nature of church	and	Apostolic reality in the community
Burdened heart, bended knee	and	Clear mind, calloused hands

It is not so hard if you are willing to give up so you can go up. Remember, until you reform you only revisit.

God never called us to be workaphobics, whether expressed in theology or in practice. Neither did He call us to be workaholics trying to prove our salvation, or to prove our value to ourselves or others. We have to be "equiliberated" from dualism and introspective specialization to have equilibrium. Equilibrium enables community transformation. If we had equilibrium, Humpty Dumpty would never have fallen.

2. Truth and consequences

The second reason the Church is incarnationally challenged is what I call the ethos of ivory towers. Earlier, I pointed out that the culture of the church has been shaped by the office of the teacher through the vehicle of seminaries and Bible schools. The ethos of most seminaries and Bible schools is Bible knowledge, Bible theory, and the propagation of their particular theology. It is the always-learning-never-able concept that Paul criticized in 2 Timothy 3:7.

There is a reason colleges, universities, seminaries, and other institutions of higher learning are called ivory towers. These well-meaning institutions, whether secular or sacred, tend to have a disconnect from real life and practical application. The professors are theory-oriented. They teach the way things ought to be or should be. In many cases, the intellectual approach to life is incomplete, disconnected, and "elitist." The intellectual "football games" between institutions of higher learning are rougher than the physical football games on the gridiron. The stadium of the mind is more adversarial than the physical stadium.

This dysfunctional academia causes the Church to separate from the community. This it's-enough-to-know ethos disables the necessary component of good works through calloused hands. Under this ethos, the Church tends to become filled with fruit eaters rather than fruit bearers. We create a culture in which we are incarnationally challenged.

The comfort of being "fed" inside the church walls creates a culture of faith without works. We eat but do not expel. We inhale but do not exhale. We become spiritually constipated. We tend to become anabolic rather than catabolic. We value the faith but shun the works. We value the intellectual but shun the actual. The ivory towers of the inside incapacitate us for the practicality of the outside. We have the answers inside the Church but will not give the answers to the outside world. The consequence of this truth/ivory tower ethos causes a disconnect from other churches and Christians as well as from community spheres of influence and the community.

Faith in church ivory towers must be accomplished by works in community steel towers. Otherwise, the church is rowing the boat with one oar. What is the solution? How about good scholarship and good workmanship for the benefit of the community? I am so thankful that Bible school and seminaries are beginning to catch on to these two worlds. When I hear academicians use terms like purpose-driven theology, it encourages my heart and gives me hope for the community. Theology was never intended to be an end in itself, but a means to an end. It is purpose-driven, a vehicle to allow people to get to know God more completely.

Would not it be great to have more Bible colleges and seminaries with a knowledge and practical application ethos? Community transformation requires more than an ivory-tower ethos. It is time to reform. A heart for the community is shifting the ivory-tower ethos to a new wineskin. I will discuss this wineskin more in Chapter 15. This new wineskin will create both good workmanship and good scholarship.

3. Why I eat French fries

The third reason the Church and church people are incarnationally challenged is that we confuse beliefs with values. This is a problem that demons have also.

> But someone may well say, "You have faith, and I have works; show me your faith without the works, and I will show you my faith by my works." You believe that God is one. You do well; the demons also believe, and shudder. But are you willing to recognize, you foolish fellow, that faith without works is useless?
>
> —James 2:18–20

Isn't this amazing? The demons believe but do not do anything about it. Demons know the truth, but will not apply it. They have a belief *but not a value.*

The same is true for me. I know I should not eat french fries. French fries are simple carbohydrates soaked in salt and fat. Science says they are unhealthy, artery-plugging time bombs. I know that. I am convinced of that. I mentally acknowledge that. Now ask me if I eat french fries.—of course I eat french fries! They taste wonderful. I love them.

What is going on here? I have a belief but not a value.

Here is another example. I *believe* I should work out. I *believe* that exercise is good. I *believe* that I would have more energy if I worked out. Now, ask me if I work out. Of course not! Working out is hard, it requires effort, and on top of that I do not like those people who look so fit!

What is going on here? I have a belief but not a value.

This truth applies to all of us. We may *believe* we should read the Bible. We may *believe* we should love one another. We may *believe* we should not gossip. We may *believe* we should give the church back to the community. The issue, as the demons show us, is not whether we have a belief, but whether the belief has become a value.

Beliefs do not necessarily express values. Remember, our values drive our behavior. That is why I wrote this book—to reveal community-transformation-core values that start with beliefs but end up in values. It is not enough to believe in community transformation, you need to value community transformation. There will be no real, tangible, and lasting community transformation without a value transformation.

In their book *Basic Christian Values*, authors Larry Richards and Norman Wakefield say the following about values:

> A value is something that is actually important enough to be expressed in my daily choices. This helps us in thinking about the nature and the role of values in our own lives. There are certain things that we recognize, or believe, are important (loving our neighbor, using time wisely, whatever). But then daily life brings

> us to points at which choices must be made. We choose either to do, or not to do, as our belief suggests. When I keep on making choices that express what I have said I believe is important so it becomes part of the habit of life I am building, then it is a significant value.
>
> How good it is to recognize, and put into practice, this simple process of growth toward godliness.
>
> I discover or state what I believe to be important.
>
> As opportunities come, I choose daily to act on what I believe is important.
>
> As I consistently make such choices, the belief becomes part of my character and lifestyle.
>
> And then it is truly a value to me, important enough to me to be consistently expressed in daily choices.[1]

This is a very crucial concept that enables us to get to productive, positive results in any area of our life. Businesses have values. Countries have values. Governments have values. Families have values. Churches have values. Communities have values. Mental assent is not application. Mental assent or belief is the alpha, but values are the omega.

Here is my point. Many Christians, churches, and church institutions have a belief in the mission of Jesus. They believe in the vision of community transformation. However, beliefs by themselves are not enough to achieve community transformation. The belief has to become a value or a set of values. To achieve you have to do more than just believe. Just ask the demons (James 2:19).

4. From a bride to a wife

Finally, the church culture is incarnationally challenged because we tend to over-spiritualize to a fault. The "Truth and Consequences" section of this chapter is about over-theorizing and over-analyzing. This section is about over-spiritualizing. We need to be equiliberated to have equilibrium in this area also. This tendency to over-spiritualize is only natural because God has assigned the church to bring spiritual awareness and wisdom to the community.

Remember, however, that good things taken to extremes can become "bad" or unproductive things. Spiritual input that is a means to an end is a good thing. When spiritualizing becomes the end rather than the means to an end, it becomes a bad thing. Over-spiritualization is a wonderful servant but a terrible master, especially in the context of community transformation. It causes us to become too spiritually minded to be any earthly good, especially in the opinion of the community. The spiritual contribution of the church starts in heaven but must end up on earth. The church exists to be God's telephone to the community.

Jesus came from heaven to earth to show the way. That is what I call incarnating. In many cases, the church is connected to God but not to the community. The result is underachieving communities. What starts in heaven must be finished on the earth.

Let's look at two verses in 1 Peter that show two different ministries of the Church regarding heaven and earth. I have borrowed from Pastor Gary Carter of Drayton Valley, Alberta, Canada, to illustrate the concept of moving from prophetic revelation to apostolic reality.

Prophetic revelation "You also, as living stones, are being built up as a spiritual house for a holy priesthood, to offer up spiritual sacrifices acceptable to God through Jesus Christ" (1 Pet. 2:5).

Apostolic reality "But you are a chosen race, a royal priesthood, a holy nation, a people for God's own possession, that you may proclaim the excellencies of Him who has called you out of darkness into His marvelous light" (1 Pet. 2:9).

Prophetic revelation has to do with the church's connection to God. It is vertical, priestly, visionary, spiritual, and prophetic in the sense that the ministry hears from God and sees what God wants to do. It is a place of ideas and God speaking through word and prayer. It is a place where churched people come and experience the presence of God. It is a place of ministry from and to God. However, we must also realize it is the starting point of ministry to the community. It was never to be the "staying" point. That comes later *after* God's vision of the earth shall be filled with the knowledge of the glory of the Lord.

If the prophetic revelation is vertical, then the apostolic reality concept is the horizontal. The cross is both vertical and horizontal. This is where God incarnates on the earth. This is the reality of the church, not just the revelation of the church. This is where God makes Himself known in and to the community. As prophetic revelation is about relationship, apostolic reality is about task, becoming real and tangible. The prophetic may see but the apostolic builds what is seen. The prophetic is about initiation but the apostolic is about completion.

Remember, the whole foundation of the church is built upon apostolic and prophetic ministry and concepts (Eph. 2:20). It takes both apostolic and prophetic concepts to transform church and community. As Paul says in Ephesians 2:21, God takes the "whole building" of the community and builds it into a "holy temple" in the Lord. Remember, the prophetic sees, the apostolic builds and completes. Without apostolic reality, the Church becomes a place of better and better ideas with less and less potential of ever being fulfilled. The Church becomes all vision and no government. The power and ability to fulfill the vision never connect. Ultimately, the Church disconnects from the community it was called to save, serve and enhance. The church becomes vertical but lacks the horizontal. This has been the problem of the church for centuries. The prophetic revelation needs to become an apostolic reality.

Pastor Bernard Sanders of Andover, England, points out that the prophetic ministry tends to be idealistic, visionary, and spiritual. For example, many prophetic church-centric people focus on the concept of the bride of Christ. They stay in the continual wedding-day-and-honeymoon stage of Christianity. He points out that the purpose or goal of becoming a bride is to become a wife. After a woman is married, she quickly finds out that it is time to grow up, mature, become productive, and complete in life what she started on her wedding day. A wife is a completed bride. That is the lesson the Shulamite woman had to learn in the Song of Songs.

Another prophetic theme is being the children of God. Sanders points out that apostolic reality transforms children into a family. A bunch of children running around doing their own thing was not God's intention. The point was for children to become a functioning family. Apostolic ministry transforms a house to a home. Apostolic ministry helps the vertical to become the horizontal also. While we are on earth, the point is not to be a habitation of God (a churchy, vertical concept). The point is to fill the earth with the knowledge of the glory! Our mission until Christ returns is for the church to incarnate on the earth in a real and tangible way. Our mission is to take what God gives us and deposit it in the community in such a way.

This does not take away from the prophetic revelation part of the church. Actually, it adds to and completes the mission. Following is a chart I made to illustrate Sanders' principle to help us integrate what we have learned into our value system:

It is time for the church to combine the spiritual and the natural. The church has to be a culture of completion. Without this core

Moving From a Prophetic Revelation to an Apostolic Reality

"and the Word Became Flesh and Dwelt Amongst Us" —John 1:14

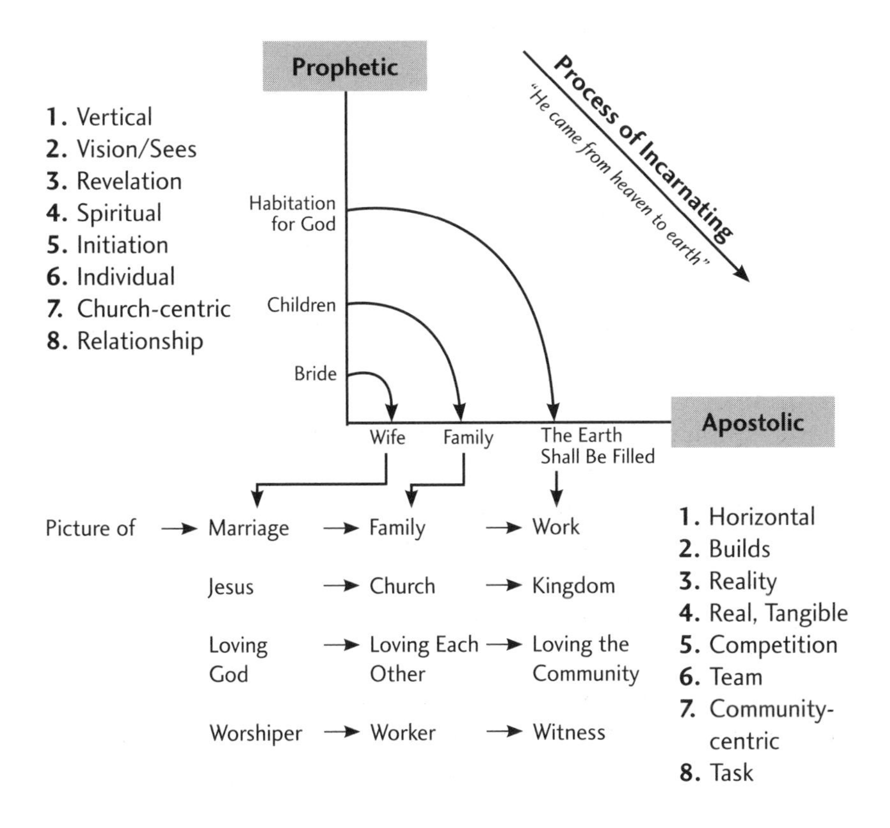

value, the potential of community transformation is greatly reduced. Business, government, education, and media/entertainment spheres of influence live in and value the culture of completion. The church needs to learn this valuable lesson also. Just as Jesus had to become "natural" in order to communicate and demonstrate heaven's reality to man, so does the church. Humpty Dumpty is waiting!

Catching the Sight of the Community

At the beginning of this chapter, I mentioned three types of good works that Jesus says "catch the sight" of the community. The potential of these "sight catchers" is staggering especially if all three of these are done simultaneously. Let's explore these concepts that have the potential to redefine the church in the eyes of the community in a positive way:

1. Peeping Toms

Do you realize the community is looking at the Church? The community (especially the community spheres of influence) are spies sent by God. I will call them Peeping Toms. The Peeping Toms are looking for good works done in the community by the church.

> Let your light shine before men in such a way that they may see your good works, and glorify your Father who is in heaven.
>
> —Matthew 5:16

These are the works I referred to earlier in this chapter. Every community, every city and every nation has something that is of vital concern to the community. It is a need in the community that most members of the community are aware of. This area of need has caught the heart of the community.

These areas of need are what Jesus tells the church to meet. These are the good works that let the church's light shine in such a way that the community responds in a powerful way. Meeting these areas of need and concern is a key into the community. There are many good works the church can do but there are also "good works in such a way." The challenge is to find the key—the good work that catches the sight of the community. Let me give you a real example of this.

A few years ago I was speaking at the church of Pastor Wilfred Lai in Mombasa, Kenya. His church is called Jesus Celebration Centre and is around twenty thousand in attendance. Wilfred and his church discovered an amazing key into the heart of the community and country of Kenya. The church's corporate offices are located on one of the main highways of Kenya. This section of highway was littered with garbage that had accumulated for years. Pastor Wilfred decided something had to be done about it. Frankly, he did not want the highway where his corporate offices were located to look like a garbage dump. What did he do to solve the problem? He gathered his twenty thousand people in the church and picked up all the garbage along four miles of the national highway. The corporate offices were centered in the middle of this project.

This project did not cost the church or the community anything. It was a matter of men, women, and children doing the work, getting the calloused hands and looking for a way into the community, not a way out. They found a need and met it. They "pitched a tent" in the neighborhood.

What was the community and country's response? Wilfred showed me a copy of the main newspaper in Mombasa. They were on the front page! It displayed pictures of the Pastor Wilfred and the church members cleaning up garbage and a wonderful article about the project. The church that did something for Kenya. Even President Moi, the president of Kenya at that time spoke about the church that cleaned up a highway of Kenya. It caught the government's attention and the media's attention. Word went out all over Kenya about this. The church tapped into the "good work in such a way" that the unchurched began glorifying God. President Moi said this is what the church should be doing. As the story was told to me, he even said that this is a physical solution that could lead to cleaning up the garbage in people's hearts in Kenya. First the natural, then the spiritual.

I was amazed as I listened to Pastor Wilfred. The accumulation of years of garbage in many areas of Kenya is on most every Kenyan citizen's mind. This is a key into the community that is not only a task but also a relationship. It is a task that needs to be done, but as a "good work in such a way," it creates a positive relationship with the community. It is both Martha and Mary. It produces favor with God and favor with man. As a result, the community has the opportunity to experience "the good part, which shall not be taken away" (Luke 10:42). And the church gets a passport into other spheres of influence in the community. The church is one of the players again in enhancing a community. As President Moi said at that time, "This is the way churches should be." Folks, that is validation and appreciation.

As a result of this, I have challenged Pastor Wilfred Lai, Pastor Thomas Muthee, and other key Kenyan leaders to start a project whereby every church in Kenya cleans up a mile of garbage on the road in front of it. It is one thing to have a passport, another to use it!

Obviously, cleaning up garbage would not be a key that would catch the community's heart in Dublin, San Francisco, or Tokyo. However, I do believe every community has a need that is a deep concern to the whole community. The community has a heart for it. This key may be discovered through prayer, through wisdom, and through the consensus of church leaders with a concern for the community. However, I believe the most effective way to discover this key is for church leaders *together* to go ask the local government, such as the mayor or town council.

In most cases, local government gets stuck with the real issues. In most cases, they need help and want help. They need the Church to help solve these real issues. Real issues require real ministry, calloused-hands stuff. This is where strategic alliances and mutual collaborations are needed to meet the needs of the community. As the church contributes its ministry to meeting these needs and relationships are established, the church may then be in a position to bring in spiritual solutions to community problems also. We cannot expect government, business, education, and media/entertainment to be spiritual at first. We must establish the relationship in the natural realm first. After we have a passport into the other spheres of influence, then we can help in the spiritual realm. In other words, you are Martha, then you are Mary! I will have more to say on this subject in the "Innovative Disruption—In the Nick of Time" chapter.

Back to the Kenyans—their community was peeping! They were waiting for the church to be the church in a real and tangible way. Just as the Kenyans were waiting, your community is waiting. While there are many tasks, works, and ministries churches can do in and for the community, such as feeding the poor and taking care of the homeless, these works may not catch the heart of the community. These works are good and necessary. By all means, the church should keep doing them. But there are works like picking up garbage along a Kenyan highway that not only accomplish a task, but also establish relationship. Community transformation initiatives could greatly benefit from targeting these key tasks.

These tasks move us from the possibility of community transformation to the probability of community transformation. The ultimate winner is the community. The result is that the earth is more filled with the glory than before. The Peeping Toms are watching for good works in such a way!

2. Peering Toms

The Peering Toms are people representing the community who are looking at the relationships and behavior among Christian people in churches. Frankly, in many cases they cannot believe what they are seeing. Relationship problems, power accumulation and preservation, factions, divorces, nasty church splits, competition, and gossip seem to be the rule of thumb in church culture, not the exception. Jesus tried to awaken the church to this reality in John 13:35:

> By this all men will know that you are My disciples, if you have love for one another.
>
> —John 13:35

How will *all men* (that is the community) know we are Christ's disciples? Jesus *said by our love for one another*. Right relationships lead to real ministry, remember? How can we say we love God and not each other? As a pastor and leader of many years, I have seen it all. When I go to Dairy Queen I do not order a banana split, I order a church split!

Do you realize there is more emotional baggage produced from broken relationships than from any other area in life? If there ever was an area where the church is incarnationally challenged, this is it. We are long on declaring love, short on living love. Why? It is our right-or-wrong orientation. We need to understand that whether we like it or not, the community is peering at the church.

Every time we travel the right-or-wrong-first road, we create the biggest public relations problem in the world. We offend God, we offend one another, and we offend the community. It is a lose/lose for the church, God and the community. We undermine real, tangible, and lasting community transformation. Frankly, there are thousands of books written on this subject, so I will be brief in this section. The issue is not one of knowledge. This issue is one of incarnation and application. We have a belief, but that belief is not a value—yet!

Jesus says that the Peering Toms could become the Praising Toms as they see love demonstrated in the church. Goodness knows they will not get love anywhere else! If the church does not incarnate love, who will? Jesus came to heal a broken relationship between God and man. Jesus is the ultimate Matchmaker and Third Party Negotiator. He came to get the two parties, God and man, back to the peace table again. He is an Ambassador of Reconciliation equipped and graced with the word of reconciliation.

Jesus spent three years with the disciples primarily on the development of relationship. Heaven is made of a relationship among the Father, Son, and Holy Spirit. These Three are so much in relationship that you cannot tell where They start or stop. They are One!

> Many will say to Me on that day, "Lord, Lord, did we not prophesy in Your name, and in Your name cast out demons, and in Your name perform many miracles?" And then I will declare to them, "I never knew you; depart from me, you who practice lawlessness."
>
> —MATTHEW 7:22–23

Here Jesus says in effect, "Depart from me because you were not relational. We never had a relationship. You were into your agenda of prophecy, deliverance and miracles. That agenda was more important to you than a relationship with me or others!"

A good question to ask is, is our agenda more important than our relationship with God and others? Is our agenda more important than how the peering Toms look at us? Even though we can cloak our relational issues in prophecy, deliverance, and miracles in the church, we cannot cloak these issues with God or the community. The right-or-wrong-first core value is never more important than the life-and-death core value. Fruit eaters eventually die, fruit bearers live on, and on through others!

Jesus came for the restoration of relationships—from bad to okay, from okay to good, and from good to great. He is the ultimate marriage counselor, conflict negotiator, bridge builder, and lover of men. He did not come for the thrill of a miracle, the study of Greek, or for correct theology. He came to seek and save the lost. He came for the complete healing of spirit, soul and body. He does not war against flesh. He brings peace on earth and good will towards men in whom He is well pleased. He represented God. He came to make His Father known.

> And I have made Thy name known to them, and will make it known; that the love wherewith Thou didst love Me may be in them, and I in them.
>
> —John 17:26

He did not advertise Himself; He came to make God known. He gave glory to God, He did not take it for Himself. You could not get Jesus to have an agenda other than God's if you wanted to. His statement, "I came to make You known," exemplifies His ministry. Make others known—that was His attitude and mindset (Philippians 2:3–8).

That is the Church's ministry also, "We came to make God known." Where? To the community! Would not it be wonderful if the Church really made God known? Jesus' love for God and for the community controlled and constrained Him to do that. That is what the Church is all about, love for God and love for the community—our priestly ministry to God and our prophetic ministry to the community. All you need is love!

Jachin Mullen of Red Deer, Alberta, Canada, has written a song called "That is What Worship Is." While the song has to do with the Church, let's extend it out a little to the community. Read it, turn its words into values and live its values out loud in the community.

The way we live
The way we love one another
The way we give
That is what worship is
Coming closer to the Father's heart
Finding a love that never stops when it starts

The way we care
Reaching out to one another
The way we share
That is what worship is
Coming closer to each others' heart
Knowing His love can never be torn apart

When we love one another
We are loving the Father
Part of His family
We are His sons and daughters
We are joined in the Spirit
By the blood of the Son
When our hearts are knit in love
We are one.

3. Pleading Toms

The Pleading Toms are people in the community who are watching the relationships among churches and denominations in the community. Their cry has been and still is "Why can't these churches get along? Why are they in competition? Why are they so individualistic?"

This problem and lack of unity is especially an issue with other community spheres of influence. They have a built-in radar and, frankly, are turned off by the lack of church unity.

> That they may all be one; even as Thou, Father, art in Me, and I in Thee, that they also may be in Us; that the world may believe that Thou didst send Me....I in them, and Thou in Me, that they may be perfected in unity, that the world may know that Thou didst send Me, and didst love them, even as Thou didst love Me.
>
> —John 17:21, 23

Jesus prayed that there will be unity among real brothers, churches, and denominations. His glory was given to produce unity. His unity was given so the world will know that God sent Jesus. Community transformation is dependent upon unity. Unity is a *prerequisite* for community transformation. When brothers dwell together in unity, *there* (at that physical spot) the Lord commands the blessing (Ps. 133).

Wouldn't it be wonderful if Baptists exemplified the same humility and unity as Jesus? In other words, what if Baptists started complementing and cooperating with other denominations instead of being self-propagating? When Baptists complement and cooperate with Assemblies of God. When Assemblies of God complement and cooperate with Presbyterians. When Presbyterians complement and cooperate with Calvary Chapels. When Calvary Chapels complement and cooperate with Baptists. When husbands complement and cooperate with their wives, and vice versa. When prophetic people complement and cooperate with pastors. When intercessors complement and cooperate with evangelists. I could go on and on.

It is time we apply what we learned in the "Dual Citizenship" chapter. Let's make the other known. That is how you turn pleading Toms who desperately want to see the "tribes become a nation" into praising Toms. We can do it and when we do, we will greatly enhance the community and one another.

Valuing Values

In conclusion, we must not just believe our beliefs, we must value our values. If a belief stays a belief and does not come to full maturity in a value, we will stay incarnationally challenged. As the Chinese say, we will be the tiger's head and the mouse's tail.

To God, real worship is both vertical and horizontal. Real worship expresses itself in the way we live. Whether it is brother to brother, sister to sister, church to church, denomination to denomination, or church to the community, the outworking of the inworking is loving God, loving ourselves and loving our neighbor (Mark 12:30–31).

Chapter 12

Clueless in Seattle:

The Principle of Redemptive Relevancy

In times of change, learners inherit the earth, while the learned find themselves perfecting, equipped to deal with a world that no longer exists.

—Eric Hoeffer

Focus is simply doing those things that need to be done now, and doing them correctly.

Awareness is a broader focus, if you will, on the factors that might affect the success of those endeavors. For example, during the Korean War, General Douglas MacArthur had just completed the destruction of the North Korean army in one of the most brilliant campaigns in American military history. His focus was winning the war in Korea, and he had done that. He neglected, however, to consider that two hundred thousand screaming Chinese just across the Yalu River were taking serious exception to his plan. He knew they were there (he was not stupid), but he either was not or refused to be aware that they might jump him. Well, they jumped him, and

MacArthur and the rest of the US forces in Korea had a very nasty time for the next few months because of his lack of awareness.

This true story illustrates a life principle I call the principle of focus and awareness. Focus is essential to doing what we need to do, but awareness is strategic in determining the way it is done. As General MacArthur discovered, focus without awareness is trouble. Focus without awareness may be unintentional, but the results can be disastrous. Awareness is the key to any good campaign or mission that we do. Awareness enhances the probability of our getting to where our focus wants us to go. Focus without awareness causes a small-picture approach to life, work, ministry, relationships, and the community.

On the other side of the coin is awareness without focus. Some people are so aware they never get anything constructive done. They do not accomplish, they ponder. It is the both/and core value that allows for both of these concepts to come together to accomplish an objective. To be successful in community transformation, the church needs to be both focused on its mission and have awareness of the community climate and culture.

X and Y Chromosomes

What do many women say about men? What do many wives say about their husbands? They just do not get it; they are clueless! Cluelessness is not the same as intentionality. Intentionality means that something is done on purpose. A husband may do things that provoke or mystify his wife, but that does not mean the husband does those things on purpose. In fact, most times he may be unaware of how his actions affect his wife. However, if he remains clueless, his wife may attribute intentionality to what He is doing. Then they have real trouble.

Cluelessness is an issue of the head; intentionality is an issue of the heart.

My advice is husbands, get smart! Get some intelligent fire, not just passionate fire. The key to a good marriage is both focus and awareness. Most men are not instinctively aware of women's needs. We need to learn about women. We need to become aware of how women view themselves and their issues. The excuse of cluelessness will not last for very long even with great focus. After twenty years of marriage I am still trying to tune into Channel Becky (my wife). I am learning that productive living is about focus *and* awareness in both the relationship and task areas of my life. The all-focus-no-awareness tendency of many men ultimately gets us, like General MacArthur, into trouble. And all the women said, *amen*!

Church Focus and Community Awareness

Just as General MacArthur was unaware of Chinese ire, and just as men are unaware of where women are coming from, most churches are unaware of where the community is coming from. A church's total focus on church culture and issues leads to a church unaware of its mission to the community. That church's attitudes and actions reflect a you-are-here-for-us mentality. People in the community perceive that that church is using them as a means to its own end. This church-centric mentality creates an image in the community's mind of one-upmanship and superiority. That is like thinking the sun revolves around the earth rather than the earth around the sun.

When the community revolves around the church rather than the church around the community, the four other spheres of influence discussed in the "Humpty Dumpty" chapter feel marginalized and "judged." The secular and sacred distinction takes the church and its relationship with the community to the only place it can go, disconnection. This is mainly an awareness problem. The church needs to stop being clueless in Seattle, Dallas, New York, London, or wherever. Our relationship with the community depends upon our being aware and open learners, like men need to be aware and open learners about their wives.

Whether intentional or not, church focus without community awareness produces the same result over a long period of time—the biggest public relations problem in the world. The Church tends to think the community knows where it is coming from, but this is naïve.

The truth is that the community will never know where the Church is coming from without a relationship. For the Church to be redefined in the community's eyes, the relationship between Church and community needs to be more real and tangible than the community's prior perception of the Church. Real and tangible relationships change negative perceptions and opinions. To do something about the problem the Church must first become aware of the problem. The Church needs to move from "Clueless in Seattle" to "Houston, we have a problem."

The purpose of this chapter is to wake up the Church, wake up pastors and leaders, and wake up those Christians imbedded in church culture. Things have changed! *Times* have changed. *Values* have changed. The *community's opinion* of the church has changed.

This is no time to be an ostrich, "sticking your head in the sand" and pretending to change things. It is time to become both aware and focused—on the *community*.

CHANGE HAPPENS

Awareness lets us know when something has changed in our context or community. Awareness wakes us up, shakes off the cobwebs, and gets us thinking. It is designed to cause us to respond to problems and come up with solutions. Awareness was never meant to paralyze us, but to motivate us to do the best we can under the circumstances. It stimulates and propels us to real and tangible actions and solutions. Awareness should never cause us to lose focus, but should allow us to get to our focus when circumstances change.

Change does not equal instability if we know how to handle and process it. To live is to grow; to grow is to change.

Below are four issues that have changed drastically in the last fifty years that I will address in this chapter:

1. The World Has Changed
2. World Values Have Changed
3. The Church's Place in Society's Eyes Has Changed
4. Therefore, Old Forms of Conducting Church Need to Change

The church today is like the prophet Daniel in the Old Testament. Remember, most of the population of Jerusalem was removed by the Babylonians and exiled to a city called Babylon. This was about the worst place and situation any God-fearing Jew could go. Daniel and his "church" culture were the majority in Jerusalem, but a minority in Babylon. When Daniel went from his society to Babylon, he went from being part of the people in authority to, at best, being an influence. He went from being the head to being the tail in Babylon's eyes. He had to learn how to live in a whole new set of circumstances where his world was not respected or the norm. Daniel had to learn how to live in Babylon and have influence in Babylon, but not let Babylon get into him. Daniel had to be aware of Babylon to influence Babylon.

The truth is, the Church has lost much of the authority and influence it once had in Western culture. In a sense, the Church is perceived by the community as a non-player. Noted researcher George Barna recently conducted a poll on the top seven influencers of United States culture. The result shocked most church-centric people: the Church was not even listed in the top seven influencers.[1] In other words, while the Church was studying Greek, having Holy Ghost meetings, conducting deeper-life sermons, and cocooned in a church-centric ethos, the world changed. Why wouldn't it? If we become a world unto ourselves, what contact can we have with the community unless it is on our terms?

If we, like Daniel, are to influence our culture back to God, we have to look at the Church more like a missions outpost than a traditional church. The same was true of the apostle Paul in Corinth or Athens. We have the message, they are the audience. Now how can we get the two groups together? Can we come out with a win for the Church and a win for the community a la Humpty Dumpty? After all, that is the goal of community transformation—favor with God and favor with men (Luke 2:52).

Like Daniel, the Church today needs to learn how to be a bridge builder rather than a bridge burner. We need to know how to live out Christian core values, yet maintain great flexibility outside of our core values. Community transformation is about having "first contact." Daniel did not sulk, he *lived*. Daniel realized he was not a native, he was an immigrant. Daniel changed, he adapted, he influenced and he even prospered in Babylon. He was looking for a way into Babylon, not a way out of Babylon. He understood that he was there for Babylon, Babylon was not there for him. He would have gotten his head cut off looking at Babylon any other way. He was aware of Babylon, but not fearful of Babylon. What was wrong with Babylon? They were missing some godly core values, and Daniel was there to give them to Babylon.

Get the message? Will we be ostriches or opportunists? Can we be relevant? Can we influence our Babylon?

Before we can influence our Babylon we had better become aware of the changes in Babylon.

THAT WAS THE WORLD THAT WAS

Let's take a look at our Babylon. In May of 2000, one of my friends attended a conference called Exploring Off the Map in Denver, Colorado. One of the speakers, Leonard Sweet, spoke about the radically different world we are facing. This is the gist of his message:

> The world is changing, and the change is not one of degree, but one of *kind.* If we do not understand this we are making a credit card call on a rotary phone. If you are under thirty-eight you are a native, if you are over thirty-eight you are an immigrant. Immigrants have three reactions when they come to a new country:
>
> They do not get it.
>
> They get it, but for some reason they cannot, or will not change.
>
> They get it, and they change.
>
> We need to understand that the world today is different than the one we grew up with and were educated in. Much of our education incapacitates us for this new world. We need to forget, so we can learn what will be required for effective ministry in the twenty-first century. The big question is this: *Is the church going to go native, or will we force the natives to become immigrants?* If we do not understand the fundamental shift that is occurring we will not see God's burning bushes in this new world.[2]

I am fifty-four years of age and I thought I was a native. I was not aware that I was an immigrant. That is the point Leonard is trying to make. The world has changed. The I'm-Okay-You're-So-So way of doing things may be wonderful for me but a total disconnect to my audience. My challenge is accepting that *my* world is not *the* world anymore.

The same is true for the Church. Are we going to make credit card calls on rotary phones? Are we going to force the natives to become immigrants? Can we relate the gospel to people other than those already in the Church for years? Can we adapt to a changed world? Can we communicate with the community?

Assistant Pastor and author Dan Scott of Christ Church in Nashville, Tennessee, has developed a chart that he calls "The Time Line of Social Organization in Western Society." This chart depicts the changes that have occurred in social organizations from the time just before Christ's birth to modern times. Notice the four categories on the left and the changes that have occurred in the passing of time:

Time Line of Social Organization

	0–1670	1670–1945	1945–Today
Community Structure	Rural	Urban	Global
Social Structure	Clan/tribe	Nuclear family; father, mother, child, dog	Autonomous self; family dispensable
Spirituality	Mythos—spiritual principles	Reason	Mythos—not reality, it's information that makes me feel comfortable
Unit of Exchange	Produce	Capital/ Product $	Information, credit cards, computers

Look at the Community Structure category. Notice the change from rural to urban to global. We do not need to agree with these changes. But we need to be aware of these changes. Everywhere I go in the world

I hear the phrase "global awareness." This phrase can be intimidating to those who are aware of the prophecies concerning one-world government, the anti-Christ and end times. However, the Church's mission here is how to connect our message with the audience of today's globally aware people. Our role is not reactive but proactive. Rather than "ostriching," let's be opportunistic. What needs do today's people have in this type of culture? How do we meet those needs? How can we help our communities cope with these changes? We have lots of opportunities if we are open to looking for the opportunities.

Now let's look at the line of social structure. Society has moved from the clan or tribe to the nuclear family, to the autonomous self with the family dispensable. That is quite a change from the old days. Many people in their fifties have seen our culture, sad as it seems, move from family-centered to self-centered. Our culture has become more teen-like than adult-like. Today, younger people individualize early in life, creating all sorts of complex issues for them and their communities to deal with. Rather than ostriching, let's be opportunistic. This is a great opportunity to help self-aware, perhaps selfish and self-centered people to learn to cope in a world of self-centered people. These people will eventually see that life was not meant to be lived out independently, but interdependently. A modern, aware, community-centric church could easily meet the needs of these people. The glass is half full, not half empty.

The spirituality line is also quite revealing. Until 1670 a.d. the world was keenly aware of the spiritual realm. Most had no problem believing in God, the devil, angels, demons and the like, and they lived their lives in that reality. With the dawn of the Industrial Revolution and rationalism in the 1670s, the Western world swung to the age of reason. Reason replaced mythos or spiritual principles in large parts of Europe, America, and western-oriented countries such as Australia, New Zealand and Canada. Religion was looked upon as more superstition than reality. Of course, some of the religions were based upon superstition and religious control, which only added to the case for rationalism.

The end of World War II brought back a degree of spiritual awareness. However, today's world (especially in the West) looks at religion as a way to medicate or become more sensitive to our environment. Eastern mystical influences such as yoga, Hinduism and New Age are ways of coping with life. These religions are not reality, but information that makes people feel more comfortable with themselves and life. The good news for today's Bible-believing church is that there is an increased hunger in the community for God and spiritual things. God is creating a need in the people. Our churches can help with that if we are aware. The awareness of the church activates the focus of the church. The church exists to make God known just like Jesus did (John 17:26).

The last line is the unit of exchange. Notice how our economy has gone from bartering to money and now is rapidly moving toward an information-based unit of exchange. The information age is here with computers, ATMs, credit cards, satellites, and other modern technology. It will not be long until we function in a cashless society. I realize that to the church-centric person this sounds the "666" alarm. The question is, will we be ostriches or opportunists at this stage of history? Can we have credit-card machines in our churches and not be "666"? I think so! At some point, we have to stop trying to make credit card calls on rotary telephones.

Western Culture or World Culture?

If you are thinking the timeline change pertains only to Western culture, I encourage you to think again. Have you been in Africa, India, Latin America or Asia lately? Have you been in China lately? Western culture is influencing the world's culture through satellite television, the Internet, mobile phones and a variety of other means. When you walk into an Internet café in Buenos Aires, Bombay, or Lagos you had better be ready. Even remote villages in Africa and India are watching CNN or the BBC. These formerly undereducated societies are catching up quickly to the West. Many of these people are better and more sophisticated in computer programming and operations than Europeans, Australians, or Americans. It is not a Western phenomenon, it is a world phenomenon. Yes, there are a few places on the earth that remain in the 0–1670 era and the 1670–1945 era, but these places are quickly becoming the exception as compared to the rule of thumb. Global awareness is here.

The question is will the Church ostrich or be opportunistic? Will we be effective, modern-day Daniels, or will we retreat to deeper life clubs, doctrine centers, or Holy Ghost parties? Will we become salt and light or hide our light under a lamp stand in the name of holiness? Will we be a holy huddle or a world-class apostolic impact center? Would Jesus come to earth in this case or would Jesus stay in heaven? What would Jesus do?

Whether we are proactive or reactive really depends upon one thing: What are our core values? Do we operate from the life-and-death core value, or from the right-or-wrong core value? Those whose behavior is determined from the life-and-death core value will be proactive and redemptive toward the community.

AN EVALUATION OF THE DEVALUATION

Following is a story about people in today's communities to which the Church has been called to preach. I chose this example because it illustrates how much United States values can change in just a few short years, and it shows the clash of values between the community and the Church. (Excerpted from *Lifestyle Evangelism* © 1981, 1993 by Joe Aldrich. Used by permission of Multnomah Publishers, Inc.)

> Come with me on an imaginary journey into the home of a non-Christian neighbor. We are invisible. In the den, a Playboy magazine tops the stack of reading material on the coffee table causing a yellow caution light to flash on our spiritual dashboard. In the corner opposite a mute TV set sprawls the man of the house, feet propped up, beer can clenched in his fist. The yellow light flashes again. Bob's tired from a rough day in the dog-eat-dog world. His mind is reliving the events of another day's scramble for the almighty dollar. A day of cutting corners, pressure, compromise, and more pressure. He is not entirely happy with what the realities of the marketplace have done to his boyhood ideals. But then, doesn't everyone have a price? He smiles when he thinks of his new Mercedes. Could not really afford it, but nobody needs to

know. Besides, if he can close the Smith deal quickly, he will make a killing. Isn't that what life's all about?

The driving beat of a rock record with its screaming vocalist has his sing-along daughter's undivided attention. The caution light flashes again. Glancing at his bookshelf, it is obvious that some of Bob's books did not come from the local library. Marian, the librarian, would have surely blushed. We do not blush—invisible people cannot—but our yellow light continues to flash. Mom (Pam) puts down her cigarette long enough to answer the phone. She explains to the caller that they will not make the bridge party. They are going to the movie with some unexpected guests. The yellow light is at it again.

Sally, the teen-age daughter, finally shuts the music off and disappears. She has a date with her steady. They are going to the disco. She is on the pill. Yellow lights flash. Jim, Bob's son from a previous marriage, bursts into the den demanding his overdue allowance. His timing is poor. Bob shares with him a piece of his mind he can ill afford to lose. His comments about Jim's shoulder length hair add fuel to the fire. There are hard words. The air turns blue. Again, our spiritual dashboards light up. No grace is offered before the meal and there is little grace expressed during it.

But things calm down. Jim retires to his room. The rock star posters (not to mention the eastern guru's grinning portrait) do a number on our spiritual dashboards. The books on transcendental meditation do not help. It is a good thing we do not see the drugs stashed away under his mattress.

Responding to the doorbell, Bob welcomes Karen and Ned, friends from way back. Bob pours them drinks as they make small talk together. Karen and Pam disappear for a few minutes, providing Bob and Ned an opportunity to exchange some off-color stories salted with four-letter words. Their boisterous laughter almost drowns out Karen and Pam's discussion of you, their next-door neighbor.

They cannot seem to figure you out. You seem to enjoy going to your church and sitting while someone preaches at you. They shake their heads at the thought. It must be a terrible waste. And you would not let your kids go to the ball game on Sunday even thought they really wanted to go. This they cannot understand. Pam shares how they had offered to take your teen-age son to

> the school dance, but you explained that you did not allow your children to dance. That was okay, but your comments about being born-again and accepting Christ and submitting to husbands did not communicate. It is almost as thought you had your own language. Your more Spartan, conservative lifestyle does not go unnoticed either. It makes Pam feel somewhat guilty about her love of flamboyant, expensive styles. But what is wrong with looking good, eating good, and living good while it all lasts. You cannot take it with you. It must be a difference in values.
>
> They consider your submission ideas to be a cop out. Your husband is viewed as a chauvinist, although he seems to be a nice guy. This "chain of command" stuff has to go.
>
> Pam says she feels you are in the Dark Ages intellectually. How can anyone believe that stuff about a virgin birth, miracles, and angels? Why would anyone involve himself with such an outdated lifestyle?
>
> Pam knows you are better than she and admits she probably needs religion. In fact, she feels uncomfortable around you. They laugh together as she describes herself as your "project" in spite of her Christian Science background.
>
> Earrings finally in place, lipstick properly applied, they rejoin their husbands and drive off to laugh through an R-rated movie. Isn't this the good life?

Just think of how much the world might change in the next ten years!

Postmodern Core Values

If we are going to reach our neighbors in the world we had better know their values. While much has been written about postmodern core values, I want to articulate a few of them. Much of what I write here came from pastors at my Pastors In Covenant group in Phoenix, Arizona. Please remember I am not necessarily endorsing these values, only identifying them.

Value 1. "I create my own truth."

To relate with me you have to accept my right to my truth. This is what is called relativism.

Value 2. "There is no such thing as truth."

Truth is how I have experienced life and how I have put it together in order to survive. You have Christ, I have Buddha—they are really the same.

Value 3. "Family is whomever I wish to relate to."

The idea here is that family is not made up of blood relatives. For example, family could be gangs, causes, or movements.

Value 4. "I can have contradictory truths."

In other words, saving a whale while aborting a baby is not a problem. If this is the stand that seems good and a just cause to a person, he is free to do as he pleases. To appeal to logic or truth holds no real value. They might say it this way, "In this area I am a Christian, in that area I am New Age."

Value 5. "There is no right or wrong."

It is "yes, I agree" or "no, I do not agree." In other words, opinion takes the place of truth. Their opinion becomes their truth. They say, "I have a choice of truths."

Value 6. "I have to be sensitive above anything else."

The issue of sensitivity is probably the main value of postmodernism at the present time. If you are not sensitive to race, gay issues, animals, the environment, women, and a host of other politically correct issues you become the worst thing anyone can be in a global culture. You are labeled as insensitive. This is especially a problem to the Church in light of its right-or-wrong ethos and of course is labeled as insensitive and prejudiced. The mentality is "you have to accept my diverseness in a non-judgmental way."

Value 7. "I feel" has more importance than "I think."

This value is based on experiential rather cognitive reasoning. Experiencing and feeling are what give life value. "My perception and feeling is what is really real; I am enlightened."

Value 8. Post-literate and high technology.

Postmodernism consists of sound bytes, moving cameras, interactive games, and *USA Today* newspapers. Long books are being replaced by shorter books. Through technology virtual reality is taking the place of reality. For example, you can change the way you look by changing your body on a computer or on an operating table.

Value 9. Leadership is by team and influence, not authority.

This might be expressed by the "I need to be heard, too" approach. Leadership is by consensus and not by the one-person-in-authority direct approach. The leader would not appear sensitive if all were not heard. The team gets the credit for good leadership decisions and shares the blame if there is a problem. No one person is singled out positively or negatively.

Perhaps some of you might be shocked, cringing, and even mad at me for bringing these values to your attention. However, for the sake of our communities, we had better be the church aware. The traditional church's us/them approach will never change anything in our communities for the better. Daniel went to the University of Babylon to learn the ways of the people he was to influence back to God. Joseph did the same. These wonderful postmodern people are not the enemy, they are victims of the enemy. How could we do anything less than Daniel or Joseph? Community transformation requires that the Word become flesh in a postmodern world.

Rubies, Robes, and Altars

As a result of these changes in the world and its values, the church's place in society has changed also. In essence, while the world has been dynamic, the Church has been static. As I mentioned earlier, the Church is not even on the list of the top seven influencers in the United States. That would be even more true in Europe, Russia, Australia, New Zealand, and Canada.

Years ago I met a pastor who told me he had done a thirteen-week series on rubies in the Bible. I was in shock. He had spoken on *Sunday mornings* for thirteen weeks on obscure verses in the Bible on rubies! He developed Christian themes from "types and shadows" that I am sure church-centric people liked, but the community would not even be able to relate to. He was relevant to a few people, but not relevant to most people. I wanted to say, "Do you realize that there are people coming to your church who are trying to figure out how to stay married for the next week, and you are talking about rubies in Obadiah?"

Rubies in Obadiah is not where today's postmodern people in the community are. Most unchurched people visit churches on Sunday morning. Why not do the ruby series on Thursday nights or some other time? That is a subject for Christians, not the community. Use Sunday morning as a time to address real-life issues for both the churched and the unchurched. Remember, the church is a lost-and-found department, not just a found department. This well-meaning pastor did not create the disconnect from the community intentionally. He is a product of the teacher-driven ethos of the Church that loves word studies, types, and shadows on rubies. The pastor was Clueless in Seattle. Unfortunately, when you are clueless, the church and the community lose. The church does not grow through new conversions, and the community does not get the benefit of Christ to help solve their problems.

Remember back in Chapter 1 the findings of George Barna in regard to "barely one-half" of the churches in America addressing September 11 "in any way"? If September 11 happened, and Lesson 7 on rubies was on September 16, 2001, that pastor's first sentence may well have been, "Open your Bible to Exodus 39:10, the row of the ruby." My assertion here is that community transformation and putting Humpty Dumpty back together again require much more than studies on rubies, robes, feasts and altars. Community transformation is about connecting the message with the audience in a way real people can identify with.

The apostle Paul says in 1 Corinthians 2:14 that natural people do not understand spiritual things. Why should they? What else would you expect? That is why the Church needs to shed its teacher-driven ethos and adopt some apostolic/evangelistic ethos also.

The Church is a "sent one" to the community. The church goes to the community, not vice versa. The Word becomes flesh and moves into the neighborhood. The Son of God became the Son of Man because the natural man needs a natural man to communicate with him in a real and tangible way. Jesus became a servant to the community. A servant will go where theology will not. Jesus was able to be both holy and relevant.

The Church's place in society has changed because the Church has not changed. Ask any citizen of your community. Ask the mayor, the university president, or key business owners in your community. Ask them, "What do you think of the Church?" Here is what most will say: "The words they use are obsolete, not relevant, judgmental, sectarian—a world unto themselves, the problem rather than the solution and uneducated."

While church people know that description is not true, that is the opinion of the church held by most people and governmental spheres. These people, by the way, are the very people God sent His Son, and now the Church, to reach. The problem is we have already been defined by many of the influencers in our communities. The Church 's reputation precedes it, and in many cases disqualifies it from being an influencer in the community.

How can the Church redefine itself in the community's eyes? How can the church reconnect with the very community it was created to serve? Can the Church be relevant? Can the Church be part of putting Humpty Dumpty back together again? Can the Church get past its right-and-wrong ethos, past its victim mentality and change its public relations image in the community? The answer is yes. Real and tangible community transformation requires it! What is the answer? Read on.

REDEMPTIVE RELEVANCY

Relevance is a major issue in the Church today. The community calls the church an irrelevant entity in today's world. Church-centric people call today's churches that attempt to be relevant "compromised." There is an indictment on relevancy issues from both sides of the continuum. One side is critical of legalism, the other side is critical of liberalism.

Relevance speaks to significance, weight, importance, consequence, and application. Therefore, relevance is an important, necessary component of reaching the community. Without relevance, we have the community leaving the church as fast as it comes in. Without relevance, there is no connection with the community. Without relevance, potential church harvests, such as those following September 11, are lost. Without relevance, the church remains safe but trapped inside the ethos it has created for itself. Relevance is a prerequisite to real, tangible, and lasting community transformation. Without relevance you cannot communicate. Without influence, you remain a wannabe, on the outside always looking in. You become a spectator rather than a player.

If the Church really adopted the life-and-death-first, right-or-wrong-second value, the church would become relevant as a result. The life-and-death core value propels you to be like the apostle Paul, who said, "To the weak I became weak, that I might win the weak; I have become all things to all men, that I may by all means save some. I do all things for the sake of the gospel, that I may become a fellow partaker of it" (1 Cor. 9:22–23).

The Church will become all things to all men that by all means some may be saved. In other words, the Church becomes relevant for the purpose of redemption. Relevancy is a means to an end, not the end in itself. To many church-centric Christians, relevancy seems like compromise. They interpret relevancy as becoming "all things to all men" rather than becoming "all things to all men so that some might be saved." There is a big difference in those two perspectives. Jesus did not become all things to all men. Jesus became all things to all men so that some might be saved. He demonstrated a purpose-driven relevancy. I call it redemptive relevancy. Jesus was relevant for the sake of redemption. Real relevancy is not church-centric. Real relevancy is community-centric. Real relevancy is favor with both God and man.

> And Jesus kept increasing in wisdom and stature, and in favor with God and men.
>
> —Luke 2:52

Do you see that? Real ministry is not just being right with God. Real ministry is about being right with God and right with man. It is not an either/or but a both/and. The early church was able to have both.

> And he must have a good reputation with those outside the church, so that he will not fall into reproach and the snare of the devil.
>
> —1 Timothy 3:7

Paul writes to Timothy that an overseer must have a good reputation with those *outside* the church. An overseer must be community-centric. Paul even implies that without contact with and a good reputation in the community, that overseer could fall into the snare of the devil. The argument that the church needs to be separate from the community or else they might get contaminated never worked with Paul. In fact, the opposite is true. Without real contact with people in the community, you can get contaminated with a religious ethos or outlook that could become a reproach to the community. Remember, favor with God *and* man.

Apostolic Awareness

As the first apostles started to spread the gospel and Christian core values from Jerusalem to the ends of the earth, they began to see the "other" cities and nations in a different way. They became aware that Jerusalem and Israel were not "the world." They became aware of different cultures, different customs and different needs among the people they were sent to reach. They had to have a global awareness in a redemptive sense. This apostolic awareness required contextualization. The challenge they faced was to incarnate faith in culture.

Contextualization is applying biblical core values to a particular culture or context. In other words, there was no compromise on the core values of Christianity. However, the way these values were expressed was in a form that communicated to the people or community they were trying to reach. This form was relevant to the people the apostles were attempting to reach with the gospel. It was not compromise; it was context and communication. It was connecting the message and the audience. It was not forcing a Jerusalem form on the Romans, but adapting to a form of communication the Romans could understand. It was being aware of Rome. The apostles practiced redemptive relevancy to *by all means win some.*

The apostles had to determine their approach to the community. They had to be aware of the community, yet focused on the character, ministry and mission of Christ. They had to have favor with God and favor with men to transform a community. From a missions perspective, apostolic awareness had "to open their eyes so that they may turn from darkness to light and from the dominion of Satan to God, in order that they may receive forgiveness of sins and an inheritance among those who have been sanctified by faith in Me" (Acts 26:18).

Notice also the principle of favor with God and man in this verse. The apostles needed "awareness" to "open their eyes" first before the "focus" in the rest of the verse. Church-centric ethos sees the last part first and the first part last. Relevancy is about "opening their eyes in order to—"

In other words, relevancy is not compromise; it is a prerequisite for community transformation. Relevancy opens the eyes of that particular culture or audience, and addresses issues and meets needs where that audience is. Relevancy moves them from knowing about God to experiencing God in a way that is meaningful to them. It is approaching them, not sorting them out. It is speaking to them, not at them. It is not the condescending one-upmanship that has been the modus operandi of many fundamental or Spirit-filled churches for many, many years.

As we said at the beginning of this chapter, focus without awareness greatly influences the outcome of our efforts. General MacArthur's lack of awareness cost him dearly. The churches' lack of awareness has cost us dearly in terms of church growth, church influence and a huge public relations problem with the community. Would you go to a store that has a reputation for factions, judging customers, overcharging and a condescending attitude, and who serves bad food? I doubt it, unless that is the only store available to you. Whether the church changes or not depends upon whether it is aware or not. The question is, what is the church more aware of, life and death or right and wrong? Your values determine your behaviors. Your function determines your form of ministry.

The Reality of Relevance

Let's review and begin to conclude this chapter with some real and tangible ways for your church to minister in a relevant manner. We have seen that the world has changed, values in the world have changed, and the church's place in the community and society has changed.

These changes require the way church is conducted to change. The Church needs to become aware that we are in the twenty-first century, not the twentieth century. The Church cannot continue making credit card calls on rotary phones. It requires contextualization; it is not compromise, it is proactive missions in action. The Church can change its forms of ministry without changing the essence of its ministry. The core values stay the same; forms can change. That is the essence of redemptive relevancy.

My good friend, Pastor David Boyd of the Jesus Family Centre Church in Cabramatta, Australia, recently told me a story that illustrates this. He said that a pastor was interested in reaching the Asian population in the Cabramatta area. Because David pastors a multicultural church with many Asians in it is congregation, this pastor asked him how he does it. David replied, "You will have to change the way you dress on Sunday mornings if you want to reach the Asians."

This pastor from Canada has a church plant in Cabramatta with an ethos of dressing "southern California cool." The pastor wears cut-offs, Hawaiian shirts, and sandals. While that style may be considered cool in southern California, it is not cool to the many Asians who have moved to Cabramatta. The Asian culture places a high value on pastors or leaders dressing up for church. California cool is not cool to the Asians.

This leads to an interesting dilemma for the California-cool pastor. Does he want to remain cool with no Asians, or does he want Asians in place of California cool? Opting for the Asians would require him to depart from the culture of his sending church in southern California. He can keep rubbing the fur the wrong way, or he can let the cat turn around. Will he change? Will he adapt? It all depends on his values. Is he willing to meet the Asians where they are at, or must the Asians meet him where he is at? Is he willing to become all things to all men so that some might be saved (even to the point of wearing a nice shirt and slacks), or will he go church-centric? It all depends upon his values. If his vision is to reach Asians, he had better have the enabling core value or government of life-and-death first, California-cool second. He had better have some intelligent fire.

EVERYTHING GETS OLD, INCLUDING WINESKINS

Remember, until you reform, you only revisit. To "ostrich" and minister in old forms to a new world in the name of the Word is foolish. The mission of Jesus requires relevant, meaningful ministry to your audience. The Church is the only organization in the world that exists primarily for its non-members. The Church is here for the community, not the community for the Church. A speaker at the Exploring Off the Map conference sums up the concept in this way:

> Leaders need a relentless focus on customer results. Jesus died for His customers. We must ask ourselves, what are we doing for our customers? What are we doing for the people in our congregations and for our lay leaders and workers?

The point is that the Church is here to serve the community, our members, and our church workers. That is awareness and focus. That is the lost and the found.

Finally, here are some real and tangible issues and approaches that will help you in reconnecting with the community. In essence, there are issues that can help you build tomorrow's church today. Applying these principles and values in your church today can put you ahead of the curve, not behind it. These five issues are:

1. Man of peace or man of war?
2. Where is a Christian a Christian?
3. We are surrounded by insurmountable opportunities—current trends of relationship and community.
4. Different strokes for different folks.
5. Daniel's church.

1. Man of Peace or Man of War?

One of the most significant values of post modernism is sensitivity. As I have stated earlier, the issue with many people today is not are you right or wrong, but are you sensitive? Do you care? Frankly, there is validity in this concept. No one likes a man of war, especially if he initiates it repeatedly. When Jesus appointed the seventy to go before him into the cities where He was to go, He sent them with a message:

> Go your ways; behold, I send you out as lambs in the midst of wolves. Carry no purse, no bag, no shoes; and greet no one on the way. And whatever house you enter, first say, "Peace be to this house." And if a man of peace is there, your peace will rest on him; but if not, it will return to you. And stay in that house, eating and drinking what they give you; for the laborer is worthy of his wages. Do not keep moving from house to house.
>
> —Luke 10:3–7

His message was peace first, not war first. If you want influence in a city (which community transformation requires), you had better be a person or leader of peace. James 3:17 says that wisdom from above is "first pure, than peaceable, gentle, reasonable, full of mercy and good fruits, unwavering, without hypocrisy." James goes on to say in verse 18, "the seed whose fruit is righteousness is sown *in* peace by those who *make* peace."

Many of the warrior types have found out by experience that walking up to a major or businessman and "binding him" is not very productive. The us/them approach lessens rather than enhances influence. David, for example, was disqualified from building God's holy temple because he was a man of war. He was a prophet, a man after God's own heart, a warrior—and he was also disqualified from building the temple of God.

David was disqualified because he went from being in war, to war being *in him*. God never supports war for war's sake. War is never the end; it is the means to an end, which is peace.

People of wisdom and peace build today's temples. Wisdom is a form of intelligent fire. Peace and wisdom find the influences and the people in a community who really want the community to be better. Effective ministry in today's world requires that the Church be as wise as a serpent, and as innocent as a dove. That is a both/and, not an either/or.

Transforming communities requires a message to the community of "Peace be to this house." A church of peace sows seeds of peace and creates a community of peace. My advice is, try a different approach than war in the community. Remember, favor with God and men.

2. Where is a Christian a Christian?

One of the biggest mistakes I made as a pastor was teaching people how to be Christians in church, but not in the community. That is a mistake many pastors make. It comes from the church-centric thinking that many the pastors learn in Bible school or seminary.

Many people are great at being Christians in church, but not very good at being Christians in their marriage. Many do not know how to be good Christian parents, employees, neighbors or friends. In other words, they are not exposed to or equipped with a community approach to Christianity. They are equipped with a church-centric approach to Christianity. They have their Sunday behavior, but it is not the same as their Monday behavior. People in our churches tend to vie for spiritual or church "badges of honor," behavior which is supported and endorsed by their churches. They end up looking good in church, but are ineffective in the community.

To transform a community requires having community transformers. In this case, they are "sent ones" who go into the community and demonstrate Christ to the community. They are Christians in their marriages and Christians in the way they bring up their children. They are Christians in the workplace and Christians in their neighborhoods. They are relevant, men and women of peace who incarnate Jesus in the community. They not only prophesy in church, they prophesy in the community. They have wisdom in the church and wisdom in the community. They are community-centric.

In order to develop these "sent ones," pastors and church leaders need to live and teach outside of their comfort zones. Rubies make wonderful sermon topics for church-centric people who have been Christians for twenty years, but what good do studies on rubies do for a marriage with young children or teenagers, or people at work? A pastor would do well to start teaching and discipling his constituents to be effective Christians outside of church also. That is where we reconnect the messenger with the audience.

3. We are surrounded by insurmountable opportunities

Let's look at some statements from some contemporary Christian thinkers on current trends in Western culture that the church should be aware of and use as points of entrance into the community. Remember that postmodern ministry is all about relationships and community.

Here are some thoughts on postmodernism and the church, excerpted from notes taken at the Exploring Off the Map conference:

> The future is less about the institution and more about community and our life in the community. Community is about relationships. The heart of genuine community is vulnerability. You are not connected if you are not vulnerable. Community is about living together. Community is about understanding our dependence on each other. Community is about asking each other—who are we? It is NOT asking 'what do we do?'
>
> —Peter Senge

> The major task of our time is to nurture the human spirit. The enterprise we are facing in the twenty-first century is the exploration of God.
>
> —Margaret Wheatley

> We must understand that the great cry of people is 'Will you know my name? Will you know that I exist?' People want to find each other and be recognized for their uniqueness. People will only stay in our church or organization when they feel seen, when they feel they are recognized, and when they feel they can contribute and be appreciated. There is nothing in the universe that is alone. Everything is in relationship. Nothing is independent. Everything is about relationships and being together.
>
> —Margaret Wheatley

> We are in an age of participation, so shine the light on others. It is only in relationships that we can discover God and each other. Doctrine is dying; relationships are living. What will save the world? Relationships or doctrine?
>
> —Leonard Sweet

These statements are outside the box for many coming from a church-centric mindset. However, the mission of Jesus Christ, community transformation, and the life-and-death-first core value propel us to see the potential for evangelism in these times. Postmodern people have a need for spirituality. Postmodern people have a need for community. Postmodern people are aware of ecology and environment. Postmodern people want leadership by influence rather than a dominating authority.

Do you realize that the Bible talks about the virtues of each of these issues? We can address these issues in a redemptive way if we can adjust our forms and approaches to ministry. Jesus came to make the Father known (John 17:26) and so can we. Ladies and gentlemen, we are surrounded with insurmountable opportunities!

4. Different strokes for different folks

Do you realize that there is no one perfect way to share the good news to all people? The Bible shows us many ways to share the good news. The key is to determine which approach is the most effective for whom you are trying to reach. Different folks require different strokes. What is relevant to an African may not be relevant to a European. The one-way-is-the-only-way approach undermines community transformation. Bill Hybels and Mark Mittelberg write about several different approaches to evangelism in their book *Becoming a Contagious Christian*.[4] I like this "both/and" approach to missions.

1. Peter's confrontational approach

> Therefore, let all Israel be assured of this: God has made this Jesus, whom you crucified, both Lord and Christ.
>
> —Acts 2:36, NIV

2. Paul's intellectual approach

> So he [Paul] reasoned in the synagogue with the Jews and God-fearing Greeks, as well as in the marketplace day by day with those who happened to be there.
>
> —Acts 17:17, NIV

3. Dorcas's service approach

Dorcas was always doing good and helping the poor.

—Acts 9:36 (author's paraphrase)

4. Blind man's testimonial approach

One thing I do know. I once was blind, but now I see.

—John 9:25, NIV

5. Matthew's friendship approach

While Jesus was having dinner at Matthew's house, many tax collectors and "sinners" came and ate with him and his disciples.

—Matthew 9:10, NIV

6. The Samaritan woman's invitational approach

Leaving her water bottle, the woman went back to town and said to the people, 'Come and see a man who told me everything I ever did.' They came out of town and made their way toward him.

—John 4:28–29

Each one of these approaches is biblical. Peter used a frontal assault after the convincing demonstrations of a language lesson. Paul used the intellectual approach in Athens to the educated elite. Dorcas knew that the language of love was tangible service to her audience. The testimony of healing opened the eyes of the unbelieving near the pool of Siloam. Matthew threw a party and invited Jesus. The Samaritan woman had connections all over town and used her "networking" and "people collecting" skills to bring people to church. Get the message? If we do not go, they will not come!

I am sure there are more than six approaches, but the point is this—find out what is most effective and fruitful to a certain person or group of persons, and use it. Relevancy requires that we be led by the Spirit, not led by a church-centric form. The Word has to become real and tangible and move into the community's neighborhood in a way that its residents can understand.

5. Daniel's church

Early in this chapter, I used the example of the prophet Daniel learning to adapt and be relevant in the "sight and sound" generation of his day. Babylon was the postmodern world of its day. Do you realize that Daniel and his three friends changed the whole city? Do you realize that God is raising up modern-day Daniels with a heart for transforming communities? Daniel worked with the government of his day and put Humpty Dumpty back together again. Daniel had more influence in Babylon than the king but never tried to be the king. Daniel changed, he adapted, he became relevant, he influenced and he prospered in Babylon. He had the wisdom to coexist rather than conform. He had favor with God and man. Daniel is the ultimate community transformer. The transformation of that community was not just "in the Spirit" but real and tangible. The Word became flesh and dwelt in the neighborhood.

How did Daniel do it? The answer is simple. He lived by a set of core values that enabled him to reach Babylon, have passport into Babylon and create "Daniel's church." Daniel's "church" was the whole community, not just a small group of people. Listed below are some core values of Daniel, as well as the corresponding Bible verses. In essence, these values summarize this whole chapter for us. Daniel was not "clueless in Babylon"! He had favor with God and favor in Babylon.

1. Daniel was a man of choice.

Daniel learned how to co-exist rather than conform. He knew his boundaries. He knew what he could and could not do for the sake of Babylon. In essence, he knew that if he compromised basic character values, it would be a detriment to both himself and Babylon.

> But Daniel made up his mind that he would not defile himself with the king's choice food or with the wine which he drank; so he sought permission from the commander of the officials that he might not defile himself.
>
> —Daniel 1:8

2. He was aware of Babylon.

Daniel knew the people, the values, the philosophies, and the culture of Babylon. He knew what strokes worked for what folks. He attended the University of Babylon to learn and become aware. If you do not understand your culture, you will never penetrate your culture. This is a far cry from the safety-oriented, fear-based church culture that is so prevalent today.

> Youths in whom was no defect, who were good-looking, showing intelligence in every branch of wisdom, endowed with understanding, and discerning knowledge, and who had ability for serving in the king's court; and he ordered him to teach them the literature and language of the Chaldeans.
>
> —Daniel 1:4

3. Daniel was relevant.

Daniel knew where the Babylonians were coming from. He spoke with and related to people in ways they could understand with wisdom and knowledge. He was well informed, up to date and wise. There was two-way communication.

> As for every matter of wisdom and understanding about which the king consulted them, he found them ten times better than all the magicians and conjurers who were in all his realm.
>
> —Daniel 1:20

4. Daniel was authentic.

Daniel did not play perfect. Daniel was not judgmental or "holier than thou." Daniel was not condescending or a man of war. Daniel was who he was. With Daniel, what you saw was what you got. He was real and transparent in the eyes of the Babylonians. Babylon, like the world today, was crying out for authenticity.

> Then these men said, "We will not find any ground of accusation against this Daniel unless we find it against him with regard to the law of his God."
>
> —Daniel 6:5

5. Daniel was not self-centered; he was community-centered.

Daniel was concerned about these Babylonians. He was even concerned about the king and the king's welfare. He did not hate the government; he honored the government. Daniel had a right to hate King Nebuchadnezzar. After all, this was the king who had separated him from his family, his friends, and his country. Yet, even with all this, he cared for the king.

Daniel was a bridge builder rather than a bridge burner. People respond to care and concern. People do not care how much you know until they know how much you care. Even when judgment was coming to the king, Daniel was compassionate. He could separate the person from the sin.

> Then Daniel, whose name is Belteshazzar, was appalled for a while as his thoughts alarmed him. The king responded and said, "Belteshazzar, do not let the dream or its interpretation alarm you." Belteshazzar answered and said, "My lord, if only the dream applied to those who hate you, and its interpretation to your adversaries!"
>
> —Daniel 4:19

6. Daniel was a person of prayer.

Remember the ingredient of the bended knee in making the cake? Just being good and concerned would not get Daniel a transformed community. Daniel got God involved through prayer. Prayer is essential in any community transformation initiative.

> Now when Daniel knew that the document was signed, he entered his house (now in his roof chamber he had windows open toward Jerusalem); and he continued kneeling on his knees three times a day, praying and giving thanks before his God, as he had been doing previously.
>
> —Daniel 6:10

7. Daniel spoke words of truth in difficult situations after the relationship was established.

Many years ago, a pastor taught me a truth that I have never forgotten: The ultimate change agent is truth spoken in the context of a loving relationship.

If you are going to tell a government official something that will be hard to swallow, you had better have a relationship built first. In other words, do not drive a ten-ton truck over a two-ton bridge. It is destructive to everyone. Belteshazzar did not reject Daniel because he had a relationship with Daniel. The truth with no relationship creates a disconnect. The Church will not influence the government or other spheres of influence in the community without establishing relationships first. Then, after the relationship is established, the Church can talk truthfully.

> Yet you, his son, Belteshazzar, have not humbled your heart, even though you knew all this.
>
> —Daniel 5:22

8. Daniel was persistent and consistent.

It takes time to reach and transform a community. Community transformation is not an event; it is a process. Church unity takes time. Effective and informed intercession takes time. Finding works in such a way that catch the attention of the community takes time. Just as it is said in the book of Daniel, Satan will seek to wear down the "saints of the Highest One." In 99.9 percent of the cases, real, tangible, and lasting community transformation will not be instantaneous.

> And he will speak out against the Most High and wear down the saints of the Highest One, and he will intend to make alterations in times and in law; and they will be given into his hand for a time, times, and half a time.
>
> —Daniel 7:25

9. Daniel found ways to bring God into the conversation.

That was a great value for Daniel and is a great value for the church today. Look for opportunities to testify, to proclaim or to bring God into your conversation. Daniel showed to Babylonians how God could answer their greatest questions and meet their greatest needs.

> Daniel answered before the king and said, "As for the mystery about which the king has inquired, neither wise men, conjurers, magicians, nor diviners are able to declare it to the king. However, there is a God in heaven who reveals mysteries, and He has made known to King Nebuchadnezzar what will take place in

> the latter days. This was your dream and the visions in your mind while on your bed."
>
> —DANIEL 2:27–28

10. Life-and-death first, right-or-wrong second.

Look at the verse below. The king wanted Arioch to destroy the wise men of Babylon, but Daniel interceded on their behalf. His response to the king was not to kill them. Most people in today's church would see these wise men as magicians, witches and the enemy. Daniel saw them as people. He lived and operated by the principle of "mercy triumphs over judgment" (James 2:13), and "the kindness of God leads you to repentance" (Rom. 2:4). Daniel knew that even the wise men could be redeemed after they experienced the kindness of the Lord. Daniel did not "right or wrong" them, he "life and deathed" them.

> Therefore, Daniel went in to Arioch, whom the king had appointed to destroy the wise men of Babylon; he went and spoke to him as follows: "Do not destroy the wise men of Babylon! Take me into the king's presence, and I will declare the interpretation to the king."
>
> —DANIEL 2:24

11. Daniel had team support—a mini-church.

Daniel also had friends he could talk to from Jerusalem. He was not the Lone Ranger. He had a team. He had accountability. He had people of refreshment. He had a church imbedded in the community that was not adversarial to the community. He was like Peter and John who "went to their own companions" after they ministered in an unfriendly community. It takes a community of churches to reach a community of people. *A* church will not transform a community, but *the* church can.

> And the king talked with them, and out of them all not one was found like Daniel, Hananiah, Mishael and Azariah; so they entered the king's personal service.
>
> —DANIEL 1:19

Are Those in the Church Willing? Are Those in the Church Ready?

I hope the application of this chapter is evident to you. Here are some questions that you need to ask yourself or your church:

- Are we ready to give the church back to the community?
- How are we similar to Daniel?
- What can we do to be more aware of our community?
- What can we do to be more relevant in our ministry?
- How can we build a bridge and with whom?
- Do we have a deep concern or burdened heart for the community?
- Are we authentic? Are we what we appear to be?
- Will we change, or "ostrich"?

Remember, impression without expression leads to depression!

Chapter 13

Innovative Disruption—In the Nick of Time: *The Principle of Spiritual Entrepreneurialism*

You will never possess what you are unwilling to pursue. Jesus knew this. He did not set up a throne in the middle of each city and say, "This is my palace. This is the only place you can see me." He went to the market place. He went to the boats of fishermen. He went to the homes of the people. He went everywhere. He "went through the towns, preaching the gospel, and healing everywhere."

—Mike Murdock

I love that term: *spiritual entrepreneurialism*. This is entrepreneurialism with a purpose. It is holistic. It is favor with God and man. It is both spiritual and natural. It is on earth as it is in heaven. This concept reflects who Jesus was on earth. Jesus started a whole new movement meant to solve Earth's problems. He was not status quo or static. Jesus was dynamic. Jesus was proactive. Jesus was entrepreneurial. He did not just talk the talk; He walked the walk.

Caring is good—doing something is better. Doing something strategically is even better. Jesus' life-and-death core value caused him to be an Innovative Disruptor and in the nick of time. He could do no less. His core values determined His actions and behavior, not others' inaction or behaviors.

The essence of community transformation is about making communities better both spiritually and naturally. Jesus proactively changed communities spiritually and naturally. He realized natural men needed to see real and tangible ministry, whether by signs and wonders or bandaging up a man by the road. Natural men needed practical teaching brought to them in ways they could understand.

Jesus proactively and innovatively connected the message with the audience. His teachings were not merely academic. They were strategic, innovative, creative and effective. He was sensitive to both God and men and had favor with God and man. He was aware and focused. Jesus was proactively looking for opportunities that would reach the heart of the community. He realized the importance of the church/community connection. Community transformation comes from addressing real problems in the community in proactive and creative ways. Community transformation is more of an entrepreneurial initiative that is about redeeming and lifting the people in a community.

The word *entrepreneur* means one who owns, organizes, manages, and assumes the risk of a business or enterprise. It comes from a derivative of the French word for undertaker. So an entrepreneur undertakes a business, cause, or enterprise. The dictionary uses words like promoter, broker, intercessor, intermediary, mediator, or middleman to describe the entrepreneur. An entrepreneur owns, launches, manages, and assumes the risks of a venture.

Using this definition of entrepreneur, I see all five of the community spheres represented. I see a complete Humpty Dumpty, not just one or two parts of Humpty Dumpty. I see intercessors involved, managers involved, mediators involved, and brokers proactively involved in a strategic alliance for the sake of the community.

Isolate or Incarnate?

The needs and problems in today's communities require action by the Church and other community spheres of influence. We need some innovative disruption in the nick of time. We need to be proactive. Now is not the time to isolate, now is the time to incarnate. The Word needs to become flesh and move into the neighborhood.

Jesus did not just stay in heaven and "isolate." Earth did not come to heaven. Heaven came to Earth. Canaan did not come to Abram. Abram had to go to Canaan. Ninevah did not come to Jonah. Jonah reluctantly went to Ninevah. The Promised Land did not come to Joshua. Joshua had to go to the Promised Land. The woman with the issue of blood pressed through the crowd to touch Jesus, not vice versa. The Queen of the South came to Solomon, not vice versa. Talk about proactive!

The apostolic concept of "sent ones" means the Church is sent. "Sent" means proactive, moving, dynamic, entrepreneurial and motivated. The Church is never fully alive until it becomes a proactive sphere of influence in the community. Unfortunately, in much of today's church culture the church is waiting for "Canaan" to come to it. Many in today's churches have become experts in justifying isolation and inaction. The endless prayer meetings, committees, feasibility studies and doctrine studies have only served to make the community worse. As I noted earlier, there are "Mary" times and there are "Martha" times. This moment in history is a "Martha" time, not a "Mary" time. That is why God is activating apostolic ministry once again. It is time to be sent, not to talk, do sermons or pray about being sent. There came a time when Abram went to Canaan. Canaan was not going to come to him.

Permission to Be Entrepreneurial

Remember the woman who sought me out in Wellington, New Zealand? Remember what she said after my message at Pastor Mike Knott's conference? She said, "You have given me permission to be entrepreneurial."

What did she mean by this? She was an entrepreneurial person in a non-entrepreneurial ethos or church ethos. Remember, church ethos has been mostly determined by the office of the teacher. Remember the chart on page 133? In most cases, the apostle is the most entrepreneurial of the five offices of the Church. The teacher tends to be the least entrepreneurial office of the five offices. As apostolic ministry and mindset is restored in the Church, entrepreneurialism will increase. Entrepreneurialism is an essential, enabling core value in the transformation of people and communities. The Church was called to go to the community, not the community to the Church. You cannot have community transformation and isolation at the same time. Otherwise, you are the Kenyan man trying to win the Olympic marathon without practicing. The core value of isolationism disables community transformation every time.

Take a look at the scarcity and abundance paradigms. Which one of these paradigms will enable community transformation and which one will disable community transformation? These paradigms have been adapted from the book *The Seven Habits of Highly Effective People* by Stephen Covey.[1]

Scarcity	Abundance
Defense	Offense
Maintain	Create
Escape Loss	Pursue Vision
Reactive	Proactive
Guard/protect	Risk/opportunity
Gifts contained	Gifts released
Stagnation	Multiplication
Paralyzed	Fluid/dynamic
Narrow/closed	Wide/open
Win-lose	Win-win
Independence	Interdependence

Which of these two paradigms reflects an apostolic ethos? Which one reflects a teacher-based ethos? I think it is obvious that the apostolic-based ethos is much more conducive to community transformation than the teacher-based traditional church ethos. As I stated earlier, the Church must shift from a teacher-based traditional church ethos to a more apostolic ethos if we truly want real, tangible, and lasting community transformation. I repeat my earlier assertion: The teachers are not the problem. What the teachers are teaching is the problem.

In leading my business and pastoring my church, I frequently explained to leadership that 80 percent of the time we wanted to be on the "abundance" side of the chart. However, at times we would need to use discretion and function on the chart's "scarcity" side. We understood that it was not an either/or but a both/and. We also understood that in order to be successful and accomplish our mission, we needed to practice many more abundance factors than scarcity factors.

DISCONNECT OR RECONNECT?

The effectiveness of community transformation initiatives depends upon operating from the abundance paradigm. That is what I love about New Zealand. Most Kiwis are entrepreneurs and initiators, and have learned to do much with limited resources. Many Kiwis appear conservative outwardly, but on the inside are "raging" entrepreneurs.

America is similar. I recently read a study that said 78 percent of Americans saw the glass as "half full." The study went on to say that only 18 percent saw "the glass as half empty." The rest were undecided. Many Americans will be reading this book, so let me make an observation on the Church's ministry in America. How does the Church expect to be relevant, have real influence and transform communities if the Church operates by the scarcity paradigm derived from the church-centric teacher ethos? How can such a negative way of looking at things communicate with a culture than is 78 percent positive? The Church seems to be trying to conform proactive, positive entrepreneurial people into defensive, reactive and negative people.

The same holds true for many other nations. How can the Church affect other community spheres of influence that tend to be positive in nature if the Church is negative in nature? The melancholy attitude and outlook frequently disqualifies the Church from real influence in the community.

It is no wonder the positive but realistic "can do" churches ministering in relevant ways are so successful in the United States. They have connected the message with the audience. They have recognized culture and how culture plays into communication. They have incarnated rather than isolated. They have adopted an apostolic ethos that enables influence in the community. They have adopted the abundance-paradigm core value and are on their way to real, tangible, and lasting community transformation. They are taking the right steps for their desired outcome. They will have a passport into their community.

Community Reformers

So we see that entrepreneurialism can be spiritual but must manifest itself in the natural. In order to redefine the Church in the eyes of the community and community spheres of influence, the Church must have relevant words backed by relevant works. The Church has the wisdom to be a problem solver rather than a problem maker. The Church was called to be innovative in problem solving and disruptive to the status quo. The community is waiting for innovative disruptions in the social, political, and family problems in today's world. Churches that are alert to these needs will be drawn to them. Nature abhors a vacuum. God is raising up community reformers who will see communities transformed before their eyes in the nick of time.

I originally thought I would name this chapter "Innovative Disruption." However, my daughter Kristin suggested something better. She said, "Why do not you call the chapter 'Innovative Disruption—in the Nick of Time'? That is really the issue."

Kristin is right. We are in a crucial time for our communities. Community reformers have a sense of timing and see the urgency of the situation. When opportunities present themselves, especially with the other spheres of influence, the Church had better be ready. The Church must be ambassadorial, and not act like a bunch of generals. The superior attitude will disable us. A servant attitude will take us much further in the community than the know-it-all attitude.

Community reformers know what communities respond to—solved problems, reduced crime, and a positive attitude in the community. Community reformers know that the Peeping Toms of the community are looking for good works in such a way that the community sees the Church meeting these needs and responds positively and appreciatively toward God. (See Matthew 5:16). This is what Pastor Greg Brown of the Skyway Church in Glendale, Arizona, calls social evangelism. In other words, the Church can combine meeting social needs, issues and concerns with evangelism. That is called favor with God and favor with men. It is redemptive relevancy.

My friend Hal Sacks of the Bridgebuilders network in the Phoenix, Arizona, area addresses this issue by saying that many have left "social-concern" churches and gone into "spiritual" churches. In other words, social-concern churches focus mainly on meeting social needs and issues, but important spiritual issues are not addressed or considered important. In an effort to learn about important spiritual issues, some members have transferred to "spiritual" churches. These "spiritual" churches, however, tend to be just as weak regarding social issues and concerns as the social-concern churches are in spiritual matters. The pendulum swings to the extremes on both sides, and so typically do the churches and their membership.

Community transformation requires that both worlds integrate. It is not an either/or; it is a both/and. One without the other is incomplete. The social without the spiritual is "favor with man." The spiritual without the social is "favor with God." Both mentalities are incomplete.

Remember, Jesus had favor with God and with man. The Word became flesh and dwelt among us. Community transformation is "on earth as it is in heaven" (Matt. 6:10). Community reformers understand this, and frankly it is just in the nick of time!

The combining of these two worlds is a great innovative disruption to the lives of church-centric people. There is a church/community connection that cannot be denied. Fight against this principle and you always lose. However, the biggest loser is the community.

Redemptive Innovations

God's heart is for these innovative disruptions in the nick of time to be redemptive innovations in the nick of time. This is not disruption for the sale of disruption but disruption for the sake of redemption. Redemptive innovations are purpose-driven; that is, these works in the community meet the needs, concerns and issues of the community in a relevant and redemptive way. These works are entrepreneurial where the church and other community spheres of influence meet crucial needs in the community. These works are strategic for both the church and the community. They have an objective that is achievable and recognizable as making a positive change in the community.

These works do not come about by luck. They happen through a desire to be a problem solver. If you want to be a problem solver in your community, go ask the mayor of your city, the school superintendent, or a business within your community how you can help. Remember, a servant will go where theology will not. Go with a servant attitude. Go with a spirit of cooperation. The result will be needs that are met, connections with government, business and other spheres of influence, a redefined church, and people glorifying God.

But it takes a strategy to do this.

My friend Grady Daniels, a retired military man, wrote a short description on objectives and strategies that he calls "Military 101." We could all benefit from what Grady has written here:

> Objective (At the highest levels, this is sometimes called Grand Strategy): What it is that you ultimately want.
>
> Strategy is the art of picking the big-picture way of obtaining your objective.
>
> Operational Art is choosing and organizing your campaigns so that they make sense and work together towards the objective and in support of your strategy.
>
> A campaign is a series of battles aimed at a specific part of the objective.
>
> Tactics is the art of winning a battle.
>
> A Battle is simply the fight you are engaged in at the moment.
>
> Now, there is nothing esoteric or arcane about any of this. Observe:
>
> Objective: Happy wife.

Strategy: Show your wife a wonderful time on your anniversary.

Operational Art: Find a good jeweler for that nice tennis bracelet you know she wants. Find a good florist in the neighborhood. Remember the name of that posh restaurant your wife has always wanted to go to (if you cannot remember, ask your kids).

Campaign: Go to the jeweler, get her a new diamond tennis bracelet, pick up roses on the way home, then take her to dinner at the posh restaurant. In that order. Going to the jeweler at 11 p.m. after dinner will not do at all, and you will not look good.

Tactics: Be sure the car has gas. Have a clean suit ready. Leave early/do not be late. Avoid the accident (that is happening just ahead of you) at the next intersection. Know what time the jeweler closes, and be there before closing. Ditto the florist. Buy roses (get more than one). Brush teeth. Be charming.

Battle: Put all of your tactics to work to win all the little battles on the way to your objective.

Here are two more strategies to consider:

Focus: Attention to what you are doing now.

Awareness: Attention to things outside the direct plan that may impact it.

Here are examples of focus and awareness that may occur at any given point in the campaign on the way to your objective of the Happy Wife:

Focus: Stick to the plan. Talk football after work another day.

Awareness: On the way to pick up your wife, do not forget to stop when the police car in front of you stops, too.

All things considered, in the end, if you worked your plan right: Voilà! A happy wife!

Obviously, there may be intermediate objectives, concurrent campaigns, supporting operations and such throughout the plan, but you get the idea. Get a strategy!

Do not just do something without a plan. Hope is not a strategy. It will take time, effort, prayer, cooperation, money, and manpower to shift your community. Find a need and meet it strategically for everyone concerned.

The Incarnation of Spiritual Entrepreneurialism

Chapter 12 introduced the principle and power of redemptive relevancy. This chapter presents the principle and power of redemptive innovations. These are relevant words backed up by relevant works. The works are "out of the box" innovations to solve problems in the community.

Because the Church tends to be verbal rather than incarnational (Remember, incarnationally challenged?), I asked leaders from around the world write about real and tangible ministry in their countries or communities. Following are a few examples of some very creative, entrepreneurial and innovative ways that churches are disrupting the works of evil in their communities. These works have created favor with God and man. I realize that many of you reading this book have your own redemptive stories to tell. To you I say, keep up the good work.

Example 1: The "Samaritan strategy" for Uganda: police appreciation day in Kampala

Dateline: Kampala, Uganda

As a modern church, we've spent a lot of time in recent years on the first part of Ephesians 4:11, arguing over who or what is a real apostle, a real prophet, etc., and not nearly enough of our energy on verse 12:

> It as he who gave some to be apostles, some to be prophets, some to be evangelists, and some to be pastors and teachers, to prepare God's people for works of service, so that the body of Christ may be built up.
>
> —Ephesians 4:11–12, NIV

In 1998 some of the staff from Kampala Pentecostal Church (KPC), Kampala, Uganda, received teaching on Wholistic Ministry and Biblical Worldview through a Samaritan Strategy/Discipling Nations Alliance Vision Conference. The church leadership had already been moving toward more "doing" in their church, and the teaching on the four areas of how Jesus grew (in wisdom, physically, spiritually, and socially) from Luke 2:52 seemed to resonate with them. Already, the church had pioneered a ministry to AIDS orphans in Uganda, and their church had given birth to the Watoto Childcare Ministries. Still, the Lord seemed to be moving them toward being agents of reconciliation in other, simple-yet-practical ways in their community.

Seven members of one small cell group at KPC were middle-aged Christian women who had known one another since their primary school days. Together, they learned of "Seed Projects," small, manageable demonstrations of the love of God to their community. After prayerful consideration, the seven of them decided to form "Harmony," a group with a mission to counsel and bring godly encouragement those in the public sector in Kampala—namely, the police.

In order to appreciate the task ahead, one must consider that only a few short years ago Uganda was ruled by the brutal, dictatorial regimes of Idi Amin and of Milton Obote. Life in Uganda under these men was difficult and often in question; gunfire echoed in the streets day after day, in daylight or after dark, and travelers were—more often than not—accosted en route from one village to another and robbed, beaten, and/or killed. The police were generally known to be untrustworthy, and they were the last people to whom the populace would turn for help. But, to seven middle-aged Christian women, one immediate way to demonstrate the love of God and to disciple their community was to hold a historic event: Police Appreciation Day.

After a year of planning, which involved meeting with the inspector general of police and with numerous, potential business sponsors, Police Appreciation Day was held on February 23, 2003. A central Kampala city park was the stage, and tents were erected to hold the hundreds of chairs needed to seat the guests of honor, the Uganda police. In attendance as well were thousands of curious citizens alongside dignitaries from the Uganda Parliament, the city government and businesses. The US Ambassador to Uganda, Jimmy Kolker, was the keynote speaker. Thousands of people turned out to witness a small group of women—who, by this time, had rallied many parts of the community in Kampala—in the act of "catching the police doing something right." They had dignitaries, luminaries, and plain-old average citizens recount acts of heroism, of selflessness, and of police doing things to ensure the safety and development of their communities all in the course of doing their jobs. The inspector general reiterated his commitment to fighting corruption within the department, and entreated the public to help him as well—noting that corruption occurred not only when an officer accepted a bribe, but also when a citizen offered one. One citizen noted that the police immediately responded and, within 24 hours, found the vehicle from which she had been carjacked at gunpoint. The thank you her harrowing story included was heartfelt and it moved the crowed to an awestricken silence.

Some local businesses had donated their wares as thank yous—dishes and gift certificates. A few businesses were bold enough to put up their advertising banners in the park. Given the climate toward the police, the reports were that all of these businesses understood they were taking a risk in putting their "stamp of approval" on such an unseemly event—appreciating the "foundation of corruption" in Uganda.

Story after story, hour after hour, these seven Christian women watched what they had been the catalyst for: discipling a nation. Teaching others to do what Jesus had taught them to do—to love their neighbors. Their inspiration had been to do something small—small, but very significant. They listened to what the Holy Spirit was saying to them, and they acted upon it, zealous for good works:

> They said, "Thank you, Police." And they really meant it.
>
> After the event, police and citizens alike were keen to recount their feelings about the day. The police officers we encountered were, without exception, beaming with pride, stunned by the outpouring of affection and appreciation. This, after they had been subject for years to ridicule and belittlement by their communities and written off as unredeemable by the citizenry of their nation. The onlookers, too, were amazed. No one had ever expected to

see other Ugandans actually appreciating the police. After hearing the stories of heroism and of duty, however, the citizens we spoke with were unanimous in their evaluation of the event, of the seed these women planted: Basic kindness could certainly change Uganda for the better. Many noted that they would now help the police to do a better job, knowing that the police were really trying.

This is not to say that Uganda's problems with police corruption are resolved. On the contrary. What has changed, however, is the perception on the part of both the police and of the people. Many departed with an understanding that, in Uganda, the "same old, same old" would never satisfy again. They are not satisfied with the status quo, and they now understand that they have the power to change it for the better.

Harmony is now making plans to hold similar "Appreciation Days" in the near future—one for the military, and one for (no kidding) taxi drivers. Both groups are generally seen as being ongoing civic troublemakers. But, instead of always "bashing" them, the ladies of Harmony and the people of Kampala Pentecostal Church will be busying themselves "catching them doing something right," adopting the "Samaritan Strategy" for Uganda. They have seen what God can do through the power of kindness.

—Tom Polsin, Harvest Foundation

Example 2: Influencing influencers

Dateline: Drayton Valley, Canada

Seven years ago we started our intercessory prayer teams. We applied Jeremiah 1 to our city. It says, "Before you were born I set you apart" with a purpose and the gifting to carry out God's purposes. We believe the Lord has a purpose for us as individuals, for our church (if it really is born of God) and for our city. We started to look for the city's redemptive purpose. It took four years of prayer and research for us to trace the cycles of community dynamics back to a point of origin. When we saw how the cycles started, we went before the Lord and asked Him to return our community to its redemptive purpose that He had from the beginning.

He had shown us that our heavy industry/resource-based community was to be a training center. We thought this was the opposite of what we had become, but we asked the Lord to anoint us as we give our lives to restore our community to His plan and purpose. Within days of this prophetic act, I was invited to sit on our mayor's advisory board. At the first meeting I attended, our mayor (who is of a Muslim faith) sat down and said that he and our council had just determined we needed to move from being a resource-based community to a training base. The spiritual climate of our community shifted so much that even the secular people noticed the change.

That same year one of our prayer teams (called "Mountain Movers") that walks every street every year proclaimed that we would have a drug-free community. They said we just were not going to tolerate it here! Within days of completing the prayer walking, our mayor made a public statement that he had chosen the platform for the upcoming elections. He said we are going to have a drug free community! "Why?" I asked him. "Are we really worse than any other heavy industry community?" He thought for a few minutes and then said no, the statistics are about the same but, "We just are not going to tolerate it here!"

There are many other tangible changes that have taken place because of the prayer ministry but I will share just one more. In March 2001, a prophet spoke over my life and said, "This year the Lord is going to place something into your hands that is bigger than our community."

In June I wrote a six-point core value system for our twenty-five-year strategy to pastor our city. My goal was to give us a common value system we could work on with all sectors and faiths. We needed some common ground or common principles to work from. These core values were not elaborate or deep spiritual revelations. They just reflected the core values of any community, such as family development or education, quality of life and so on.

Later that month, we had a ministerial luncheon meeting with our mayor at which I gave him a copy of my core value idea. About an hour after this meeting I got a call form the mayor's office and he said he had something for me and wanted to bring it by my office. He came into my office and put into my hands a program he had found called the International Association of Character Cities. This is a citywide program that promotes forty-nine Bible-based character qualities. (Remember, our mayor is a Muslim, and our town manager is East Indian). He asked if I would look into this program and see if it was what I was looking for.

In 2002 Drayton Valley became Canada's First Character City. We are still in the process of implementation, but it has opened the doors of relationship across the boundaries of politics, business, education and faith! If you are interested in this program, it is from the Character Training Institute on Oklahoma City. Tell them I told you to call. We are still in the process of transforming our community, but we have seen significant changes already. People are getting saved, churches are being blessed and the whole community is going forward into its redemptive purpose that the Lord had for it before it was even born!

—Gary Carter, Drayton Valley Word of Life Centre

Example 3: Coldwater Christmas

Dateline: Phoenix, Arizona, USA

Every year at Christmastime, many people feel compelled in their heart to help their fellow man. Most people want to participate in the process, not just donate funds. These uncommon acts of love spring up throughout cities and towns each year, helping the less fortunate find relief from the hardships of life. The story of Coldwater Christmas comes from a setting just like this.

In the West Valley of the Greater Phoenix area, several groups were working independently of one another trying to make a difference in the lives of the poor. Some groups were led by local businesses, local churches, schools, and even the city. Each group worked independently, not knowing the dates and locations of others' activities unless they happened upon each other.

In 2000, that is what happened, and I felt compelled to talk to these leaders about working together and doing something far greater together than anything we were able to do individually. This message was met with great excitement and acceptance, and we all agreed that the following year, 2001, would be a Christmas party for the poor like they have never witnessed before. We reserved the largest park in the community, Coldwater Park, only a short distance from the poorest of the poor in our city.

The word went out to the local high schools, the business community, churches, and our city government. We created a steering team that met weekly to pool our ideas, establish leadership, design our layout for the event and pray to meet our city's needs. We put the word out through local agencies and prepared to love our city.

As the day started, a St. Mary's Food Bank truck rolled out with twenty thousand pounds of food. The tables were manned with people who smiled and loved each one who walked through the line. Local high school lettermen in football and wrestling carried food boxes to the recipients' cars. In less than two hours, the food was distributed to more than three hundred families who were assured to have provisions in their homes for that week.

The children and parents were welcome to come and enjoy a special free Christmas party planned just for them. There were booths for face painting done by the caring hands of teenage artists, and there were booths for children to creatively decorate cookies. The cold morning made the hot cider especially appealing. It was strategically placed next to fifteen tons of snow we trucked in for the kids to play in! A small train gave kids rides around the park, while the older ones took turns climbing a rock wall. In the middle of it all was a mechanical bull, and everyone tried to stay on!

Praise teams and soloists played music all morning. The main stage held events like break dancing for the kids, and a power team demonstration told them about the power of Jesus Christ. The Bible and prayer booth never lacked a line. While the kids needed to have fun, their parents recognized that they had spiritual needs. This was a day for meeting both. Finally the main event brought everyone together at one place: the high wire act of Tino Wallenda. As everyone looked up at the thirty-foot wire, Tino told the crowd about Jesus, who was born as a man and came to save us from our sins. Tino led the people in the sinner's prayer while standing on a chair balanced on the wire.

Once the show was over, we began to give out gifts. We had huge covered wagons filled with presents and toys. Each wagon was set up for specific age groups. The children waited in line with hopeful anticipation. They each wanted that special toy. By God's grace they all received something far more special than they had expected. One-year-olds held by their loving mothers picked out stuffed toys. Eighteen-year-olds picked out cool remote-controlled cars. Everyone received a high-quality present. The smiles on the children were outdone only by the smiles on the volunteers giving out the gifts.

More than one hundred volunteers joined together to provide 1,500 toys for children. More than three thousand people came out to experience a wonderful morning of joy, love and laughter. It was gratifying to see the variety of folks who pulled together to help our brothers and sisters in need. I was personally filled with a great sense of satisfaction. The Christian volunteers from our church worked alongside people who did not attend church. What we all accomplished together was far more successful than anything we could have done separately. Together we celebrated the birth of Christ in a way that made people's lives better. On that day, the Church went to the people.

We now hold this event annually. It is officially recognized by the City of Avondale as The Community Christmas Party. We all agree this is one way that working together is far more effective than working alone.

This single event designed to spread love is now connecting these same groups for other purposes. The City of Avondale has requested Nick Hill, one of Skyway Church's staff pastors, to join in on the City Revitalization Board. The Church is being viewed as a helpful resource for bringing volunteers and ideas to improve the city. Our actions are now speaking louder than our words, and the community is starting to listen.

—Greg Brown, Senior Pastor, Skyway Church of the West Valley

Example 4: The church of youth and doctors

Dateline: Wellington, New Zealand

We are a church of many nations in the capital city of New Zealand. There is excellent unity among the churches here, and we have some powerful times of prayer together with Members of Parliament in the Government Building, with University Christian groups on campus, and around the various church centers in the city. Our vision as a church is to make Jesus known,

From the Nations in the Capital

To the Nations of the World

We hope to do so by strategic prayer, ministries and partnerships—intelligent fire!

Partnership

One of the benefits of longevity in ministry is the opportunity to gain respect and then build partnerships with agencies in the local community. This has resulted in partnerships with police, schools, university, health agencies, museums trust, and with the local council.

Our young people have established an annual citywide concert featuring Christian artists from the Wellington Region. Last year the city council, having seen both the quality and the impact of these events, asked us to run a similar event for them, featuring young talent from the area. They offered $10,000 in funding for the event. On learning of this, we made it a matter of prayer as we felt that a greater amount would enable us to do a better job. Our Young People's leader, Salote, put together the programme and presented it to the council. They decided that we would need at least $20,000!

The event was a huge success, and they were very impressed with the way it was so professionally run and was totally problem-free.

This year we planned a similar event, but with a desire to preach the gospel and see young people saved. Salote told the council of our plan, and said that we wanted to see a permanent change in young people's lives and that we would not accept any funding if we were not able to preach the gospel. They went away to think about it, but came back with a positive response. So this year the council funded our outreach—how about that! Numbers of young people gave their lives to Jesus.

Capital Care Health: Vision

Capital Care is a Pro-life Medical Centre with a Vision to provide Christian-based Health Care and Social Services to people who are not already adequately catered for by existing services, whether because of religious persuasion, socio-economic status, difficulty with English, or otherwise.

Story

In response to a vision given to the senior minister, a meeting of interested parties, on August 10, 1994, decided that the initial focus would be on establishing a crisis pregnancy centre and an elderly support service. Health Check programmes were also planned. Our Practice Nurse/Pregnancy Counsellor commenced in May 1995, along with several trained volunteers.

September of that year was a significant month with the first baby saved from abortion, the first refugee contact and the first off-site clinic for the elderly. Soon after, we received our first abusive phone call! The Centre was able to expand from the original one room/one phone/one desk and although simpler than it is now, we thought our Centre magnificent. Member of Parliament, Whetu Tirikatene-Sullivan officially opened it in December 1995.

We had only part-time doctors until Dr. Max Stevenson commenced full-time practice in July 1997. The health centre is now led by Dr. Samantha Murton, with several thousand non-churched, (80 percent), and Christian patients visiting our doctors, nurses and other services.

We still have our pregnancy focus with antenatal care and many happy births. YES! As far as our crisis-pregnancy counselling is concerned we have seen hundreds of babies saved who would otherwise have been aborted. We are networking with other pro-life groups in Wellington. Our Health Centre is now a hub of activity, outreach and blessing. We give thanks to the Lord for this.

We have a vision for more medical centres like this to be launched, and so far have had two requests to this end. Also we would like to see medical teams serving not only in our city, but nationwide and overseas.

We would like to continue with our efforts along with *other pro-life agencies* to influence change in current abortion laws and practice. The centre is a gateway of blessing into people's lives, a bridge into the community, and a platform to speak into issues of health and welfare in the nation.

So much has happened. We have so much potential. We give our wonderful God all the praise and all the glory and thank so many who have supported us.

—Mike Knott, Elim International Christian Church

Example 5: City transformation involves the total church

Dateline: Sydney and Bendigo, Australia

In Australia the move towards community transformation has been facilitated in many places by the ministry of the Australian Prayer Network. The strategy used by this ministry in facilitating a citywide initiative amongst the churches is to appoint a Servant Leadership Team that will be responsible, under the authority of the city pastors, for facilitating the vision and strategy that is given by God for their community.

In the early stages of this ministry, the Servant Leadership Team was made up exclusively of pastors. However, it was discovered that when the city is seen only through pastoral eyes it is confronted by the can's and cannot's peculiar to pastoral ministry. In other words, the view of the city is slanted toward what has worked or not worked in the past rather than gaining fresh insight into new strategies that could move the church and the city beyond the extent of their reach under old paradigms.

The understanding of the make-up of a city Servant Leadership Team has now expanded to take in not only pastoral leadership but a spread of Christian leaders representing the total life of the Church and the city. A typical team will now by made up of 50 percent pastors and 50 percent other ministry leaders representing men, women, youth, intercessors, business leaders and Christian leaders in the secular and governmental areas of the life of the city.

What they have found as a result of this is that a much more progressive view of the city is obtained and the ministry to the city and strategy developed by the Servant Leadership Team is more widely representative of a total Church view and not that solely from the pastoral viewpoint.

BENDIGO, AUSTRALIA

The Church in the city of Bendigo, Australia, was confronted with the collapse of a Christian school in their city due to the misappropriation of a large sum of money by one of the board members of the school.

Some of the city intercessors were researching the history of their city and discovered that the demise of Christian schools in their city seemed to recur every twenty to thirty years throughout the 150-year history of the city. It was also noted that the demise was usually as a result of financial mismanagement or fraud/misappropriation of funds.

The pastors became interested and asked for research to be done back to the foundations of the city in an endeavour to find the root cause of this recurring problem. After some weeks of research, the intercessors reported that they had located a newspaper editorial some 150 years old, which stated, "The Church should be held to account by the Government for the misappropriation of public funds given to them by the Government to assist with the building of Christian schools in their city but which they instead had used to build their own Churches."

This gave a clue as to an original sin that had never been dealt with that the enemy could have been using against the Christian school system ever since, and which was again manifesting before their very eyes. The pastors gathered for a day of prayer to seek the face of God on the problem and felt the Lord challenging them to deal with the issue by repenting to the Government for the sin committed by the Church leaders 150 years ago. They felt also there needed to be some form of restitution for the funds misappropriated.

After struggling as to how much the restitution should be, they remembered that a team of intercessors had taken up an offering when they had been praying at the school some weeks before and had given it to the pastors for, at that stage, an unknown purpose. The Lord quickened to them that the small sum of $150 taken up was to be the token restitution they were to offer to the Government.

They made an appointment with the Minister for Education in their State Parliament and confessed to him the sin of the Church in previous generations. He accepted their repentance, forgave through absolving them of their responsibility for the misappropriation of funds and encouraged them to give the money they offered him to a local school to buy material for the school that could be used by disadvantaged students.

At the completion of this process, the Church firmly believes it has broken a curse over Christian education in their city that manifested each generation through financial disasters of various kinds that had been occurring ever since that original sin had taken place. The lesson learned was that the affairs of today can be affected by the sins of the past if they are ignored or not dealt with in a full and proper way.

I hope these ideas will help people understand issues related to City Transformation.

—Brian Pickering, National Coordinator, Australian Prayer Network

Example 6: The other Las Vegas

Dateline: Las Vegas, New Mexico

The first night of the conference our mayor, Henry Sanchez, was in attendance and immediately after you finished he came and apologized for not being able to show up the next day then said, "I want to see you in my office this week." That Thursday afternoon he takes me into his office and starts off by asking what does the church want to do for the city and my response was, you tell us what you want the church to do which led into his felt need, many elderly residents on fixed incomes have a hard time paying their utility bills in the winter and what could we do. So we wrote a letter to all the churches in our town inviting them to a meeting in the council chambers. The first week at least twelve people showed and the discussion started with the idea of taking up second offerings during our Sunday services which probably would not raise enough money or awareness. The final outcome was the Love Your Neighbor Fund, each church contributed to a fund to purchase envelopes addressed to the Salvation Army and a letter from the mayor that was added to every utility bill (eight thousand a month). In the first month we raised over $2,000 dollars and over fourteen churches and charitable organizations have partnered to make this happen. The city did not have to spend one penny to fund this initiative and many people from our churches helped Salvation Army interview applicants, keep the books, and meet with the committee to drive this project. Since then we have continued meeting and discussing other needs in our city. One Tuesday the local paper showed up and gave the Love Your Neighbor Fund front page coverage. Other outreaches that have developed since you were in town were:

Cleaning yards of our elderly residents keeping them in compliance with the local ordinance.

Meeting with the social department of Highlands University to start using graduate students as interns.

Our city helped host a Juvenile Justice Forum for youth at risk.

Partnering with the Salvation Army for their Christmas projects.

Responding to our Chief of Police to start a chaplaincy program. All this and more happened in less than ninety days after our Community Transformation Conference, what a return on our investment! Humpty Dumpty is coming together!

—Pastor Mark Saiz, Cornerstone Church

Example 7: 96744

Dateline: Kaneohe, Hawaii

Here is another example of a group of churches that got together and adopted the zip code they were located in that is unique. Talk about impacting a community! Read on as Pastor Rob Gross of the Mountain View Community Church gives us a brief story of what has happened in Kaneohe, Hawaii.

In the spring of 2003 I commissioned our church to begin praying daily for every student and faculty member of Kapunahala school-the elementary school where we gather every week to worship God. In order to accomplish this we acquired a copy of the school's year book and photo copied every page that had faces and names. Every member of our congregation then committed themselves during a commissioning service to pray five times a week for thirty people each (one page of faces/names). I explained to our people that each face and name represented a family of at least five to six people and that by praying for thirty people/page they were really praying for thirty families or 150 people each.

Later that year I felt led to form a pastoral team that would pastor the principal of our school. First, I asked her for an appointment. Second, I asked a key lay leader from another church who was already very involved with helping the school to join our team. I did this because this man had already earned, through countless acts of service, the respect of the principal and her administration. Third, I asked my personal church administrator if she would act as a liaison between the school and our church to receive prayer requests the school would ask for. And finally, I asked our key logistics guy if he would join the team to ensure that school requests for help such as school clean ups would be carried out quickly.

Finally, we all met with the school principal and what we learned was phenomenal. First she acknowledged that because of our prayers the school was prospering tremendously. These are a "few" of the things she said had happened to the school because of our prayers:

A colonel from the nearby marine corps base called to volunteer, for two years six hundred of his men for "anything" the school needed in terms of manpower for fix up projects. This was amazing because the Colonel had called eight other schools in the district to volunteer his help but only one school responded—Kapunahala.

The school received a $200,000 reading grant.

The school was vaulted from sixth place on a state waiting list to first to receive substantial funding for the overhaul of their aging computer system.

After the principal shared everything that was happening to her school she gave God all the credit—SHE IS NOT A BELIEVER (YET)! We then asked her what we could be praying for and she made three very simple requests:

For the health of her students (apparently the flu bug was hitting the school hard).

For students' test scores to go up in 2004.

For a member of her faculty who was struggling to get along with others.

So, we prayed for her and she was visibly touched. Following this meeting with her we forwarded her prayer requests to our two intercessory groups who have since been praying regularly for God to answer her requests. One of these groups meets "on" the campus once a week.

Rob writes on about some very real actions that the 96744 churches did in the community:

Twenty churches from across Oahu gave $11,000 to Castle High School last year, and you should have seen the look on the principal's face when presented with the check.

Our church helped fund along with another Kaneohe church a brand new batting cage for Castle High's baseball program. This year we are looking at footing the bill for brand new dugouts or possibly underwriting their end of the year awards banquet.

Remarkably, a year ago Castle High's varsity football team made it to the Hawaii state finals as a very strong chaplaincy team ministered to the boys on a weekly basis. The head coach received Christ and attributed his team's success to divine help. Castle had never been in the finals before. We even saw gifts of healing manifest regularly as we prayed for kids in the training room (many of the boys were healed).

This year Castle has had both boys and girls varsity soccer teams in first place. God has truly been touching Castle athletics. Now more of the coaches are requesting chaplains.

Amazingly, the head coach of the boys varsity team invited my wife and I to attend their daughter's birthday party and say the dinner blessing. Today, God has given me tremendous favor with this man, and I look forward to the coming baseball season.

Two years ago we gave $2,000 to Kaneohe Little League. This really opened doors with the entire Kaneohe baseball community which is very strong.

Last year after five hundred of us gathered to pray over the grounds of Castle High School, three "major" drug dealers were busted.

—Pastor Rob Gross,
Mountain View Community Church

All these true examples have one thing in common: These innovative disruptions come from leaders who see the community in a different way. They realize they are in a community for the benefit of the community. They realize the way they see the community is the way the community sees them. They understand the significant and strategic words of Jesus in Luke 6:38:

> Give, and it will be given to you; good measure, pressed down, shaken together, running over, they will pour into your lap. For by your standard of measure it will be measured to you in return.
>
> —Luke 6:38

Notice the last part of this verse: "For by your standard of measure it will be measured to you in return." In other words, whatever you give you get in return. If you honor the community, the community will honor you. If you ignore the community, the community will ignore you. If you are neutral toward the community, the community will be neutral toward you. If you demonize the community, the community will demonize you.

Recently, my friend Apostle John Kelly spoke with me about this principle. His concept was that whatever you dishonor, you will never have. If the Church honors the government like the apostle Peter suggested in 1 Peter 2:17, the honors open the possibility of the government honoring you. If you honor the community by serving the community, the community honors you. Actually, we see this concept at work in the Old Testament when the man of God spoke to Eli the priest. The problem was that Eli was honoring his very disobedient sons above God. The man of God declared in 1 Samuel 2:30:

> Therefore the Lord God of Israel declares, "I did indeed say that your house and the house of your father should walk before Me forever"; but now the Lord declares, "Far be it from Me—for those who honor Me I will honor, and those who despise Me will be lightly esteemed."
>
> —1 Samuel 2:30

If the Church lightly esteems the community that God has called it to serve, the Church will be lightly esteemed.

The above six examples show leaders who honor the community, honor the government, honor the police, honor other community spheres of influence, honor the poor and needy, and honor God. The honoring ethos they exhibit opens the gates of the community that the King of Glory may come in. These leaders see the community differently, think about the community differently, and pray about the community differently. Therefore, they serve the community differently and redemptively. They have wisdom. They have focus and awareness. They incarnate. They present the whole Church to the community. The life-and-death core value that drives their behaviors allows them to do no less.

Remember what Mike Murdock said at the beginning of this chapter? You will never possess what you are unwilling to pursue. The world needs more spiritual entrepreneurialism in the Church. The early Church consisted of innovative disrupters and spiritual entrepreneurs of that day. How about this day? I still believe and always will that if we can make the Church a little better, we can help the community to be a lot better. We will never possess what we are unwilling to pursue. The way we see the community is the way the community sees you!

Activating Spiritual Entrepreneurialism

How about you? Are you ready to see an entrepreneurial church? Are you ready to see a church with core values like I have been writing about? Are you ready to shed that teacher-only, church-centric ethos? Are you ready to get outside of the four walls? Are you ready to do the work of an evangelist rather than hide behind your gift or theology? Are you ready to get off the exercise bicycle and get on a real bike and go somewhere? Are you ready to do more than talk?

If you have been praying about this, let me give you a word of advice. The answer to your prayer is *you*. If you have been studying about this, the answer to your study is *you*. If you have been preaching about this, you answer your own altar call!

The timing is right, the harvest is ripe, doors are open, and the community is ready. Pray and clothe yourself with the spirit of entrepreneurialism both "naturally" and "spiritually." Put off the right-or-wrong-first ethos and put on the life-and-death-first ethos!

> *God, activate the spirit of entrepreneurialism in these wonderful readers and community transformers! God, give them the objectives, strategies, operational arts, and plans to transform communities and impact cities and nations!*

Chapter 14

GUESS WHO'S COMING TO DINNER?

The Principle of Stature and Influence: Positioning Christian Influencers Into Positions of Influence

Solomon is a type of Church, and the Queen of the South is a type of community sphere of influence. It took some time, but she realized there was something Solomon had that she needed. In these very unique days, the lack of wisdom and real answers to real problems will become increasingly apparent to all in the community. I believe the Church was called to have influence in the community through the vehicle of wisdom. The community has knowledge—what is needed is wisdom. The successful navigation of "storms" of problems on the "sea" of the community comes through wisdom. Therein lies a secret in real community transformation: God's wisdom was designed to be made known through the Church. Wisdom is the Church's contribution to the community and a pearl of great price. However, having wisdom and being in a position to influence the community through wisdom are two different things. To influence, the Church must be like Jesus and grow in stature with God and men.

—ED DELPH

> The Queen of the South shall rise up with this generation at the judgment and shall condemn it, because she came from the ends of the earth to hear the wisdom of Solomon; and behold, something greater than Solomon is here.
>
> —Matthew 12:42

> And Jesus kept increasing in wisdom and stature, and in favor with God and men.
>
> —Luke 2:52

Do you realize that every miracle started with a problem? Have you thought about that? Every solution started with something that needed solving. Every answer started with a question and every need met started with a need not met. In other words, it takes a problem to have a miracle. It takes a question to have any answer. It takes a need to bring a solution.

Remember Pastor Bruce Benge's statement from the introduction to this book: "There is a stronghold of opportunity in your community and I want you to take a strong hold of it." I believe the lack of wisdom in today's communities worldwide are causing more and more complex problems that cannot be solved by conventional knowledge. The prophet Daniel was certainly correct when he said in Daniel 12:4:

> But as for you, Daniel, conceal these words and seal up the book until the end of time; many will go back and forth, and knowledge will increase.
>
> —Daniel 12:4

Notice the end of the verse. He says many will go back and forth and *knowledge will increase.* That statement accurately describes the ethos of today's communities. People are overloaded with knowledge. This is the information and technology-explosion age, even in the remotest parts of the earth. This explosion of knowledge is fueled by the media/entertainment sphere of influence. Every incident on earth that is considered newsworthy is reported, with news media often making mountains out of molehills. *The problems in today's world and communities are constantly bombarding the community through the media or eye-gates of the community.* As a result, many are overwhelmed, overstimulated, and not prepared to cope with the problems of the day.

If people add those problems to their problems, their lives can become depressing and complex. Many have given up hope. There is an inability to cope. The more we try to be inclusive and diverse to a fault, the more problems we create. The more sensitive to an extreme we try to become, the less sensitive it seems we are to others. The more politically correct we try to be, the more politically incorrect we become. The community is beginning to see that knowledge and education alone will not make everything better. That is not an indictment on knowledge or education, but knowledge alone is not adequate to solve the problems we all want to see solved. In order to do that, we need wisdom. Lack of wisdom is creating a stronghold of opportunity for the Church that the Church had better take hold of. The Church's role in a community is primarily a wisdom-based contribution, not a knowledge-based contribution.

Innovative Wisdom in the Nick of Time

Remember, every solution starts with a problem. In the midst of the darkness of real problems and concerns comes the light of innovative and redemptive wisdom in the nick of time. This wisdom was never meant to control, it was meant to influence.

> And those who have insight will shine brightly like the brightness of the expanse of heaven, and those who lead the many to righteousness, like the stars forever and ever.
>
> —Daniel 12:3

The Community needs wisdom, and wisdom is a birthright of the Church.

> But by His doing you are in Christ Jesus, who became to us wisdom from God, and righteousness and sanctification, and redemption.
>
> —1 Corinthians 1:30

Jesus Christ became to us wisdom. The verse in Daniel 12:3 says in the midst of knowledge-oriented, educated, and fast-paced societies those who have wisdom will shine like the sun. That verse assumes that whoever has the wisdom will be in a position to use the wisdom. Daniel certainly was:

> The queen entered the banquet hall because of the words of the king and his nobles; the queen spoke and said, "O king, live forever! Do not let your thoughts alarm you or your face be pale. There is a man in your kingdom in whom is a spirit of the holy gods; and in the days of your father, illumination, insight, and wisdom like the wisdom of the gods were found in him. And King Nebuchadnezzar, your father, your father the king, appointed him chief of the magicians, conjurers, Chaldeans and diviners. This was because an extraordinary spirit, knowledge and insight, interpretation of dreams, explanation of enigmas, and solving of difficult problems were found in this Daniel, whom the king named Belteshazzar. Let Daniel now be summoned, and he will declare the interpretation."
>
> —DANIEL 5:10–12

Daniel had an extraordinary spirit that stood out among the crowd of magicians and soothsayers. His wisdom made him a person of influence in Babylon to the benefit of all in Babylon. The king recognized Daniel's gift of wisdom and accessed it. There were problems in Babylon that needed solving, and in the end wisdom solved them.

The same is true for our communities today. I believe that innovative wisdom will come through the Church in the nick of time for the benefit of all in the community. Pastor David Dishroon of the Tauranga Worship Centre in Tauranga, New Zealand, believes the key spiritual gifts in the Third Millennium will be the word of wisdom, the word of knowledge and the discerning of spirits.

Why would God feature these gifts at this time? The answer is simple: we need these three gifts the most in the context of the community. Remember, every miracle starts with a problem. Every solution starts with a problem that needs solving. "Daniel's church" has the wisdom and people of an extraordinary spirit embedded in the community.

Our communities need help, not condemnation. Our communities' leaders and community spheres of influence need wisdom, not war.

The Church is called to engage the community, not enrage the community. The Church's contribution of wisdom is absolutely essential to the destiny and purpose of the community. However, having wisdom and using wisdom are two different things. Let me say it this way: before the Church can use wisdom in the community, the Church had better have wisdom with itself. We had better have wisdom with the brothers so we can have wisdom with the "others."

Everybody Loves—Wisdom

I love word concepts that are positive and true. Wisdom is such a concept. It is a concept that most people in the community can accept as a noble attribute to have. Wisdom has not been politicized yet. Most politicians would still say they desire wisdom. Most business people and educators see wisdom as a noble virtue. Media representatives would have a hard time being critical of wisdom. Whether young or old, rich or poor, male or female, everyone loves wisdom.

What is wisdom? Wisdom is the proper *application* of knowledge through understanding. Wisdom implies awareness and focus. It sees the short and long-term effects of a decision. It looks to build, not destroy. Wisdom draws from experience and revelation and comes up with understanding. It is proactive, planned, and not reactionary.

Wisdom is building-oriented, and sees the big picture. It realizes you may have to choose your fights. It can integrate the both/and factors of life; it is primarily inductive rather than deductive. Wisdom is an apostolic virtue that enabled the early church to grow, prosper, and influence the community. It is a passport into the community.

If the Church comes to the community with Bible knowledge only, the result will be a disconnect from the community. The Church will appear arrogant, judgmental, and superior (1 Corinthians 8:1). The community needs help, not judgment. Wisdom allows the Church to "be shrewd as serpents, and innocent as doves" (Matt. 10:16). It allows the Church to contribute its part to a community, and to take a strong hold of the strongholds of opportunity in our community.

Wisdom engages the community, to enrage the community. Yes, there will be times when the Church cannot compromise but, let's be honest, those times are few and far between if the Church is wise. Just ask Daniel or Joseph! After all, Joseph's name means "he shall add wisdom." Daniel and Joseph were known for their wisdom, not their knowledge. They had wisdom about how to co-exist with and yet influence others in some very difficult situations. Pharaoh loved wisdom. So did Nebuchadnezzar. So does your community! Everyone loves wisdom.

The Three-Legged Stool: Wisdom, Understanding, and Knowledge

Let's look at the following verses:

> By wisdom a house is built, and by understanding it is established; and by knowledge the rooms are filled with all precious and pleasant riches.
>
> —Proverbs 24:3–4

I will use the analogy of a three-legged stool to show how wisdom, understanding, and knowledge work together:

- Knowledge is *What.*
- Understanding is *Why.*
- Wisdom is *How.*

All of the legs need to be present or the stool falls down. Proverbs 24:3 says that wisdom is the house. It is the place to which we want to get. It is the end, not the means to an end. It is the main course, not the appetizer. It is the tree of life, not the tree of knowledge. Wisdom changes your destiny; just ask Adam and Eve. Wisdom is the *how* to live up to your full potential. It is God's highest and utmost.

> How blessed is the man who finds wisdom, and the man who gains understanding.
>
> —Proverbs 3:13

> The beginning of wisdom is: acquire wisdom; and with all your acquiring, get understanding.
>
> —Proverbs 4:7

Wisdom Has Real Answers to Real Problems for Yourself and Others

Understanding is the "why" leg of the three legs. It is important to know why God gives a "what." Understanding is revelation power. Once we know why God gives a command, a truth, a principle or a problem, we can begin to apply the "what." Understanding is *power*. People and communities will not respond to a plethora of do's and do nots in today's world.

Most people are educated, aware and free to make their own choices. I often say that a church that teaches the what is will be a small church. The church that reveals the whys will be a big church. The "always learning but never able" wineskin of yesterday's churches will have very limited impact on today's community. A long time ago I heard Ed Cole say something to the effect of, "The man who knows *what* will be a good employee, the man who knows *why* will be his boss." Why is the principle on which Jesus builds His kingdom in Matthew 16:17–19:

> And Jesus said to him, "Blessed are you, Simon Barjona, because flesh and blood did not reveal this to you, but My Father who is in heaven. And I also say to you that you are Peter, and upon this rock I will build My church; and the gates of Hades shall not overpower it. I will give you the keys of the kingdom of heaven; and whatever you shall bind on earth shall be bound in heaven, and whatever you loose on earth shall be loosed in heaven."
>
> —Matthew 16:17–19

Knowledge is the "what" leg of the three-legged stool. Knowledge is called, in my words, the furniture in the room. Knowledge fills the rooms, but knowledge needs a context. Knowledge was never the end in itself; it was designed to be the means to an end. Knowledge is purpose-driven.

Knowledge is a building block and a necessary component of wisdom just as bricks are a necessary component of a house. Knowledge is where you start but not where you finish. Eve ate the apple from the tree of the knowledge of good and evil because it was desirable to make her wise in her eyes (Genesis 3:6). She used knowledge as a source of significance and security rather than what knowledge was designed for. What is that, you ask. The answer is, to be a building block for wisdom. Our communities are in trouble because everyone is judging the other. People are calling their opinions fact and the facts opinions. Everyone is wise in his own eyes, and why should not they be? It is in their family line.

Remember, wisdom is the proper application of knowledge through understanding. Wisdom considers all the sides and comes up with what is best for the community. Knowledge can take us to extremes. Knowledge without wisdom and understanding is incomplete and ultimately causes all to underachieve. A river without borders is a swamp. Knowledge without understanding and wisdom is a swamp. Every great river has borders. The borders may be broad, yet still channel the flow of waters. On other hand, a river should not be an inch wide and a mile deep. Wisdom allows for rivers that are *deep and wide* for the sake of all in the community.

God Has a Strategy

I believe wisdom is God's strategy to pull the community out of the problems it has created. Wisdom builds the house and wisdom can rebuild the house. However, each of the spheres of influence in our communities will have to embrace wisdom for itself and the community. Embracing knowledge takes all of the community spheres of influence to the "Never Land" of opinion and separation.

Wisdom is about perspective, peace, and purpose. It builds and does not tear down arbitrarily or unnecessarily. Wisdom is honoring and esteeming one another even when you may not agree with each other. Wisdom is a magnet to those looking for real answers to life's deepest problems. Unfortunately, many of our community and country leaders in today's world want an issue, not a solution to a problem. It is time for all the community spheres of influence including the Church to fix the problems of our community, not push a self-serving agenda. That is wisdom.

Herein lies a huge stronghold of opportunity, and the Church must take a strong hold of it: In all your acquiring, acquire wisdom. It is a strategy of God that creates a passport of influence into the community. Let me say that another way: as wisdom in the worldly sense decreases, church growth and personal living strategies will come through wisdom. This shows a need for you and me in our daily lives to acquire wisdom.

Wisdom is the power of God for the community today. Those who have wisdom and solutions to the complex problems of our day will "shine like the sun." That is intelligent fire in the nick of time.

You Say You Want a Revelation

You may be wondering about the title of this chapter, "Guess Who's Coming to Dinner?" I am referring to the story of the queen of Sheba in 1 Kings 10:1–13, to which Jesus refers in Matthew 12:42:

> Now when the queen of Sheba heard about the fame of Solomon concerning the name of the Lord, she came to test him with difficult questions. So she came to Jerusalem with a very large retinue, with camels carrying spices and very much gold and precious stones. When she came to Solomon, she spoke with him about all that was in her heart. Solomon answered all her questions; nothing was hidden from the king which he did not explain to her. When the queen of Sheba perceived all the wisdom of Solomon, the house that he had built, the food of his table, the seating of his servants, the attendance of his waiters and their attire, his cupbearers, and his stairway by which he went up to the house of the Lord, there was no more spirit in her. Then she said to the king, "It was a true report which I heard in my own land about your words and your wisdom.
>
> Nevertheless I did not believe the reports, until I came and my eyes had seen it. And behold, the half was not told me. You exceed in wisdom and prosperity the report which I heard. How blessed are your men, how blessed are these your servants who stand before you continually and hear your wisdom. Blessed be the Lord your God who delighted in you to set you on the throne of Israel; because the Lord loved Israel forever, therefore He made you king, to do justice and righteousness. And she

> gave the king one hundred and twenty talents of gold, and a very great amount of spices and precious stones. Never again did such abundance of spices come in as that which the queen of Sheba gave King Solomon.
>
> And also the ships of Hiram, which brought gold from Ophir, brought in from Ophir a very great number of almug trees and precious stones. And the king made of the almug trees supports for the house of the LORD and for the king's house, also lyres and harps for the singers; such almug trees have not come in again, nor have they been seen to this day.
>
> And King Solomon gave to the queen of Sheba all her desire which she requested, besides what he gave her according to his royal bounty. Then she turned and went to her own land together with her servants.
>
> —1 KINGS 10:1–13

This historical account has a timely and prophetic message to us today. The queen came from the south to see for herself the Jerusalem that wisdom built. The amazing thing to her was that the accounts she heard of Jerusalem were not hyped. As she says, "Behold the half was not told me. You exceed in wisdom and prosperity the report which I heard" (1 Kings 10:7). As a result of the overwhelming riches and revelation of wisdom, "there was no more spirit in her."

That is what wisdom or the proper application of knowledge through understanding can do to the community. The queen of Sheba came to Solomon because she could not find real wisdom anywhere else. She came to him because he had a real, tangible, and lasting example of community transformation. Wisdom moved Jerusalem from dream to done. Wisdom moved Jerusalem from revelation to reality. It was, to quote Josh McDowell, "evidence that demanded a verdict." She came to dinner at Solomon's and she was not shortchanged. She even talked about dinner, "the food at his table." This was no exercise bicycle—this was a *real* bicycle.

As I mentioned earlier, Solomon is a type of Church and the queen of the South is a type of community. Solomon's wisdom was not merely "in the Spirit"—it was real and tangible in the form of a city. Jerusalem at that time was an example of God's wisdom made known through a man in a natural way. Natural people like the queen of Sheba need natural examples; after all, they are natural. The size, revelation, and splendor of Solomon's wisdom drew her to him. Somebodies draw somebodies, and people of influence attract people of influence.

As the Church builds its house by wisdom and it operates in wisdom with the other community spheres of influence like Sheba, influence with influencers will happen. It is God's strategy for such a time as this. Today's "queens of the South" are looking for a revelation on how to live life and succeed. They want real answers to real problems in their lives, families and communities. They are going to go to dinner somewhere. Why not go to people who are as wise as a serpent but gentle as a dove? After all, wisdom is better than warfare (Ecclesiastes 9:18). Wisdom is influence.

The Magnetic Power of Incarnated Wisdom

Let's outline this amazing historical event and see some principles of the magnetic power of wisdom at work in a community. I will draw out five principles then develop each one for us. "She" in this outline refers to the queen of Sheba, and "he" refers to King Solomon.

- She heard because he had (verse 1).
- Because she was a seeker, she came (verse 2).
- She brought something (verse 2).
- She gave her heart and possessions (verses 10-11).
- She received answers, prosperity and peace with God (verse 13).

An important aspect of this event is that Solomon had wisdom incarnated, not *wish*dom hoped for. He *gave* wisdom because he *had* wisdom. At this point in his life, he was not a wisdom wannabe. He was not a wisdom professor; he was a wisdom possessor. His wisdom was not an academic wisdom. His wisdom was a strategic wisdom.

Like Jesus, Solomon was able to grow in stature and favor with God and men.

We all know that a little later in his life, Solomon was not perfect. The same is true of David, Abraham, Peter and Moses. There are no perfect men, only a perfect God. The important thing to see is the power of wisdom at work through a weak man like Solomon. If he can do it, perhaps we can also.

1. She heard because he had (verse 1).

> Now when the queen of Sheba heard about the fame of Solomon concerning the name of the Lord, she came to test him with difficult questions.
>
> —1 Kings 10:1

The queen of Sheba came to Jerusalem to meet Solomon because she had heard that something about this city was different than other cities. This was the city that wisdom and peace built. When wisdom and peace work together, prosperity is the result. Solomon's name means "peaceable." Earlier in Solomon's life, God had asked him what he would like as the king. God, in essence, gave him a blank check and said, "Write in what you want." Solomon chose wisdom and wisdom is what he received (see I Kings 3:3–14). This is an Old Testament example of the New Testament truth in James 1:5:

> But if any of you lacks wisdom, let him ask of God, who gives to all generously and without reproach, and it will be given to him.
>
> —James 1:5

So Solomon received wisdom from God but he also received a side benefit, prosperity. Look at the fallowing verse:

> And God said to him, "Because you have asked this thing and have not asked for yourself long life, nor have asked riches for yourself, nor have you asked for the life of your enemies, but have asked for yourself discernment to understand justice, behold, I have done according to your words. Behold, I have given you a wise and discerning heart, so that there has been no one like you before you, nor shall one like you arise after you.

> And I have also given you what you have not asked, both riches and honor, so that there will not be any among the kings like you all your days."
>
> —1 KINGS 3:11–13

Is not that interesting? Men of war ask for weapons, but men of peace ask for wisdom. The wisdom that this man of peace asked for resulted in prosperity for the community. In Proverbs 8:18, wisdom is speaking and says, "Riches and honor are with me, enduring wealth and righteousness."

Proverbs 8:21 repeats the same concept: "To endow those who love me with wealth, that I may fill their treasuries."

So we see that peace, wisdom and prosperity in a community are connected. This is another "three-legged stool." Now I will tie together all three of these components:

> The fear of the Lord is to hate evil; pride and arrogance and the evil way, and the perverted mouth, I hate. Counsel is mine and sound wisdom; I am understanding, power is mine. By me kings reign, and rulers decree justice. By me princes rule, and nobles, all who judge rightly. I love those who love me; and those who diligently seek me will find me.
>
> —PROVERBS 8:13–17

In verse 13 we have wisdom. In verse 16 we have riches and honor (favor and stature), and in verse 17 we have peace.

So the queen of Sheba came to a city of peace (Jerusalem) whose king's name was "peaceable." He was wisdom-driven, and the result was a prosperous city that was known all over the world. This city of influence drew people of influence. Remember, somebodies draw somebodies.

No one wants to follow a failure. Remember, success draws success. Solomon made a deposit of wisdom and got a return of wisdom from God. With the return of wisdom from God, he reinvested wisdom in the city and that deposit of wisdom produced a return from the nations. Her name was Sheba. This is wealth by wisdom. Solomon was wise in the community's and nation's eyes. The Book of Proverbs says in chapter 1, verse 20, "Wisdom shouts in the streets," and the queen of the South heard it.

I believe this is very prophetic for the Church and people in our churches. God's primary strategy in this hour is wisdom. The Church as an institution and as an organism needs wisdom in this hour for the sake of the community. Wisdom is shouting from the streets. Do you hear what I hear? The community needs churches that are full of wise people embedded in the community. We need to position people of influence into positions of influence. Having influence in the Church and being in a position to use influence within the community are two different things. The Church needs people of peace, men of peace, as Luke 10:6 says, who are prosperous and wise. The reason much of the Church is poor today is because she keeps going to the wrong tree. The tree of knowledge produces fruit eaters and fruit ingesters like Adam and Eve. The tree of life produces wisdom and fruit bearers like Solomon at that time of his life.

> She [wisdom] is a tree of life to those who take hold of her.
>
> —PROVERBS 3:18

Wisdom is shouting in the streets. The community will be coming. Hopefully, the Church will be a reflection of wisdom through Christ (1 Cor. 1:30). However, if they came and we do not have what we say we have, the "queens" will leave and never come back. In other words, the Church must have real answers to real questions. The Church had better not be shooting blanks. Solomon was not. The queen came because of the *fame* of Solomon and the *name* of the Lord. What a great model for today's Church!

2. Because she was a seeker, she came (verse 2).

> So she came to Jerusalem with a very large retinue, with camels carrying spices and very much gold and precious stones. When she came to Solomon, she spoke with him about all that was in her heart.
>
> —1 KINGS 10:2

Imagine how Solomon felt when the queen came. She had a very large retinue. Solomon treated her wisely. He was not afraid of her past, her country, her upbringing or her motives. He did not say, "Queen, I bind you, you son of Belial." Solomon was gentle, considerate and well mannered. He was an ambassador, not an army general. He was the King of Hearts working with the Queen of Hearts.

They were two different spheres of influence that honored one another. Solomon did not have a critical attitude toward her. She was sincere. She felt safe. She was a seeker looking for wisdom to solve difficult questions and problems. He had the wisdom to answer "all that was in her heart." The Bible says "nothing was hidden from the king that he did not explain to her." I call that the word of wisdom, the word of knowledge, and the discerning of spirits, or discernment in action. That is gifts of the Spirit being used in a redemptive way for the betterment of the community. After all, if you influence the queen of Sheba, you influence her whole country.

How many seekers are there in your community who would come to a church like Jerusalem in Solomon's day? This truly was a city whose architect and builder was God. Tomorrow's churches today need wisdom, and peace with one another and the community, and they need to be models of respect and influence in the community. Then, the queens of the South will come from afar to hear (and experience) the wisdom of Solomon.

3. She brought something (verse 2).

This is very important. The queen of Sheba knew the principle of "no deposit, no return." She knew how to receive so she brought spices, gold, precious stones and even almug trees that would later be supports in the house of God. In other words, God wanted to use her and her possessions to be a part of the temple of God. This concept is what many churched people dream about—the wealth of the Gentiles stored up for the righteous. (See Proverbs 13:22.)

Notice, however, that Solomon gave first, not Sheba. Sheba tested him with difficult questions to see if Solomon really "had the goods." She knew the difference between rhetoric and reality. After all, she was a person of the world. Maybe she was from Missouri, the "show me" state. She was omega-oriented, not alpha-oriented. She did not want to hear declarations "in the Spirit." She wanted to see the Word become flesh and dwell among us. She wanted to know, "Is this guy real?"

Solomon did not mind making the first move and the first deposit. That was his role. He was fulfilling his purpose and destiny. He made his contribution of wisdom into the community first, then awaited the response. The first move was his, not Sheba's. Sheba was willing to give, but needed the real and tangible proof in order to give. Being a worldly person, she was not going to follow a failure.

How does this apply to the Church?

The first move is up to the Church, not the community. God made the first move towards man, not vice versa. The "Shebas" of the community are willing to give and become a part of the Church, but is the Church who and what it appears to be.? The Shebas of the country want to bring their hearts and their possessions. God wants to use them to build His house. However, the Church needs to be proactive, sincere, and credible. Wisdom dictates that. The community needs for the Church to make its God-given contribution in the areas in which the whole community underachieves. However, the first move is the Church's, not the community's. The truth is no deposit, no return. Solomon's deposit of wisdom brought the return of the nations. The community is looking for a two-way relationship, not a one-way relationship.

4. She gave her heart and her possessions (vv. 10–11).

> She gave the king a hundred and twenty talents of gold, and a very great amount of spices and precious stones. Never again did such abundance of spices come in as that which the queen of Sheba gave King Solomon.
>
> —1 KINGS 10:10

As Solomon's gift of wisdom operated in the life of the queen, she responded in a real and tangible way. She gave her heart and her possessions. Why would not she? How could she resist? She saw the work of wisdom in her life, in Solomon's life, and in Jerusalem's life. Now she was the one who made a deposit, but more out of awe than an investment strategy. She sought first the Kingdom of God for God's sake, not hers. She was grateful. She found answers to life. She found a king who was for her and not against her. She found a confidant, a friend, a counselor and a consultant. She found acceptance, not condemnation.

Her response was "I want to be part of this." She probably did not understand everything about Israel, the Jews and Jerusalem, but she knew this was God and this was real. She was in a real two-way relationship. She was not being used for her money. She was being honored as someone important and significant in her own right.

She had a purpose and contribution in her sphere of influence also. Solomon had the wisdom to look for a win/win, not a win/lose situation. This was not a "Me Tarzan, you Jane" relationship. This was not one-upmanship, a one-way relationship or a trivial pursuit to see who has the bigger kingdom. This relationship was not a means to an end. It was not about who was richer or had more people in his or her kingdom. This was not about who was right and who was wrong. This was about helping someone both spiritually and naturally. This was the Queen of Hearts honoring the King of Hearts after the King of Hearts displayed that he was who he said he was. This is how real influence influences. It is a two-way relationship for the sake of a cause higher than you are.

What Solomon was to the queen of the South, the Church needs to be to the community. Remember, whatever you honor you can have. Whatever you dishonor, you will not have. The Church needs to be a friend, a confidant, a wisdom provider, and a patient, non-judgmental sphere of influence in the community. Otherwise, how will we put the pieces of our communities back together again?

5. She received answers, more prosperity, and peace with God (v. 13).

Here is the principle of "you cannot out-give God" in action. Sheba gave her bounty, and then Solomon gave back to her "according to his royal bounty." Even after she tested him and responded with her gifts, Solomon trumped her again. This shows the heart of God toward seekers who find and knockers who knock on doors until the doors open. God loves to give to those who seek Him. She made a deposit and got a return. When she let go of what was in her hand, God let go of what was in His hand.

However, God operates through people in the Church. People in the

Church give God a face in the community. Solomon allowed God to work through him. He was God's face and an example of God's grace on the earth to Sheba. In the same way, the Church is God's face and grace to the Shebas of our day. God wants to bless the people in our communities, not curse them. Really, God wants people in the community to build their houses with wisdom. The result will be greater peace and prosperity. Nothing will ever be perfect on the earth but we can redeem and improve it. Would not it be wonderful for many more of the Shebas of this world to discover that you cannot out-give God? I will return to this idea later.

How to Make Queens Faint

Here is a wisdom principle for those of you who pastor churches, own businesses, or are involved in any of the five community spheres of influence. It has to do with growth and influence. Solomon, who was the wisest man ever to live, understood the principle of both/and. He understood the principle of growing up into all aspects and combining all the elements of an initiative to bring the initiation to fullness and completion. Here I am speaking in reference to the Church, but the same principle applies to business.

Let me ask you a couple of questions: What three elements need to come together in a church for the church to influence or have the potential to change a community for the better? What three elements made the queen of Sheba lightheaded? Let's look at the following verses and draw out another "three-legged stool" of wisdom.

> So King Solomon became greater than all the kings of the earth in riches and in wisdom.
>
> —1 KINGS 10:23

> All the earth was seeking the presence of Solomon, to hear his wisdom which God had put in his heart.
>
> —1 KINGS 10:24

> When the queen of Sheba perceived all the wisdom of Solomon, the house that he had built.
>
> —1 KINGS 10:4

The three elements are:

- Revelation
- Model
- Platform

Let's explore the first element of revelation. First of all, Solomon had a revelation regarding wisdom. He had illumination on the concept of wisdom. Flesh and blood did not reveal wisdom to him. Like Peter did in Matthew 16:17, Solomon received his revelation directly from God. The concept of wisdom went from his head to his heart and then to his feet. I call that the "head-heart-feet" principle. The Word became flesh and dwelt among them. It started from heaven but ended up in a real and tangible way on earth. God's revelation to Solomon gave him something to say and something to do. Revelation works that way.

Solomon's life was purpose-driven around wisdom. He incarnated wisdom. He was not some academic who professed or spoke about wisdom; he was a practitioner of wisdom. The world needed answers and Solomon had the answers. He had something special that was uniquely his, and he lived it. The Scripture above says that all the earth came to hear the wisdom God had put into his heart. If Solomon had lived in New Testament times, we could say that he was "making known the manifold wisdom of God through the Church to the rulers and authorities in heavenly places" (Eph. 3:10). Solomon had a *revelation* on wisdom. However, a revelation on wisdom and a house built on wisdom are two different things.

The second element in making the "queens" of our communities and countries faint is *model*. Solomon did not merely talk about a model; he had a model that legitimized his revelation on wisdom. The Queen of Sheba perceived all the wisdom of Solomon (revelation) and then saw ("my eyes had seen it," v. 7) that his revelation worked. This was not theory or hopeful thinking. Solomon possessed both revelation and reality. He made the intangible tangible. The incredible became credible. His evidence demanded a verdict. As Proverbs 9:1 says, wisdom has built her house and boy, was it awesome!

Revelation without model will not influence the influencers of the earth. Revelation must be backed up by model. People of wisdom know this.

The third element in making queens faint is what I call *platform*. Platform is the ability to get the word out into the community about the revelation and model. It is a media issue for the Church, business or revelation. In the case of Solomon, the word-of-mouth method was used and "*all the earth* was seeking the presence of Solomon."

Did you see that? All the earth was coming for a "home tour" of the house that wisdom built. Solomon had the ability and model to get the word out into all the world. The model was not an end in itself, it was meant to influence the influencers of the world to God. The wisdom of God became real and tangible to the whole world.

This was not about Solomon; it was about a deposit of wisdom into the world. The return was the queen of the South hearing about the fame of Solomon concerning the name of the Lord. Solomon, like Jesus, grew in stature and favor with God and men. As a result, he influenced the influencers in a redemptive way. It was a way that the earth could be filled with the glory of God. *Platform* is absolutely essential in creating a "community shift" back to God.

INFLUENCE THROUGH EXCELLENCE

I do not know about you, but I would have liked to have seen Jerusalem in the days of Solomon. I would have loved to have seen and experienced the convergence of revelation, model and platform all at the same time. Solomon had all the tools in the toolbox. Wisdom understands excellence. Wisdom also understands that no one person or no single Church can be excellent in all areas all the time. However, we can pursue excellence, and excellence draws people.

The Church today needs to have these three elements working together to influence the queens of Sheba back to God. Possessing one or two of the elements is incomplete. I have been to many churches that have a great "revelation," yet experience church split after church split. The model is not one that draws healthy people, only dysfunctional people looking for a source of significance and security. Other churches are stable and may even be known nationally, but possess very little revelation. Still others have revelation and even a good model, but no one has ever heard of them. They might have favor with God, but not favor with men. This is not wise.

Do you see the principle? More importantly, do you have a revelation of the strategy of wisdom in the context of the community? Do you understand how revelation, model and platform work together? Just ask Pastor Bill Hybels, Pastor Rick Warren, Pastor Brian Houston, or Pastor Tommy Barnett. These pastors and their churches have learned the strategy of stature and influence. Each of these pastors' churches has a revelation worth hearing about and a model to substantiate the revelation, and as a result, the platform has gone out to reach the whole world.

However, your church does not have to be a mega church to influence your community. All you have to do is have a revelation model and platform to get the influencers of your community accessing wisdom from the Solomons of the community. Churches of influence in a small community will be much smaller yet equally as powerful and effective when revelation, model and influence are joined together in the context of their community. The pursuit of excellence in these three areas is a prerequisite to real, tangible, and lasting community transformation in most cases.

A word to those of you in business or other spheres of influence: this principle is true for you also. Your business can grow and thrive if you have a revelation or something that you do that is uniquely yours. Your business needs to be a good model and as well managed as possible. Finally, you need to advertise and get the word out about your business. When you combine revelation, model, and platform, you will usually have success and influence.

Community-centric Wisdom

I will wrap up this chapter with what I call community-centric wisdom. I am writing these points mainly to church leaders, but these points could relate to all community spheres of influence as well. Let's look at some intelligent fire for the sake of the community.

Do not just grow a church; grow a community.

At a recent conference in Dallas, Texas I heard former television station owner Linda Rios Brook say something like, "Do not try to change the church, change the world." That is good advice. Pastors and church leaders equip the saints to do the work of *their* ministry, not yours. Equip people to change the world. Do not conform the saints into a church ethos; conform them into a community ethos. Help them to grow in stature and wisdom, which puts Christ back into the workplace. Remember, give the church back to the community.

Give back to the community.

If you take from the community, you need to give back to the community. The people who tithe and serve in your church live in your community. Not only is it wrong to take from the community without returning something to the community, it is not strategic. Remember the principle of no deposit, no return. It does not take our communities long to figure out the reality of a one-way relationship. If you take from the community, you need to give back to the community. In other words, have a two-way relationship in a real and tangible way.

Pastor Gary Kinnaman of The Word of Grace Church in Mesa, Arizona, serves one day each week at a community food box ministry where he helps in assessing needs and distributing food. Keep in mind that Gary leads a church of over four thousand people. He understands the reality of being a community church. The community is not here for his church; his church is here for the community. Word of Grace also has another great tradition that exemplifies intelligent fire and wisdom in the community. All of the change that is received in the offerings each month is saved and then matched by the church. The change offering is then given to a community-service agency in the area. These agencies do not have to be "Christian" agencies. The church gives to the whole community, not just part of the community.

Influence influencers; somebodies attract somebodies.

Do you remember the verse in Psalm 133 that says Aaron's anointing oil flows from the head through the beard and ultimately to the end of the robe? In other words, the anointing flows downward. The more you reach the influencers of any area of influence, the greater the probability of reaching all in that area of influence. Most significant shifts start with influencers. Why? Because influencers have influence and leadership; and somebodies draw somebodies. Reach the influencers of a community, city or country, and you can shift your context quickly and redemptively. Remember, whoever defines the church wins. The ones who define the church are influencers. If you are not influencing, you are not defining or redefining. The answer to your prayer is you.

The city in which I live, Phoenix, Arizona has a ministry designed to reach the top one percent of the influencers in all the city's community spheres. The ministry is called the Pinnacle Forum, and was started by Jerry Colangelo, the owner of our local professional baseball and basketball teams. In my opinion, a "Pinnacle Forum" is needed in every city and community. Strategic! That is intelligent fire and the clear mind principle of Nehemiah at work. The way one impacts community is to influence influencers. Somebodies attract somebodies from which momentum is created.

Stature comes from wisdom, which creates influence.

Let's look at James 3:13, 17–18:

> Who among you is wise and understanding? Let him show by his good behavior his deeds in the gentleness of wisdom.... But the wisdom from above is first pure, then peaceable, gentle, reasonable, full of mercy and good fruits, unwavering, without hypocrisy. And the seed whose fruit is righteousness is sown in peace by those who make peace.

Those who live in wisdom in a community look for causes and needs to meet in the community. They look to enhance the community. They serve God by serving the community, and the result is influence and stature in the community. The result is a win-win for God, the Church and the community. Wisdom is ambassadorial, and wars are won by men of peace. Wisdom looks for a way in, not a way out. Stature comes from solving problems not pointing fingers or creating problems.

Frankly, too many churches have been fruit inspectors, judging all the actions of their community's leaders. They are not tangibly involved in the community and yet they judge everything in the community and live off the community (fruit eaters). Perhaps it is time to be a blessing in the community rather than curse the community. It is better to light a light than to curse the darkness.

Joseph, Daniel, Jesus, and Solomon reveal to us the intelligent fire principle of wisdom in action. Perhaps it is time for the Church to become fruit bearers in the community rather than fruit inspectors or fruit eaters in the community. I say that to government, business, education and media/entertainment also. The community is not the means to your end or agenda. If we continue using, confusing and abusing the community, we will lose influence in the community.

Wisdom says the Church needs real answers to the questions and problems of our communities. While many churches say they have the answers, which may be true, they do not know how to communicate those answers. They know the what, but not the why and how. Wisdom is the how. Wisdom says, learn how to help people, not just point out their flaws. Learn to live in the whole community, not just in the Church. A key to community transformation is the Church having real answers, not religious rhetoric for the problems in today's communities. The Church's wisdom from God regarding problems and question of the heart brings stature and influence in a community. This is redemptive relevancy.

Wisdom is our warfare.

Do you realize that wisdom is the Church's war strategy in these times? Wisdom is better than war. Wisdom is ambassadorial. Wisdom is peace, patience and time. Wars are a process; battles are an event. Wisdom leads by influence, not authority. The old authority paradigm of the post World War II time will never influence today's generation of people, at least not for long. It took years for the Church to lose its influence in Western culture and it will take time to get it back. Wisdom is there for the long term.

Wisdom is not without borders, but wisdom has large borders. Wisdom is not a mile deep and an inch wide. Wisdom has boundaries that protect it. The problem with Solomon is that he did not have a

Nathan like David did. However, the endless fruit inspecting within the Church has to stop. The fruit inspecting with the community has to stop. Otherwise, the Church will not have favor with God and favor with men. Here is my advice: Solve community problems; do not push your agenda. Win souls, not debates!

Chapter 15

The Return of the Kings: *The Principle of the Eleven-Twelfths Church*

There is nothing so powerful as a people *whose time has come.*

Victor Hugo is quoted, "There is nothing so powerful as an idea whose time has come." In this chapter we will talk about the power of a people whose time has come!

Like Jesus with the wine at the wedding in Cana, I have purposefully saved the best part of this book for the last. In this chapter I will answer the question "Who are the King's men (and women) who can put the pieces of our communities back together again?" I will propose the solution to the problem addressed in Chapter 3, "The Fall and Rise of Humpty Dumpty." I believe a solution exists for the underachieving communities of the world. That is why I wrote this book. We will probably never see the perfect community, but we can greatly improve and even transform our communities.

However, before I answer the who-are-the-King's-men question, let's review the principles I have stated so far. In Chapter 1, I introduced the concept of intelligent fire. Chapter 2 focused on the principle of the recipe, or components that work together to make something bigger than the individual parts. I stated that real community transformation requires that we have a sufficient burden for our communities, sufficient prayer for our communities, a clear strategy to transform the community and finally, people who have "calloused hands," who will give God a force and do the work of the ministry in their community. The purpose of intelligent fire, as you recall, is to focus especially on the last two ingredients in the recipe. Those are the "clear or strategic mind" and the "calloused hands" ingredients.

In Chapter 3, I addressed the problem that causes communities to underachieve and fail to reach their full potential: Community spheres of influence are largely separated from one another. Chapter 4, "Giving the Church Back to the Community," explored God's vision for communities and countries. Chapters 5 and 6 discussed principles of vision and values. I stressed that in order to accomplish the vision of community transformation, you need to possess corresponding enabling values to accomplish the vision. The key to understanding this book is identifying, adopting and applying the eight intelligent fire core values of community transformation outlined in chapters 7 through 14.

The King's Men and Women

The King's men and women who put our communities back together again need to have both the vision and values of community transformation integrated into their lives. Vision gets you started, but values enable you to finish. The King's men and women need to be aware that there are many components and issues in community transformation. They have to be people who have grown up into all aspects of the complex issues involved in community transformation. They have to be aware of the community. They cannot be one-dimensional. They cannot be one-solution-fixes-every-problem types of people. They need to be people who live community transformation values "out loud." They need to adjust, be flexible, and be redemptively relevant. Their goal must be to grow the community, not just grow a church. Their life-blood is to see the community be all that it can be even if it means change. They must not be participating in community transformation just to prove their favorite Christian emphasis is more spiritual than someone else's. They must be in the community for the sake of the community.

I have illustrated what I am saying above by the following graph.

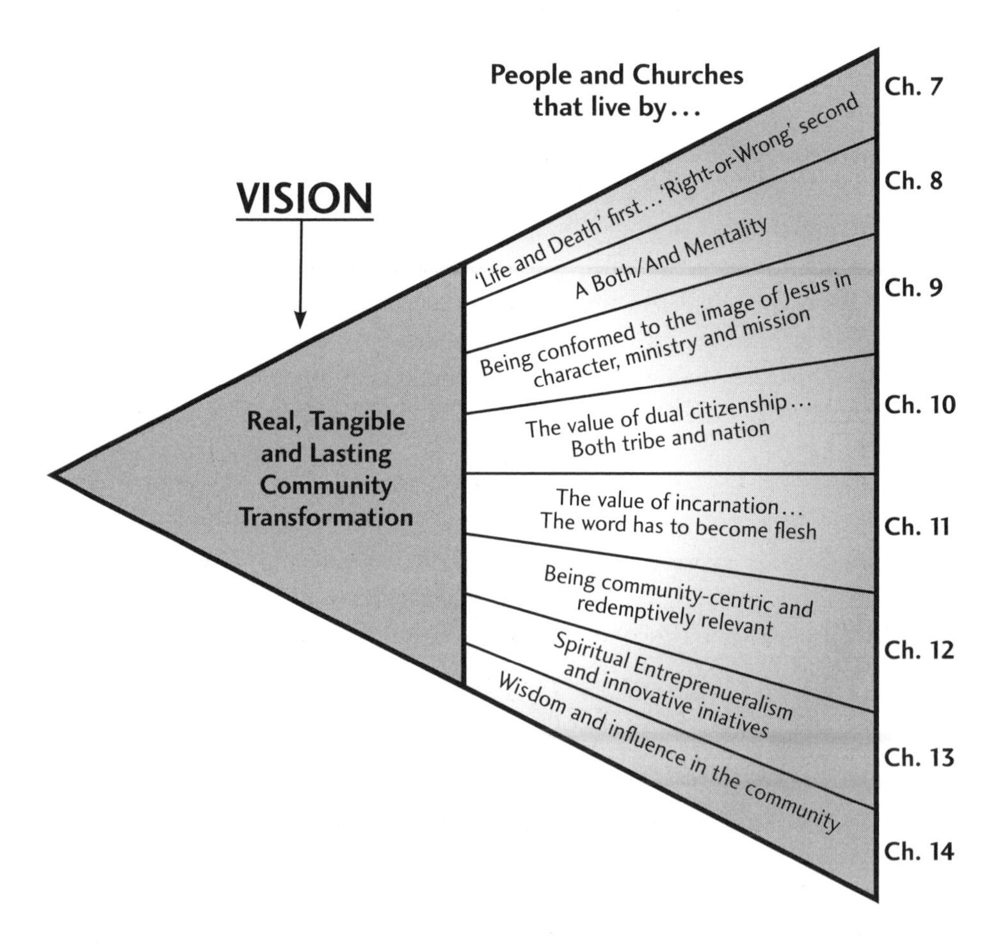

I call this the "Ax" principle: The vision of community transformation and the values of community transformation working together for the sake of the community. The vision is the cutting edge, and the values are the mass behind the cutting edge. As both the cutting edge and the mass are connected, the "ax" becomes effective. However, without mass behind the cutting edge, no trees will be chopped down.

The King's men and women will be life-and-death first, right-and-wrong second. They will be both/and-oriented people who steer clear of dualism if they can. The King's men and women are not theme or emphasis-based, but Christians who have "grown up into all aspects into Him" as the apostle Paul writes in Ephesians 4:15. They are taught by more than one office, such as a pastor/teacher, producing a more complete view of Christianity. They are apostolic in nature and community-centric.

The King's men and women are builders of unity and understand that *their* "tribe," whether it be their denomination or church, is not *the* tribe. They understand that it takes a community of churches to reach a community of peoples. They contend *for* the faith (Jude 3), not *in* the faith. They major on the ABCs, not the XYZs, of Christianity. They refuse to strain at a gnat and swallow a camel (Matthew 23:24). They finish what they start. They do not fall into the trap of always learning, never able. They understand that declaring is not the same as doing.

They understand the principle of the Son of God becoming the Son of Man to communicate to man. They let their light shine in order to get mayors, businessmen and educators to glorify God. They are not incarnationally challenged. They have values, not just beliefs. The King's men and women are not churches in Seattle, Tokyo or anywhere else. They do whatever is necessary to have favor with God and favor with man. They became all things to all men so that some may be saved. They are initiators and entrepreneurs, focused and yet aware.

They look for strongholds of opportunity in their communities and seize moments of open doors in the community. They look for a way in, not a way out. They are as wise as serpents and as innocent as doves. They are spiritually intriguing and mystifying to community leaders. They have real answers to the communities deepest needs and problems. They are known for their wisdom, not their doctrine. They are history makers, influencing the queens of the South and the world. They redeem, not condemn. They engage the community, not enrage the community. They love it when "the desired of the nations" come into the Kingdom of God. They can influence influencers. They can lead leaders. They have the power to create wealth.

They may govern governors. They may educate educators. They may raise nations and businesses from the dead. They understand the principle of strategic alliances and mutual collaborations. They have burdened hearts, bended knees, clear minds, and they are not too spiritual to have calloused hands.

They realize the answer to their prayer is themselves. They understand and can relate to both brothers and others. They realize their lives are about giving the church back to the community in their area of influence. They realize that their role in the community is to look like Jesus in character, ministry and mission. They are community-centric, not church-centric. They are today's leaders and influencers sitting in church who are becoming tomorrow's leaders and influencers in the community. They have intelligent fire core values.

Who are these people? Who are the King's men and women? "They" are *you* and "they" are *I*. However, please read on. I am not going where you may think I am going.

Personal Epiphanies

In October 2003, Pastor Richard Norman of Kapiti Christian Centre and I were having dinner with two business owners at a restaurant in Wellington, New Zealand. The business owners, John Roche and Wayne Douglas, were discussing the role of businessmen in the traditional church. They were lamenting the you-have-really-made-it-if-you-are-in-full-time-ministry-in-the-church mentality that so often reflects the values of the church. There is that "Me Tarzan, you Jane" culture again at work. We began discussing some pertinent and strategic questions regarding those in full-time ministry in the church and church attendees. Here are some of the questions put to Richard and me that evening by John and Wayne:

- Why are you here (on earth)?
- Why are you a businessperson? A government official? A teacher?
- If business were "unholy," why would you be a businessperson?
- If you are supposed to be "holy," why would you participate in something "unholy"?
- Why are you in business as a churched or unchurched person?
- What is full-time ministry?
- What is my role as a businessperson in the community?
- Is profit unholy?
- What and where is church?
- What is "secular" and what is "sacred"?

On another occasion, speaking with the owner of a construction company in Peoria, Arizona I heard similar questions asked in a different manner. His observation after attending a mega-church in Phoenix was this: "It seems to me I was at this church for four reasons: to serve at church, to spend all my time at church, to give my money to the church, and to be a salesman for the church." Ouch! I might add none of these business owners were particularly hurt or vengeful. They were "just wondering."

These are challenging, real questions. The right answers to these questions could change entire communities, cities and countries. The right answers to these questions could enable community transformation in a way and to a degree that the Church has seldom experienced. The Holy Spirit is bringing these questions to the forefront of Christianity all over the world. Let's take a close look at these questions and see if we can redefine "church" as most know it.

This is a time of epiphany in the Church for the sake of those outside the Church. It is time to close the gap between the Church and the community. It is time to be community-centric.

A NATION OF KINGS AND PRIESTS

> To Him who loves us, and has freed us from our sins by His blood, and He has made us to be a kingdom, priests to serve His God and Father; to Him be glory and dominion forever and ever. Amen.
>
> —REVELATION 1:5–6

> You have made them to be a kingdom and priests to serve our God, and they will reign on the earth.
>
> —REVELATION 5:10, NIV

> But you are a chosen people, a royal priesthood, a holy nation, a people belonging to God, that you may declare the praises of him who called you out of darkness into his wonderful light.
>
> —1 PETER 2:9, NIV

In a spiritual sense, every believer in Christ is both a king and a priest. That is quite a privilege and an honor, is not it? However, let's look at this principle in a functional sense. I believe by taking a look at Israel, the "congregation in the wilderness" (Acts 7:38), we can draw out a vital principle regarding community transformation.

You recall that twelve tribes made up the nation of Israel. One of the tribes, Levi, was set apart for full-time ministry inside the temple. Levi was actually a small tribe whose job was to hear from God, and share the vision and passions of God. Levi was to keep the other eleven tribes in touch with God. The Levites were the priests. They were provided for by the tithes and offerings of the other eleven tribes. Their role, function, and calling was full-time ministry in the temple.

The other eleven tribes' role, function or calling was full-time ministry outside the temple. They were God's people embedded in the community. The eleven-twelfths were involved in government, business, education and media/entertainment outside the temple. In other words, in role, function and calling they were to be the kings.

The apostle Peter confirms this principle in 1 Peter 2:9 by pointing out this pattern in the New Testament church. He uses the language of a "royal priesthood" a "holy nation." Remember twelve tribes comprised the nation of Israel—eleven were kings and one were priests. The term "royal priesthood" suggests kings (royal) and priests (priesthood). As I said earlier, spiritually, New Testament believers may be both simultaneously. However, New Testament believers will function more as one than as the other. Both the apostle Peter and the apostle John apply the term king first and then priest because eleven-twelfths of the church function as kings.

So the Church was designed to have eleven-twelfths of its members in full-time ministry in the community and one-twelfth of its members in full-time ministry within the Church (or temple). I have heard Dr. C. Peter Wagner call this concept "the nuclear church" and "the extended church." The nuclear church, akin to the temple priests, is made up of those in full-time ministry within a church staff. The extended church, like Old Testament kings, is made up of those in full-time ministry beyond a church's professional staff positions.

Church Is Everywhere You Are!

Do you realize that if you are a "king," your employer is paying you to be in full-time ministry? If you work for American Express, they are paying you to be in full-time ministry. The traditional church you attend does not have to raise the funds to pay you to be in full-time ministry! If Ford Motor Company is your employer, then they are paying you to be in full-time ministry. That is the wealth of the gentiles being stored for the righteous (Proverbs 13:22).

The role of kings is to govern, create wealth, have influence outside the temple, and define the Church in the eyes of the community. The King's men give the King a face in the community. The King's men and women touch the walls outside the church. They are mayors, lawyers, newscasters, business owners, employers, teachers, electricians, and plumbers. God designed them to be "sent ones" into the community. Their "turf" is the community. They are community transformers, not Church transformers. Church is everywhere they go. Their businesses are their churches. The companies they work in are their churches. Their neighborhoods are their churches. Their church is wherever their sphere of influence is. They are not limited to the walls of a traditional church—they are the kings of the community. This is the primary role of eleven-twelfths of the people who are believers. They were not called to full-time ministry in the Church; they were called to full-time ministry in the community.

THE "NUCLEAR" IMPLOSION

The traditional church ethos has magnified the priestly role and minimized the kingly role. The priests or those in full-time ministry in the local church, whether intentionally or unintentionally, have created a culture and mindset of "you have really arrived when you are in full-time ministry in the church." This mindset comes from the teacher-driven ethos of the local church presented in Chapter 7. The priests have created a priest-only ethos and have tried to make the kings into priests. This, in effect, has undermined the testimony of the Church to the community. In effect, eleven-twelfths of the Church has been neutralized, creating a huge church/community separation. The priests have made the Church the community. They have made *their* world the world. That is like a twelve-cylinder engine firing on one cylinder. One cylinder out of twelve firing is called underachieving. The real loser is the community.

Ed Silvoso, the author of *Anointed for Business*,[1] perfectly captured the essence of the priest bias in a mailing piece I received from his office one day. One section of the mailer was called "Four Lethal Misbeliefs Debunked in *Anointed for Business*." The four misbeliefs were:

1. There is a God-ordained division between clergy and laity.

2. The church is called to operate primarily inside a building often referred to as the temple.

3. People involved in business cannot be as spiritual as those serving in traditional church ministry.

4. The primary role of marketplace Christians is to make money to support the vision of those "in the ministry."

Ed then goes on to say "False" to all of these statements. I highly recommend Ed's book for another perspective on the king's men and women who can put Humpty Dumpty back together again.

I would like to add another five misbeliefs that are severely limiting the community *and* the Church:

1. "You have really made it if you are in full-time ministry in the church."

2. The community is evil; the church is holy.

3. Being entrepreneurial, making a profit and being wealthy is unholy. Work is part of the curse.

4. The anointing lies only on those "in ministry" in the temple.

5. Only priests are "elders at the gates."

My answer to all nine of these misbeliefs is "False" also. The result has been a nuclear church implosion.

God has always intended a nation of kings *and* priests, not kings or priests.

From Priests to Kings and Priests

Now, here is some good news. God is activating the eleven-twelfths church so that twelve out of twelve cylinders on the engine will be firing. God is raising the kings from the dead. God is creating room in the Church for the kings once again. Why? The King's men are the ones who will put the pieces of communities back together again. Priests grow churches; kings grow communities that reflect the king. Why? That is their role and ministry. The kings' calling and ministry is primarily to the community, not to the traditional church. They serve at church, but minister in the community. They are God's instruments to transform a community. They are the "harvesters" that Jesus asked his intercessors to pray for.

I suppose you have heard of the 10/40 Window. This geographic "window" is drawn on the globe from ten degrees north latitude to forty degrees north latitude and represents mainly the worlds of Islam, Hinduism, and Buddhism. Intercessors have been praying for this area of the world for years. Oz Hillman, who speaks on the activation of kings, says we need to pray for and open up the 9:00 a.m. to 5:00 p.m. Window. I like that. The "9-to-5 Window" has the potential to shift communities for the better. Intercessors, why not pray through the "9-to-5 Window"?

Not since the book of Acts have we seen the power of kings and priests working together. In a real way, priests represent favor with God, and kings represent favor with men when wisdom is applied. The result is growing in stature and favor with the community. It takes both favor with man and favor with God to transform a community. The Church alone will seldom transform a city.

Touch Not the Lord's Anointed Businessman

Do you realize Jesus was both a king and a priest? Over 50 percent of Jesus' life was spent working in a "secular" job. Of the 132 stories in the gospels, 122 took place in the marketplace. Of the fifty-two parables, forty-five happened in the marketplace. Of the forty recorded miracles of Jesus, thirty-nine happened in the marketplace. The temple was not the issue, the community was the issue. The war was over the community, not the Church. After all, "the earth is the Lord's, and the fullness thereof" (Ps. 24:1, kjv).

Now let me ask you a question: Which role, king or priest, has the calling and anointing to transform a community? I believe that role is primarily the king's. Thus the anointing to transform a community goes with the calling. Traditional church leaders and "men of God" have often used the story of David and his statement about Saul in 1 Samuel 24. These leaders are saying, in effect, "I am in full-time ministry in the church; I am a priest; I am a prophet—do not touch me."

The implication is that a person is the "Lord's anointed" if he is the pastor. Although that is true, it is also incomplete. Kings were anointed also. The Lord's anointed may be a businessman, a king called to pastor a business. The Lord's anointed could be a mayor called to pastor a city. The Lord's anointed could be a teacher in a school who is mentoring twelve-year-olds. Anyone who has a position of influence in the community could be the Lord's anointed. Many, many times the priests have marginalized the kings and "touched" them, hurting both parties. The ultimate loser is the community. It is time for the priests to honor and include in a real and tangible way the eleven-twelfths of the Church through whom they receive their support. Do not touch the Lord's anointed businessman, teacher, mayor, or newscaster—as well as the pastor.

I will summarize with some brief statements to the eleven-twelfths church:

If you are an employer, your business, your employees, your customers and the community you serve is your "church." Enthusiastically serve your employees, your customers, your suppliers and the community. In a very real sense, you are a king in a priest's role to your community.

As an employer you have an advantage over a traditional church—you are with your employees, your customers and your community up to forty hours per week. Simply put, you have a greater ability to influence than a traditional church's one to two hours per week.

The same is true for employees—your work, neighborhood, school, or business is your "church."

You are anointed for business, government, education, and media/entertainment. Your calling carries the anointing.

You have permission from heaven to be entrepreneurial, make a profit, advance, succeed, and be promoted for influencing the influencers of a community and blessing the community. You are blessed to be a blessing to the community.

Your place in the community is strategic for redefining the Church, redefining God, and redefining Jesus in the community's eyes. Raise businesses from the dead, help blind educators see, help deaf newscasters hear, release and set free the proconsuls. Put your community back together again.

The elder at the gates of the city will be more king than priest. Take your place of influence in the city by serving the city. Community-transformation initiatives must include both kings and priests, not just priests.

You are totally and strategically in God's will to be a "sent one" into the community. You are apostolic lawyers, teachers, businessmen, etc., embedded in the community. At least eleven out of twelve believers have been called to a ministry like yours.

You serve at church, but you minister in the community.

You can either use leadership or be used by leadership. The community is waiting for the core values and wisdom which you have been called to contribute into the community.

THE POWER TO CREATE WEALTH

> But you shall remember the LORD your God, for it is He who is giving you power to make wealth, that He may confirm His covenant which He swore to your fathers, as it is this day.
>
> —DEUTERONOMY 8:18

Do you realize the primary vehicle that God uses for advancing His Kingdom (establishing His covenant) is wealth? God gave the Israelites the power to create wealth. In other words, God many times uses wealth before he uses signs and wonders. This perhaps is why many Jewish people and the nation of Israel are prosperous even today. God gave first Israel and then the Church the power to create wealth. If this is true, then why are so many churches under-financed? Perhaps it is because the "kings" have the anointing to prosper.

When the Levites prospered, it was because Israel's kings prospered. If, however, the "kings" in a church have been marginalized, it only stands to reason that it will affect that church in a negative way. I believe the restoration of kings to the Church in a real and tangible way will have a wonderful effect on both the Church and the community. Both will benefit from the return of the kings.

Many years ago I was speaking in Bangalore, India at a traditional pastors conference. My subject was "Kings and Priests" and how they work together in the Church. I was very aware that most of the pastors had the priestly bias against businessmen, government officials and the like, and probably with good cause. After all, money is power and power can corrupt. However, I was also aware that none of these pastors' churches had any finances, either. Bangalore is the "Silicon Valley" of India and a fairly well-to-do area, so I knew there were believers with wealth and influence in these pastors' proximity.

The more I talked about the role of kings, the more uncomfortable the pastors became. As I became aware of this, I helped them to see this important principle: while there are people who abuse wealth and power, that is no reason to reject the true kings God has placed in our churches. Frankly speaking, most priests and temples do not have wealth because of the superior/inferior attitude they have toward kings. I encouraged these pastors to not "throw out the baby with the bathwater" and to learn the power of wisdom. One bad king does not equal all kings. The Church needs the power to create wealth if it is going to advance the Kingdom of God by reaching the community. The priests would be wise to understand the calling, wisdom, and wealth of the kings. It is a partnership, not a sole proprietorship.

KINGDOMNOMICS

Two of my favorite kings in the Phoenix area are Dr. Dick Drake, the provost of the Phoenix University of Theology, and Dr. Lee Melby, the president of the United Community Fund. These men have created some financial principles they call Kingdomnomics. These principles come from the idea of the power to create wealth in the context of the Church and community. These concepts are biblical and also entrepreneurial. They add wealth to both the Church and the community. Let's look at a few of the concepts they share:

1. The church should not be just a recipient of charity; it should be a dispenser of charity.

2. The church is built by prosperity, not charity.

3. God causes kings to prosper, but requires them to tithe. Tithing is not an act of charity, but an act of obedience.

Although strategically fundamental, these statements are often overlooked. The Church has tended to be more of a recipient from the community than a contributor to the community. Many times the community looks at the Church the same way it does a charity. The Church was designed by God to have the wealth to do good works in a community. The Church does not just take from the community; it gives back to the community! In fact, if the Church gets tithes and offerings from people in the community, it needs to give back finances, services, goods and spiritual input. Also the kings need to see this very important principle: The church is not a tax deduction; the church is an instrument of blessing to the community.

These next concepts will require you to think, pray and apply. In some circles, the concepts will provoke some healthy discussion and perhaps even change.

Kings in one church can work with other kings in other churches to create business "engines" in the community.

These engines produce wealth and an increase in size and influence. They create momentum and awareness in the community of the church in a positive way. Remember, in most communities, size equals influence. This may not seem too spiritual, but it is a reality that the Church needs to adjust to. That is why big churches or big businesses grow and grow. Their size gives them influence, respect, and passport into the community. It is wise to understand the principle and use it to the glory of God.

The creation of wealth is a means to an end: to establish His covenant (Deut. 8:18).

Remember, money is a wonderful servant but a terrible master. However, it is a servant whose role is to serve in the advancement of the Kingdom of God and the community. Money used the right way has all kinds of benefits. The Church can invest in the community by investing in business, creating other revenue streams. With many, those in the church can influence and reach the "up and outers" so the "down and outers" may be reached and helped.

Kings in the church should not just give to the church, but give to the community.

This may upset a few of the "priests" in the temple, but this concept is strategic. As God prospers the eleven-twelfths, it is important for them remain part of the community and not give everything to the Church. If you are a businessperson making a profit in your business from the community, be sure to give back to the community. Give to God and give to men. The king's benevolence is needed in the community also. The community will hold you in high esteem just as they did in Acts 5:13. In the community transformation context, we need to hold Christian "kings" in high esteem. Why? That is what gives God a face in the community! Both are important—the Church and the community. It is not an either/or; it is a both/and. As kings and priests, we give to our significant brothers and to our significant others. The Church is called to reach the wealthy, help the poor, generate wealth, increase productivity, make a profit, educate people on how to achieve, and influence influencers.

Venus and Mars, Revisited

I once heard someone say opposites attract and then negotiate the differences. Why does God do this? It is because both have what the other needs. Eve was God's solution to Adam's blind spots. However, Eve needed Adam for her blind spots. The same is true for kings and priests. Each has what the other needs to produce a complete picture. Each has a measure of grace that, when combined, turns into grace without measure. Where two or more are in agreement, there God is. Remember the principle—agreement, unity, abundance! The two become one; the one becomes many.

I have experienced it many times. The priests do not understand the kings, and the kings do not understand the priests. Many times the most miserable person in the church is a king on the church board. His ethos is business, He is a producer, he lives in a world where respect is paramount and inefficiency is sin.

I have heard it said, "Kings are horses, but the priests think they are sheep." You do not treat a horse the way you treat a sheep. The priest, however, is in a sheep's world. Relationship is more important than respect or achievement. In a priest's world, inefficiency does not equal sin. Does this sound familiar? The priests speak a different language than the kings. Their numbers and bottom lines come from two different worlds. The kings are task-oriented and the priests are relationship-oriented. Who is right? Who is wrong? The truth is both are right—partially.

Like two oxen in a yoke, kings and priests are meant to pull together, not pull apart. How do you train oxen to pull together? First of all, both had better follow the instructions of the Plowman. Neither ox determines the direction, the Plowman does. Secondly, the oxen have to learn how to work with each other. That means negotiation, give and take, respect, cooperation and time. As they work together they begin to understand one another. Each has to learn how to say, "Oh, it is a king thing," or "Oh, it is a priest thing." They will learn to choose their battles, not fight over every little thing. When the return of the kings comes to the Church, watch out world!

A Word to the Priests—Equip!

> And He gave some as apostles, and some as prophets, and some as evangelists, and some as pastors and teachers, for the equipping of the saints for the work of service, to the building up of the body of Christ.
>
> —Ephesians 4:11–12

Why do 10 percent of the people in the Church do 90 percent of the work in the Church? My answer is, because God designed it that way. Remember, eleven-twelfths of all believers will be in full-time ministry in the community. Kings serve in church but their ministry is in the community. It may seem noble for a bank president to serve as an usher in the church, but it is not very strategic. That bank president is much more strategic for the Kingdom of God ministering to other bank presidents. He is an influencer called to bring salt and light into the community. Kings will underachieve and never reach their potential as community transformers if they "live in the church."

Pastors, equip your people to do the work of *their* ministry in the community, not just *your* ministry in your church. That is a much wiser use of talent and resources. Equip them to be kings in the community. Equip them to be successful in all realms of life, not just in the temple realm. Release the entrepreneurial spirit in them. The king's role in your church is to be a somebody who influences somebodies.

The kings are your extensions into the community. They have the grace to be in government, business, education and media/entertainment. They are ministers of commerce. They bring essential core values and wisdom into their spheres of influence in the community. They are the parts of Humpty Dumpty that priests will never be. The priests have to equip the kings so the Church as a whole can grow up into all aspects of the community, not just one aspect of the community. The priestly wisdom and favor with God you have is transformed to the entire community through the kings. They are the Word becoming flesh in the community.

Priests, you have to give the Church back to the community. How? Through the return of the kings *through* the Church *to* the community. Priests influence the Church, but kings influence the world. Remember, trying to make a king into a priest has been the Church's problem for 1,700 years. That is why we have very little influence in the community. The priests need to become centrifugal rather than centripetal.

Another word of wisdom to those in traditional ministry in the temple is "In order to serve a king, learn to think like a king." For the sake of the community, shed that teacher-driven-church-ethos way of thinking. Learn to become a priest in king's clothing. You will never serve whom you do not understand. You cannot think outside of the box and live inside the box. Become more entrepreneurial. Learn the king's world. Learn how to talk to a mayor, a college provost, or a car dealership owner. Do not just speak at him; speak to him. Have a two-way relationship with him.

Usually priests look at kings as a means to an end. Do not do that! The king can add to your world. You can learn from him also. Priests need favor with God and men also. The priest in today's world who is equipped to be only a priest will be mono-cultural and largely ineffective. Today's effective leaders in churches are able to work in both the kings' and the priests' world. The one way-only world of those in traditional ministry is not a spiritual badge of honor. It is a recipe for failure. Let's grow up into Him in all aspects.

What causes this departure from the normal way of doing church? The answer is simple. It is the life-and-death-first core value. One becomes willing to become all things to all men so that some might be saved. The mission of Christ requires it

KINGS IN PRIESTS' CLOTHING

Today's largest or most influential churches in the world are mostly led by kings in priests' clothing. If you look at Rick Warren, Bill Hybels, Tommy Barnett, former pastor John Maxwell, Jack Hayford, and countless others, they could all be CEOs of large corporations. They understand both the king's world and the priest's world. They can organize. They can write. They can create wealth. They can lead. They can communicate the Bible in a very effective way. They evangelize. They have great spiritual influence. They can talk with kings in the community, as well as priests in the church.

They equip rather than inform. They address "why" and "how" issues, not just "what" issues. These kings in priests' clothing are comfortable in any setting. They have contact and communication without contamination. They are kings in priests' clothing in the church context, and priests in kings' clothing in the community context. In the church context they are kings, but in the community context they take on the role of a priest. They represent the Church to the other spheres of influence in the community. They understand both worlds. They have favor with God and man. Perhaps that is why they are so successful. While they may be primarily kings, they have learned the role of a priest to be effective in both church and community.

Priests, this principle is for you also. Learn a lesson from these kings. You can learn to thrive like kings also. Your wisdom and love for the Lord is needed in your community, not just in your church. Heaven knows we need both groups to transform our communities.

I saw this principle at work in November 2003 in Auckland, New

Zealand. I had been invited by the Associated Pentecostal Churches of New Zealand (APCNZ) to speak on the church/community connection. The APCNZ meets once a year for one day. This group consisted of the forty largest or most influential "Spirit-filled" churches in New Zealand.

As I looked at the attendees I noticed that most of them were kings in priests' clothing. The church leaders there, like Peter Mortlock, Brian Tamaki, John Walton, Luke Brough, Brent Douglas, Max Palmer, and Trevor Yaxley represent this new type of leader that is emerging in tomorrow's church today. They are the King's men who will ride again. They are the ones who, along with traditional pastors, can put the pieces of our communities back together again. Frankly, it takes the King's horses, not sheep, to put Humpty Dumpty back together again.

These leaders think like kings because they are kings. They are leaders first and pastors second. They have values that are very similar to the eight intelligent fire core values I have written about in this book. They are the eleven-twelfths church. They exemplify Church@Community.

Raising Kings From the Dead for the Sake of Community

It is one thing to have a resource. It is another thing to use a resource effectively. Do you realize trying to make kings into priests is spiritual abuse? Kings are the way they are because of why they are! That is why Paul emphatically states equip the saints to do the work of "their" ministry, not "your" ministry. The activation of destiny in people should be the primary concern of every church leader. Everyone in a church and in the community has a desire to believe, belong and become. If the church continues with the practice of turning kings into priests, the church, the kings and the community all lose. I predict activity the destiny of kings in the church for the sake of the community will be the next move of the Spirit of God. In doing that, eleven-twelfths of the church will be raised from the dead. Let's allow eleven-twelfths of the church to believe, belong, and become! That will move us from the possibility of community transformation to the probability of community transformation! Lazarus—come forth!

Kings in Church, Priests in the Community

Do you realize that kings in the church sphere are priests in the community because priests are representatives of God to those in commerce in the community. To the mayor, provost, or business owner who is unchurched, kings in church represent God in the community. The kings give God a face in the community. God has strategically designed it this way. Kings speak the language of kings. Most priests do not. They are able to act as an interpreter for priests in church. They know both the language of the priest and the language of the king. They have the wisdom to take spiritual concepts and translate the concepts into the language of the community. They are mediators between the church and the community. They have the respect of the kings in commerce as well as priests in church. They are the mediators, communicators, peacemakers, and connectors of the church to the community. They put Humpty Dumpty back together again. They have the calling and empowerment to connect the church and the community. It is their destiny! The priest has a calling to the church, the kings in the church have a calling to the community. Many priests do not know how to speak the language of the community. It is not the job of the priest to change the community. His job is primarily the temple. The priests in the church require the kings to transform the community. The priest "coaches" the kings in church. The kings in church "coach" the kings in the community. The king's in the church calling is to create the church/community connection. They are today's elders at the gates of the city.

The Return of the Kings

The eleven-twelfths church consists of people whose time has come—to complete the priests, not compete with the priests. These are transformational people in the community. They are able to put Humpty Dumpty back together again. They are kings in the context of the church. They also are priests in the context of the community. In the community transformation context, they influence the kings. They give wisdom to the kings. They are Daniels to the Nebuchadnezzars, and Josephs to the pharaohs. They are Nehemiahs to Artaxerxeses, and Esthers to the Ahasueruses.

They represent God to the kings in their communities. They have the wisdom to fill the earth with the knowledge of the glory of the Lord in a way the earth can understand. They have the favor of God and the wisdom of God, and are strategically placed in the community to use that favor and wisdom. They have intelligent fire core values. They have a Church@Community mindset. They have a strategy. They are a prepared people for a prepared place at a prepared time with prepared values to carry out God's prepared vision. They make and complete the church/community connection. There is nothing so powerful as a people whose time has come!

Chapter 16

Church@Community:

The Principle of Tomorrow's Church Today

Real transformation is about the process of seeing, embracing, confessing, and doing. Any revelation must move from the head to the heart to the feet—from knowing, to being, to doing. Only then does the belief become a value.

In Chapter 3 we left Humpty Dumpty, or the community, in pieces. In this chapter, we will put Humpty Dumpty back together again. I believe it takes both the Church and the other community spheres of influence working together to see a community transformed. The Church cannot do it alone. It takes a strategic alliance or mutual collaboration among all five spheres of influence. Each has a contribution. Each has a calling. Each has a role or responsibility in enhancing the community.

The Church is essential in this process. What we need is all twelve twelfths of the people in the Church doing their part. We need tomorrow's church today helping create tomorrow's community today.

Notice I did not say today's community tomorrow. It is time to put the pieces of our communities back together again. It is time to see the churches' role in their communities in a whole different way. It is time for the Church to see the community in a whole new way. I hope that after reading this book you will never see the community the same way again!

A Church and Community Whose Time Has Come

Let's review. It is important that we retrace the steps of our quest for community transformation. I will use our initial concept: Community transformation is an idea or concept whose time has come. I said in the Introduction that worldwide the Holy Spirit is moving the Church from "church-centric" to "community-centric." Then I presented God's vision of giving the church back to the community. Next I described the four major ingredients and the recipe of community transformation. After that I discussed the problem of matching the right values with the right vision, or community-transformation values whose time has come. Next followed the concept of the King's men, a people whose time has come. I will close with a final chapter about a Church and community whose time has come. Here is an outline:

- Community Transformation: An Idea Whose Time Has Come
- Nehemiah's Recipe: Four Ingredients Whose Time Has Come
- Giving the Church Back to the Community: A Vision Whose Time Has Come.
- Intelligent Fire Core Values: Eight Core Values Whose Time Has Come.
- The Return of the Kings: A People Whose Time Has Come.
- The Eleven-Twelfths Church: A Church Whose Time Has Come

These will combine to produce...

- Tomorrow's Community Today: A Community Whose Time Has Come.

Community transformation is much more complex than most of us originally thought. However, as we pursue God's vision of community transformation, the pieces of communities are coming back together again

THE "PRIESTS'" GREATEST HOUR

Let's "flesh out" tomorrow's Church today. What does it look like? How does it equip "kings" in the Church? What is its culture? How do the priests enable and empower today's leaders and influencers in the Church to be tomorrow's leaders and influencers in the community? How do priests help position Christian people of influence into positions of influence in their communities? In a real sense this could be the priests' greatest hour. It also will stretch the priests to new heights, new realms and new dimensions.

Those in full-time ministry in our churches will need to teach more strategically than academically. They will have to be more implementation-oriented than teacher-oriented. They will need to be more formation-oriented than information-oriented. They will need to let go. They will need to be more wisdom-oriented than knowledge-oriented. They will have to speak more life-application messages and fewer "doctrinal" messages. They will need to let the eleven-twelfths emerge into their purpose, calling, vision and destiny. They will need to embrace change more often. They will need to create a leadership culture, not a follower culture. They will have to be able to show the way, not just talk the way. They will need to be more about being and doing than knowing. They will need to leave the ivory towers of theory and the way it ought to be behind. They will have to embrace what is effective.

They will have to focus and become aware of the ABCs, not XYZs. (However, talking about this and doing it are two different things.) They will need to become more kingly. How does a priest become more kingly? The answer is simple. The first step is embracing the life-or-death-first core value. People's lives are dependent on it. Community transformation requires it. The mission of Jesus Christ demands it. When one embraces the life-or-death-first core value, he becomes willing to become all things to all men that some may be saved. After this value is embraced, the other intelligent fire core values can be embraced.

Tomorrow's Church Today—A Transformational Church

Pastor Lee Pace of the River Church in Phoenix, Arizona, created this slogan for his church: "Tomorrow's Church Today." The River is a true community church and a type of tomorrow's church today.

It takes a transformational church to transform a community. Laurie Beth Jones in her book *Teaching Your Team to Fish* talks about the difference between a transaction and a transformation.[1] She says "transactions are lateral exchanges between people—be it goods and service." In contrast, she says "transformations are invisible, uplifting, transcendent experiences that involve a fundamental shift or change." I say that a transaction is a touch, a transformation is a change. If we are really honest about most churches and church services, we would say they are transactional.

Most church services and churches have been existing by transactions for years. People come, get a sermon, give money, and then go home. There was a transaction but not a transformation. The pastor taught the way, not showed the way. The problem is, that is what happens at a grocery store, pharmacy, or gas station. It is a transaction, not a transformation.

Transformations are what Jesus is all about. Encounters with Jesus were not only transactions, they were transformations. Just ask the woman at the well, Zacheaus, or Peter. When they met Jesus it was a transaction that took you several levels higher than you were! Laurie Beth Jones calls this "uplifting"! A transaction that takes you several levels higher or enhances your life is called a transformation. It is more than a classroom, more than a sermon, more than a degree. Transformation is life imparting and life impacting! It takes you higher! Transformational people and transformational churches are what transform communities. That is tomorrow's church today! That is what the community is looking for. They want tomorrow's church today, not yesterday's church today. To live is to grow, to grow is to change!

What should tomorrow's church today look like? Tomorrow's church today is a community-centric church. It is based on reaching the community. It ministers according to Ephesians 3:10—Christ to the church, then Christ through the Church. It envisions, empowers, and equips those in the Church to be fully devoted followers of Christ who have redemptive influence in the community. It holds classes and groups on leadership in the community. It offers sermons and classes on character and wisdom in the community context. It provides classes on honoring the role of the other spheres of influence in the community as well as in the church. It offers classes and sermons on citizenship and how to meet needs in the community.

It emphasizes every church member discovering and fulfilling his or her purpose, calling and destiny. For example, bankers may mentor those who want to become bankers in the future, whether they are churched or unchurched. These king's men may mentor others on how to work with the influencers in the business, education, government and media/entertainment areas who are not churched. The eleven-twelfths church equips church members for life in the community as well as life in the church. Tomorrow's church today involves all the aspects of mentoring. It teaches, equips, models, conducts field trips, debriefs, and even participates in real-life situations. Its model of teaching is Hebrew, not Greek—that is, it is both relational and intellectual, it has faith that engages the culture in a redemptive way. This form of mentoring is much more transformational than informational.

Tomorrow's church today reflects the value of "the church is here to serve its people" not just "its people exist to serve the church." It is a two-way relationship, not just a one-way relationship. It is about helping people to be better in all realms of life. It is a partner in enhancing the community. It has good spiritual training as well as life training. It is relevant, it is concerned for the community, and its actions demonstrate it. It has favor with God and men, whether in the church or the community. It mentors and equips the king's men to ride again. It has intelligent fire core values and lives by them. It envisions and empowers today's leaders and influencers in the church to be tomorrow's leaders and influencers in the community.

What If?

Let's dream for a moment. It is time to stop walking into the future backwards. We cannot think outside of the box while living inside the box. While many try to be modern, their approach is ancient. Many times churches have a vision that is outside of the box, but the church suffers from beliefs that are outside of the box, but values that are inside the box. Let me ask you some questions beginning with: What if?

- What if there was a church that envisioned, empowered and equipped Christians for life—not just church life?
- What if there was a church that envisioned, empowered, and equipped Christians to be competent in family, business, church, and the community?
- What if there were more community churches than Christian fellowships?
- What if there were churches that were effective in meshing faith and culture—church@community?
- What if there were pastors who equipped the saints to do the work of community ministry, not just church ministry?
- What if there were churches really concerned for the community to the point of doing something for the community?
- What if there were churches that were concerned about how the community could be different because of them?
- What if there were churches that equipped their people for careers and how to influence others for Jesus in their careers?

- What if there were churches that had a community-eye view of the community, not just a church-eye view of the country?
- What if the community really knew by many church's actions that the church was there for the community?
- What if churches trained their people to be volunteers, neighborhood activists, community advocates, and servants in and to the community?
- What if there were churches that had the wisdom necessary to work with other leaders in the community?
- What if there was a church that was ahead of the community, not lagging behind the community?
- What if there were a significant number of churches in a community that were proactive, aware, and equipping their people to be a people for the community?
- What if the church equipped people to be transformational in the community, not just transactional in the community?
- What if there were churches that had real favor with God and man?
- What if there was a church that let go of their people and positioned their people of influence into positions of influence in the community?
- How would this affect pastors?
- How would this affect elders or the church board?
- How would this affect people inside the church?
- And most importantly, how would this affect the community?

CHURCH@COMMUNITY

What would a 'What If" church look like? What would they teach? How would they equip? How would they enable their congregation to engage the community redemptively?

Remember, when Jesus was talking about salt and light He was talking about the church in the community. If the church would be salt and light in the community, the community would be "lit" and "salted" in the church. However, the church engages the community first, not vice versa. There will be no transformation without incarnation. The church has been without incarnation, equipping its members for favor with God for hundreds of years. The problem for many churches has been in the favor with man area. So let's explore some church curriculum for favor with man. I see this strategic equipping in five areas:

1. Envisioning, empowering, and equipping for careers in the community.
2. Envisioning, empowering, and equipping for leadership and influence in the community.
3. Envisioning, empowering, and equipping opportunity seekers for service opportunity seekers in the community.
4. Envisioning, empowering, and equipping for problem solving and prevention in the community.
5. Envisioning, empowering, and equipping for the spirit and truth in the community.

1. Kingly careers in the community

Tomorrow's church today envisions, empowers and equips its congregation for success in all realms of life, not just church life. Remember, eleven-twelfths of the church's congregation is called to ministry in the community. The kings are the middlemen between the priests and the community. Their role is strategic in transforming a community.

A wise church would encourage every member to discover their purpose, calling and destiny, and fulfill it. For example, rather than having a successful banker teach a home study on Ephesians, have him mentor those in the church that want to become bankers in the future. This could be an equipping study for both the churched and unchurched. Other successful "kings' in the church could mentor the college/career people in all sectors of the community. Successful teachers could mentor future teachers. Those in government could mentor future politicians. The eleven-twelfths church would equip members for life as well as church life. They would teach, equip, model, conduct field trips, debrief, and even participate in real life situations. Their model of teaching would be both Greek and Hebrew. This type of mentoring is much more transformational than informational. It is show more than tell. It is transformational, not transactional.

The Word of Life Centre in Red Deer, Canada has started what they call The Millionaire's Club. Mike Furst, the head of their marketplace leaders describes this club.

> The Millionaire's Club is reserved for those that are millionaires or anyone desiring to become one. They desire to live according to the principles of God's word and are willing to shoulder the load of the Kingdom. They mentor business people to carry the ministry of the local church into the community. There is a peer leader that is designated to lead a group of three to five business people; they meet once a month for a meal, where they discuss the issues and obstacles that each member may be facing that month and set their goals for the next month. There is prayer, a prophetic word given, and a time of council. The leader usually opens with a word for the business sector of what he sees God is doing in the church. They bring the mandate of God for the nation's businessmen and women. We believe that matching people at a peer level equals a higher level of agreement. Success for these people is not from a leader teaching but comes when relationships grow in love and fellowship, prayer and support. There is no set curriculum. The church basically provides an environment of agreement, strength and support. A couple of the

> books we have incorporated for study and discussion are *Anointed for Business* by Ed Silvoso and *God at Work* by Rich Marshall.

As of February 2004, the church had three groups going and just had developed their first millionaire through these groups.

This is wonderful. The church is here to serve people, redeem, and then lift them. If you make people better and you make the community better. You build effective communities by building effective people. Career training can come from both college and the church. Two are better than one.

Many church leaders have tried to get successful business people to be teachers of the Word. Some have done well, but most do not. Why? It is not his calling. Pastors, if you want to see that businessperson come alive, have him mentor people for careers. Both you and the businessperson will be happier and more effective. Please activate the lawyers, provosts, teachers, nurses, politicians, newscasters, business owners, writers, and community advocates in your church to train others that they might be able to train others. Help a person and you help the community.

2. Intelligent influence

Tomorrow's church today realizes that envisioning, empowering, and equipping Christian influencers is absolutely essential in transforming a community. Remember, the kings in church are meant to be godly influencers in the community. As the church raises up people of influence they will assume positions of influence in the community. A wise leader would not only equip people for careers but also equip them how to use their influence through wisdom and servanthood to the community. The leader would equip them to increase in wisdom and stature. A humble, successful Christian king who gives God the glory is a much stronger influencer than a self-made, boastful king. Just ask Daniel, Joseph, or Esther. The church struggles with positioning people of influence in positions of influence. The next millionaires need to be aware of Who creates wealth and why wealth is created. Growing in stature is a key to community transformation. Somebodies hang with somebodies. We might as well have Christian somebodies influence community somebodies.

How do you teach this? Find a king who has influence and have him share his secrets with other influencers. It is more caught than taught. Let him show the way, not just teach the way. Remember, kings understand kings. Kings engage the community every day. They have "street wisdom." They speak "community-ese." That is wisdom.

Do you realize that God is raising new types of seminaries to educate Christian kings for the work of their ministry? It's time we accredited, educated, empowered, and validated these very strategic kingly community influencers. We need to raise up the experts and doctorates in engaging faith in culture. Doctors of church and community ministry: Dr. Dick Drake, the provost of the Phoenix University of Theology, has created such a department and degree. At this university, one can receive a masters or doctorate in faith in culture. These types of innovative disruptions can shape a whole generation of new ministers in and to the community. The potential is staggering. We need to make ministry outside of the church walls just as significant as ministry inside the church. We need the Return of the Kings with church validation for influencing and shaping the community.

3. Strongholds of opportunity through community service

At the beginning of this book I said Jesus was the ultimate neighborhood activist. Jesus was for communities. Jesus left His church for those in earth's neighborhood. He came as a servant to the community. He had wisdom. He had answers. He had passion. He looked for a way in, not a way out of the community. That is what tomorrow's church does today. Pastor Tommy Barnett of the Phoenix First Assembly of God Church in Phoenix, Arizona says find a need, and meet it. Become a community activist. There are opportunities for service and volunteering in the community everywhere. Hospitals, libraries, community action programs, politics, or soup kitchens, are just a few of the areas looking for volunteers. Find a cause that you have a passion for and serve Christ in it. I know of churches that encourage all their members to be volunteers on election day. Learn to volunteer and serve in some place other than the church. Learn to be a people for your community. A church does not need to buy or advertise their way into the community. Why not serve or volunteer your way into the community? Someone needs to recapture the volunteering attribute our communities once had. Why can't that someone be those in the church? Remember, church is everywhere you are. One aspect of the church is to be an army of volunteers for the benefit of the community. Your gift makes room for you...in the community.

4. Problem solving and problem prevention churches

One of the most crucial needs in today's communities is that of problem solving and prevention. Wisdom is absolutely essential in problem solving and prevention. Who has the wisdom needed for solutions to these problems? My conviction is that in many instances the church has the wisdom. Tomorrow's church today is a church that is ahead of the community, not behind the community. It is provocative, aware, and rejoices in being a people for the community. It is a place of neighborhood activists and community advocates. Tomorrow's church today may volunteer their church buildings for community events, election days, city council meetings, community plays or dramas, concerts, and other community events. It is involved in solving community problems, not creating more problems. It takes a stand for both God and the community. Tomorrow's church today is involved in politics and education through service.

If youth is a problem in the community, the church, working along with the other four community spheres of influence, can work together to solve the problems. The same would be true for other need areas in the community The key to this type of ministry is being in a position to contribute, help, strategize, serve and problem solve. Tomorrow's church today is God's chamber of commerce to the community.

5. Gifts that make room for the Church

One of my favorite proverbs is Proverbs 18:16:

> A man's gift makes room for him, and brings him before great men.

What about the gifts of the Spirit as well as our natural talents and abilities in the context of the community? If you are Pentecostal or Spirit-filled, what does your gift look like with your neighbors, the mayor, the board of education, or a sports personality? Think about what prophesy, healing, miracles, or word of knowledge look like in the community. If you are a fundamentalist, what does all your Bible knowledge or theology look like in the context of the community? Would you give them the truth in seminary jargon, or in real life words? Whatever part of the church you are from, God gave you a gift that makes room for you in the community. This gift puts you in the presence of other great men (kings). Your gift makes room for you and puts you before great men…in the community. That gift produces influence. That gift solves problems, prevents problems, and gives you the solutions to strongholds of opportunity in the community. It makes room for you. It produces favor with God and man.

You may have to change your religious language to relevant language but that is no problem. Tomorrow's churches today are willing to do that because life or death is more important than right or wrong. Tomorrow's churches today are willing to become all things to all men so some might be saved. Remember, God puts into you what He wants out of you in both the church and the community. The community needs what God gave the church and you!

GETTING OFF THE EXERCISE BIKE

Many times traditional churches are like an exercise bike at the gym. There is a lot of work activity and perspiration but it is not taking you anywhere. Whether you push easy or push hard, it is still getting you nowhere. All preparation but no application. God is raising up leaders and churches that can get you from A to B, not leave you at A and promise B. God is raising up churches that are equipping people for life, not just church life. God is raising up churches who are getting off the exercise bike and on to real bikes. As I have said before, impression without expression leads to depression and regression. It is time to quit putting $5.00 worth of effort into the church to get $4.00 of return. Seminary did not teach you about this. Seminary prepared you for church issues, not community issues. Tomorrow's church today is about being wisdom-driven, not knowledge-driven. Tomorrow's church today is about shifting the church from "What if" to "What is." It is real! It is relatable! It is contemporary! It is relevant! It is purpose driven! It is productive! It is effective! It is community-oriented!

It is redemptive! It is influential! In order to experience community transformation, we are going to have to get off the exercise bike. The real bike awaits. Real bikes ride in the community while exercise bikes sit in buildings. Our communities hang in the balance.

What Matters?

In May of 2004, I was ministering in the Doxa Deo movement in Pretoria, South Africa. During that conference, Pastor Alan Platt also ministered and summarized Tomorrow's Church Today in a clarion way. His message was about the type of church needed to affect a community in a real and tangible way. According to Alan, in order to maximize the impact of the church on our communities, the church needs the following power shifts or value shifts.

From being concerned to have compassion for your community

Mark 6:34, NIV: "When Jesus landed and saw the large crowd, he had compassion on them." The disciples were driven by concern, but Jesus was driven by compassion.

From condemning your city to blessing your city

Jeremiah 29:7, NIV: "Also, seek the peace and prosperity of the city to which I have carried you into exile. Pray to the Lord for it, because if it prospers, you too will prosper."

For too long we as the church have positioned ourselves as adversaries to our communities. We are called to serve and bless our cities. Eventually we get the city we deserve!

From building walls to building bridges

Matthew 5:13–14: "You are the salt of the earth.... You are the light of the world."

The first paradigm shift pertains to where we as the church see ourselves in relation to our communities. We cannot remain outside of the community inviting people in, but we must go to our communities and take responsibility in order to make a difference.

From measuring size to measuring impact

Matthew 13:33, NIV: "The Kingdom of heaven is like yeast...mixed into a large amount of flour until it worked all through the dough."

The question: "how big is your church?" should be replaced with: "what impact and influence does your church have in your community?" The question is: If your church ceases to exist, will the community be touched by it in any way?

From encouraging the saints to attend the service to equipping the saints for works of service

Ephesians 4:12, NIV: "To prepare God's people for works of service."

There needs to be a transition in the minds of our people that ministry is not restricted to spiritual and pulpit activities. Calling must be understood in the context of where each person is placed by God.

From positioning against to partnering with other ministries

Ecclesiastes 4:9: "Two are better than one, because they have a good return for their work."

We need to set aside our theological differences and move to strategic partnering based on love and commitment for one another and our communities. For transformation of communities we focus on absolutes and not on interpretation of assumptions.

From being a minister in a congregation to being a spiritual leader in a geographical region

Luke 19:41: "As Jesus approached Jerusalem and saw the city, he wept over it."

We must understand that our responsibility as spiritual leaders do not end with our local congregation. We are placed like Adam in a garden (the city or geographical area where we are situated) and we need to take responsibility for that area and take care of it. Our communities are that area.

Alan could not have said it better. These are not beliefs, but values. These values are about how we act, not what we say. Your church can change! Your church can be more effective! How? By majoring on what matters the most.

Putting the Pieces of Our Communities Back Together Again

Community transformation is about Christians in church, business, government, education and media/entertainment having real influence and giving God a face in their part of the community. Like Joseph with Pharaoh, or Daniel with Nebuchadnezzar, the kings in the Church take on the role of priest. While they are kings in the context of the church, they are priests in the context of the community. They represent God in the context of the community. Their contribution is wisdom, character core values and spiritual awareness. They are ambassadors of grace in and with the other spheres of influence in the community. Any other approach with the four other spheres will be problematic. An adversarial approach should be used only as a last resort.

After all, Jesus deals with us this way. His approach to guiding nations, cities, communities, and people is *influence, not authority*. He is waiting until "the end of the book" to exert his full authority in judgment. His grace is amazing indeed. The eleven-twelfths church consists of those who are like Jesus. They have "stature and wisdom" and will grow in favor with God and man. God will exalt these kings in the Church and put them in places of influence to work with other influencers. Jesus will give them the grace and love for the community. The Holy Spirit will give them the wisdom and the right words to say.

The king's men will not just be doing their jobs. They will be doing the work of their ministry. Having a job and using that job for the glory of God are two different things. We are now beginning to see Christian "kings" being positioned into positions of influence in the community. Not for the Church's benefit, but for the community's benefit. That is what this book is all about. Along with many others I am attempting to put the Church back into a position of influence for the sake of the community. The Church was not called to do what the other spheres of influence were called to do. The Church was called to make its contribution into the community along with the other spheres of influence. It is a "war" of peace. The result is a redefined Church that is there for the community. After all, whoever defines the Church wins—at least until Jesus returns. And the kings are the ones who define the Church to the community.

As the king's men work with the other spheres of influence in the community, they redefine the Church through their service. Their role in this is not to dominate but to serve. They contribute, not control. The idea is contribution, not conquest. They facilitate cooperation among all the entities to the end of enhancing the community. Their service will range from creating an economic base in the community to helping the poor. The king's men are called to put Humpty Dumpty back together again. They impact nations and transform cities. They know how to take a strong hold of strongholds of opportunity for the glory of God. They help create tomorrow's communities today. They put Humpty Dumpty back together again. They are the ultimate elders at the gates.

UNTIL THE PAIN EXCEEDS THE FEAR, THERE WILL BE NO CHANGE

Early in this book, I said until you reform you only revisit. The church-centric approach has to merge into the community-centric approach or we will only continually revisit the lack of influence in our communities the Church is experiencing today. In many ways we are like Abraham while he was in Ur of the Chaldees. God said to Abram, "Look up...see those stars...so shall your descendants be...now go from where you are to where those descendents are" (Gen. 12:1; 13:14, author's paraphrase). Please notice, God did not bring Canaan to Abraham; Abraham had to go to Canaan. Jesus' call was similar. Jesus came to earth; earth did not come to Jesus. Likewise, the Church today needs to leave the familiar and seize the future. God has a vision but the Church has a comfort zone. Now is the time for the Church to go into its land of promise.

How does it accomplish that? The answer is in Hebrews 11:13 (emphasis added):

> All these died in faith, without receiving the promises, but having *seen* them and having *welcomed* them from a distance, and having *confessed* that they were strangers and exiles on the earth.

I once heard Apostle Emmanuel Cannistraci speak on this verse. He emphasized three points that Abraham embraced to propel him into his future. The points were as follows:

Abraham had to—

- See it.
- Welcome or embrace it.
- Confess it.

All of us who really want transformed communities will need to

1. See the vision and values of community transformation.

2. Embrace the vision and values of community transformation.

3. Confess the vision and values of community transformation.

My concern is to make sure we see, embrace, and confess the values of community transformation. These values must make the transition from our head to our heart to our feet. We must go from knowing to being to doing. We must live the values, not just know the values. Beliefs will not be enough. Intelligent fire core values are at the very heart of community transformation. It is time to live the values out loud! No longer can the Church be incarnationally challenged.

Let me ask you church leaders a couple of questions. Do you want to grow a large church? Do you want church growth? If so, try building your church with the values I have presented in this book. The values will enable your vision. These values are designed to help you grow both your community and your church. These values will enable you to grow a community church, not just a Christian fellowship. Those of you who see the values, embrace the values, confess the values and live the values out loud will once again create a church/community connection. The church will take its place as an influencer and vision caster in the community. I will say it again—build your church with Church@Community principles. Until the pain of seeing the community not reached exceeds the fear of letting go, there will be no change.

Quests Take Time

The only problem with becoming a community transforming church is that it involves change. It requires a value shift. It requires leaving Ur of the Chaldeans to go to a place you have never gone before. Change clashes with the teacher-driven church ethos I addressed in Chapter 7. Most of the people in your church will be resistant to a change of any type, especially if it involves the community. After all, once any culture or ethos is set, it is hard to change. That is why it is always wise to make any change slowly and purposefully. Do not change too fast.

Do not read this book and adopt what I have said overnight. You will lose people in your church you do not need to lose. Plan for the change. As the late Donald McGavarn said when asked how to change the church, "Through the gradual dissemination of information when and where it matters."

Communicate with your leaders. Recommend they read this book. Discuss with your leaders what they liked or disliked about this book. Help them process the values. Explain to them how these values may change the morning services, the home groups, and the church in its involvement in the community. Start with your leaders and then go to the rest of the church. Speak on the values. Show the advantages. Keep communication going both ways. Insist on two-way communication. Make sure you take the time, prayer, study and application to make sure *within yourself* that these values move from your head, to your heart and to your feet. It has to be a *value* in you, not just a belief.

Remember the process. Move yourself, your leaders and your church from knowing to being to doing. That is a process. Adopting a program or behaviors without having it in your heart or your church 's heart greatly reduces your effectiveness and greatly increases your chance of potential problems and misunderstandings.

Remember, some people will adopt these values very quickly. Some will need more time and explanation. Some will be very slow in adopting these values. Frankly, some will never adopt these values. The key is in preparation of a plan of change and executing the plan purposefully, prayerfully and sensitively. Some of your people will just take more time and processing, but they will come along if you lead them, not "drive" them. Let's not have this shift from church-centric to community-centric leave a lot of "road kill." Remember, a quest takes time but it takes you to new heights, new realms and new dimensions.

Praying in the Values

In the introduction to this book, I challenged those involved in intercession to pray in the values. Intercessors, let's do exactly that. Pray that churches all over the world will live by the eight intelligent fire core values proposed in this book. Many of you have been praying for revival. Many of you have been praying for community transformation. Remember the principles of this book. We need to have the right values that enable the vision of community transformation. The key lies more in the values than the vision. Let's pray in the right "government" for the vision of community transformation.

Let's pray for the welfare of our communities, for in their welfare the churches will have welfare (Jer. 29:7). Pray that the Lord of the Harvest would send harvesters into the harvest (Luke 10:2). Pray that God would raise up the Josephs, Daniels, and Esthers to influence the kings of today's communities. Pray for the activation of the eleven-twelfths church. Most of all, pray that in today's churches the life-or-death-first core value would once again take its place as the central core value.

Strongholds of Opportunity

This book is about taking a strong hold of strongholds of opportunity. It is only fitting this word should come from a pastor in New Zealand because this book is dedicated to New Zealand. Remember, this book is a next step in the progressive revelation of community transformation. We are building this "airplane" while it is flying. There may be more steps. There may be more values than I have listed. In fact, originally I had twelve values. I wanted to write a chapter on relationships as well as a chapter on leadership styles necessary to reach today's culture. Perhaps I will do that in my next book.

I desire desperately for you who have read this book to see the community in a whole new way. I want to give you a revelation on the community that you will never forget. Frankly, I hope you will never see the community the same way again! My desire is for that revelation to be so impacting that it will create a shift in your thinking and priorities. I want the King's men to ride again and not be stuck the rest of their lives trying to put Humpty Dumpty back together again. My desire is for action and to help create churches up to the challenge of ministry in the twenty-first century. Hundreds of thousands of future church people are ready to become *present* church. As churched people, the answer to our prayer is us!

NOTES

Chapter 1

DIVINELY INSPIRED, SPECIFICALLY LED:
THE PRINCIPLE OF INTELLIGENT FIRE

1. See www.barna.org, accessed 10/29/04.
2. Rick Page, *Hope Is Not a Strategy* (New York: McGraw Hill, 2003).

Chapter Two

RECIPES AND REBUILDING WALLS:
THE PRINCIPLE OF RECIPE

1. George Otis Jr., Transformation videos
2. See http://firsthand.org/outreach/martyrs.htm, accessed 2/24/05.

Chapter 3

THE FALL AND RISE OF HUMPTY DUMPTY:
THE PRINCIPLE OF STRATEGIC ALLIANCES, MUTUAL COLLABORATIONS, AND SUPPORTING CASTS

1. See www.characterfirst.com, accessed 2/17/05.
2. Kelly Varner, *The Corporate Anointing* (Shippensburg: Destiny Image, 1998).
3. See www.barna.org, accessed 2/17/05.

Chapter 8

A MILE DEEP AND AN INCH WIDE:
THE PRINCIPLE OF BOTH/AND

1. Jim Collins, *Built to Last* (New York: Harper Business, 2002).

Chapter 9

SACRED COWS MAKE THE BEST HAMBURGER: THE PRINCIPLE OF WONDERFUL SERVANTS, TERRIBLE MASTERS

1. Richard Foster, *Renovare: Bringing the Church to the Churches.* Renovare, 8 Inverness Drive East, Suite 102, Englewood, CO 80112-5624.

2. John Noble, *The Shaking* (Oxford, England: Monarch Books, 2002). Used by permission.

Chapter 10

I'M OK, YOU'RE SO-SO: THE PRINCIPLE OF DUAL CITIZENSHIP— BOTH TRIBE AND NATION

1. See www.bible.org/page.asp?page_id=1474, accessed 2/24/05.

2. John Walton, *The Protocol of the APCNZ* (New Zealand: Associated Pentecostal Churches of New Zealand). Used by permission.

Chapter 11

INCARNATIONALLY CHALLENGED: THE PRINCIPLE OF THE TIGER'S HEAD AND THE MOUSE'S TAIL

1. Larry Richards, *Basic Christian Values* (Grand Rapids: Zondervan, 1981).

Chapter 12

CLUELESS IN SEATTLE: THE PRINCIPLE OF REDEMPTIVE RELEVANCY

1. See www.barna.org, accessed 2/17/05.

2. For more information about Leonard Sweet's ministry, see www.leonardsweet.com.

3. Joseph Aldrich, *Lifestyle Evangelism* (Sisters, OR: Multnomah Publishers, 1981), 55. Used by permission.

4. Bill Hybels and Mark Mittelberg, *Becoming a Contagious Christian* (Grand Rapids, MI: Zondervan, 1995).

Chapter 13

Innovative Disruption—In the Nick of Time
The Principle of Spiritual Entrepreneurialism

1. Stephen Covey, *The Seven Habits of Highly Effective People* (New York: Free Press, 1990).

Chapter 15

The Return of the Kings:
The Principle of the Eleven-Twelfths Church

1. Ed Silvoso, *Anointed for Business* (Ventura, CA: Regal Books, 2002).

Chapter 16

Church@Community:
The Principle of Tomorrow's Church Today

1. Laurie Beth Jones, *Teach Your Team to Fish* (New York, Random House, 2002), 111.

To Contact the Author

NATIONStrategy
7145 W. Mariposa Grande Lane
Peoria, AZ 85383

www.nationstrategy.com
nationstrategy@cs.com